SHOULDN'T
I BE *Happy?*

SHOULDN'T
I BE *Happy?*

Emotional Problems of
Pregnant and Postpartum Women

Shaila Misri, M.D.

THE FREE PRESS
NEW YORK   LONDON   TORONTO   SYDNEY   TOKYO   SINGAPORE

The Free Press
A Division of Simon & Schuster Inc.
1230 Avenue of the Americas
New York, N.Y. 10020

Printed in the United States of America

printing number
1   2   3   4   5   6   7   8   9   10

Library of Congress Cataloging-in-Publication Data

Misri, Shaila.
    Shouldn't I be happy?: emotional problems of pregnant and
postpartum women / Shaila Misri.
        p.   cm.
    Includes index.
    ISBN 0-02-921405-X
    1. Mental illness in pregnancy—Popular works.   2. Postpartum
psychiatric disorders—Popular works.   3. Pregnancy—Psychological
aspects.   I. Title.
RG588.M55   1995
618.2'0019—dc20   95-2848
                                                          CIP

This book is for my own sons,
Nathaniel and Nicholas,
my husband,
my mother,
and my late father

CONTENTS

FOREWORD

In this book, Dr. Shaila Misri has done a remarkable job of presenting the normal and not so normal concerns and difficulties of pregnancy. Her vast clinical experience and expertise are communicated clearly and empathically through her interactions with her patients and in her careful discussion of their problems and answers to their questions. In addition to considering some major psychiatric disorders of pregnant and postpartum women, Dr. Misri provides an understanding of such problems as emotional distress about breastfeeding, marital tension, and the tragedies of miscarriage and infant death. She offers valuable guidelines about when and how to seek therapy and to take medication. This book is unique: it deals with many questions that are rarely answered so directly.

Why is pregnancy so important to women and to society?

Reproductive health is important to every woman and her family as well as to future generations, who are dependent on the health of today's women and on the reproductive choices that they make. Because women bear this responsibility, their lives and their health are intimately intertwined with the concerns of society. It has been stated,

> Social response to women's reproductive abilities typically has made their bodies part of the public domain in a way that men's are not. . . . And as wombs have become increasingly public spaces medically, they have also become increasingly public politically; women's choices, not only about how they manage their pregnancies, but also about how they will manage their work, their leisure, their use of both legal and illegal drugs, and their sexuality, are further subject to society's scrutiny and to the law's constraints. (Nelson, 1992, p. 14)

The idea that psychological forces affect bodily functions and processes is as old as history, but in the past 50 years more serious attention has been paid to this interaction between mind and body. With more research in this area, we have been able to dispel a number of myths and beliefs in favor of factual evidence. Although much remains to be done, we have come a long way from the time when most reproductuve disorders were oversimplified, pejoratively labeled "psychogenic," and considered to be in some way related to a woman's ambivalence about her femininity or about childbearing. We no longer label those women who hae difficulties with pregnancy as immature or emotionally disturbed, without serious regard for their problems.

Clearly, every pregnancy, planned or unplanned, is motivated by complex factors, among them the need to love and be loved, to give expression to nurturant wishes, to confirm femininity, and sometimes to restitute previous losses or master earlier life trauma. Pregnancy can be seen as a normal developmental experience for some women that is accompanied by ambivalence and conflict. Although, as Dr. Misri tells us, pregnancy is accompanied by a low incidence of psychiatric disorders, there are some that we should be aware of, especially in the postpartum period. Pregnancy loss, whether planned or unplanned, is also important because of the risk of accompanying psychiatric disorders, including depression, but it is often not taken seriously enough.

Dr. Misri has taken all of these and a myriad of other issues very seriously. She has listened to her patients' questions and shared her answers with us in this unique and fascinating book. No other book provides as much important information and states it so candidly and empathically.

CAROL C. NADELSON, M.D.
Former President,
American Psychiatric Association;
Editor in chief,
American Psychiatric Press, Inc.

ACKNOWLEDGMENTS

I wish to express my warm appreciation to Kelly Talayco for staying with me throughout my book, for her invaluable input and for her thoughtful, encouraging feedback. Without her, this book would not have been a reality. John Talayco, I want to acknowledge how patient you have been with transporting the manuscripts back and forth for months on end.

I would especially like to thank Susan Arellano, my editor at The Free Press, for guiding the work to completion.

I want to thank my patients for whom this book is primarily written; many of you have given me your constructive reactions to my work, for which I remain grateful.

This book is a good place to mention BC Women's, which is a maternity hospital in British Columbia. The stories you will read in my book are about patients I have seen at this hospital over a number of years.

The support of my colleagues and friends has been tremendous during the preparation of this book. My special thanks to the following doctors who reviewed some of my chapters, offered encouragement, and provided useful suggestions: Diana Carter, Lee Cohen, Duncan Farquharson, Vera Frinton, Ron Gibson, Michael Myers, Ron Remick, Kamal Rungta, Dorothy Shaw, Kristin Sivertz, Patrick Taylor, and Douglas Wilson. In addition, Lori D'Agincourt, Mark Fleming, and Brian Harrigan also were kind enough to spare their time in reviewing some chapters.

Sharon Staceson, Director of the British Columbia Reproductive Care Program, deserves a special mention; her contribution to the book has been significant.

I wish to extend my thanks to my colleagues at St. Paul's Hospital for accommodating me and my schedule when I took leaves of absence to work on my writing—in particular, Dr. Steve Kline, whose encouragement and belief in me have helped me achieve my goal. I also want to thank Dr. Penny Ballem for her ongoing support.

I don't want to forget any member of my family—both the Kulkarnises and the Misris—who patiently heard about my book every time I met them, whether on holidays or at family gatherings. Their support has been very important to me.

Lastly, I would like to thank Liezel Mae Waechter, who organized and reorganized my patients' schedules so that I had enough time to concentrate on this book.

INTRODUCTION

MY PERSONAL JOURNEY TOWARD WRITING THIS BOOK

I began my work relating to pregnancy and postpartum disorders in 1979, and this area continues to be the focus of my psychiatric practice today. I am the director of the Reproductive Psychiatry Program at St. Paul's Hospital and the codirector of the Reproductive Psychiatry Program at a maternity hospital in Vancouver called BC Women's. The term "reproductive psychiatry" refers to the care of women who have psychiatric symptoms related to the reproductive cycle. Premenstruum, pregnancy, postpartum, and menopause are times of specific vulnerability for some women. The majority of patients in our program are seen on an outpatient basis, but I do consult to and look after patients admitted to hospital as well.

The patients referred to my service typically come from two sources—inpatients admitted to BC Women's in Vancouver and outpatients from the southwestern part of British Columbia and even referrals from as far away as northern Washington State. The outpatient population varies in age, marital status, social class, and so on; we studied referral patterns at our clinic three years ago, and found that our patients typically range in age from 25 to 45, are more likely married than single, and have at least a high school education. Fifty percent of them work outside of the home, while the other half are stay-at-home mothers.

When it comes to the outpatient population, I am convinced that many of my patients are actually going to grow old with me because they have already been in my practice for a number of years. For example, a woman who was first referred to me for treatment of depression after the birth of her first child may then decide to have one or two more children, a process that may take eight to ten years. Then she may come back to me again when she is experiencing mood swings during menopause. I tend to function as a bridge between an obstetrician and a primary care physician for many of these patients.

The inpatient population at BC Women's is also quite varied, and this is the source of many of my referrals. Commonly today, a woman's psychiatric history will be noted on her prenatal labor/delivery chart, and provides some advance notice that a psychiatrist's care may be helpful. On the other hand, I may have to respond to a sudden telephone call from an obstetrician or a family physician, telling me that a woman has had an acute psychotic episode following the birth of her baby or is acutely suicidal. Fortunately, this scenario is less and less common today; it is not unusual for me to see patients who request psychiatric referral themselves or are referred by the staff looking after them on the ward. But most of my referrals come from the family doctors or obstetricians looking after the patient at BC Women's.

Even at the age of ten, it was my ambition to become an obstetrician/gynecologist. I dreamed of following the footsteps of my paternal uncles, in whose maternity nursing home I worked during summer holidays; in fact, I held my first retractor in the operating room when I was 16! After finishing medical training, I worked in a department of obstetrics and gynecology in a hospital in West Germany. I eagerly anticipated Monday evening "pre-op" rounds, when I would go and talk to my patients about the surgery they were to undergo the next day. An anesthetist colleague pointed out to me that I was just as good at listening to my patients' fears and anxieties as I was in the operating room—a casual remark that would later have a tremendous impact on my professional life.

After finishing a year of specialization in the field of obstetrics/gynecology, I emigrated to Canada and applied for further training at the University of British Columbia. My application was for training in two specialties—either psychiatry or obstetrics/gynecology. It was simply a matter of timing that I got accepted in psychiatry earlier. After only a few months, however, I knew that this was where I belonged. I was fortunate enough to be able to combine my expertise in both psychiatry and obstetrics/gynecology and to serve the selective group of patients whose care is at the intersection of both these specialties.

Over these years, I have come to feel that the unique problems of pregnant women and mothers suffering emotional disorders should receive greater attention. Practitioners need not necessarily treat them differently from other patients, but they must recognize the particular "stigma" applied to the *mother* who is suffering a mental illness.

After all, a mother is expected to "handle" things, isn't she? She is expected to have special resources of emotional strength, to be ready, willing, and able to sacrifice her own needs to her family's well-being. A mother who is herself in emotional distress is a picture we do not want to see. Faced with these internalized societal expectations, many of my patients believe that they could control their problems by themselves, if only they exerted enough effort—without realizing that the problems could have a psychological or hormonal basis. With this view, they typically take on the full responsibility for suffering their condition—whether the most benign postpartum "blues" or a full-blown postpartum psychosis—in isolation.

In the past few years, a number of my patients have asked me to give them "something to read" that they could take home with them and share with their husbands so that their illness could be "legitimized." One of the reasons I undertook the writing of this book is that I was not easily able to recommend reading material for my patients and their families because few books are available to the public on the subject of emotional disorders in postpartum and pregnancy.

The idea of writing my own book began slowly to appeal to me. I started to imagine a pregnant woman entering a bookstore and looking for books on the subject because she'd had a depression that went untreated in an earlier pregnancy and is afraid that she will have the same frightening symptoms this time. Perhaps like so many of my patients on their first visit, she is afraid to share her fears with her husband and uncertain whether to discuss her worries with her doctor.

Could this woman in fact go to a bookstore and find a book about postpartum problems? Could she thus gain some knowledge about the experience of other women? Could she then find the courage to identify with these symptoms and approach her doctor for help? These are the kinds of questions I came to mull over. Eventually, the answer was obvious—a book of this kind could indeed be helpful to patients, their husbands, and other professional caregivers in the field.

Over several years, I made a number of starts on the project, but my two sons were quite small and I felt unable to take time away from our family life to work on the manuscript. Then my father died, and I suddenly realized how short life is and that if one wants to do something, the time is now—or even yesterday. Another legacy from that period was a personal lesson in vulnerability and distress. Throughout my own two pregnancies, I had had support from family and friends and had not personally experienced the traumas of many of my patients. My father's death, however, affected me deeply, and I found that I needed extra support and help to regain an even balance. It is strange, perhaps, that it was the death of a loved one that gave me the courage and insight to proceed with this project. The time seemed right, and I took a leave of absence to work seriously on the task of bringing my thoughts together in a book.

MY CROSS-CULTURAL EXPERIENCE

As a psychiatrist specializing in emotional illnesses related to reproduction, I have often had reason to reflect on my personal experience in giving birth to two sons. When my first child was born, I had the unique opportunity to observe the process and my own reactions from two quite different viewpoints. On the one hand, I was a medical doctor whose psychiatric training took place in Canadian medical schools and who had lived virtually all of my adult life in the Western world. On the other hand, I am Indian by birth, and when I became a mother, I received the same postpartum care that women in my homeland have received for centuries.

Following the birth of my first son, my mother flew from India to stay with me for six months, bringing with her a woman who has been a member of my parents' household for over thirty years. This woman is a specialist in the traditional rituals and practices associated with childbirth and postpartum care in the culture in which I had been born. During the first thirty days after birth, both the mother and the baby receive special daily massages, which help heal the body. Ritualistic baths are given to both mother and baby to relax and soothe them. The mother's diet is monitored very carefully, and she is encouraged to eat foods that help produce an abundant milk supply and bring less colic to the infant. All of this makes for an atmosphere in which a new mother is accorded special consideration of her needs, a designated time of rest and recovery, and a great deal of personal support in learning to breastfeed and to care for her new infant. There is also a very special continuity of experience across generations since my mother, in her time, had received this very same care.

My purpose in relating my experience is not to promote the traditional rituals of India—although I am personally very grateful to have had this nurturing and supportive postpartum experience. However, I think we in the industrialized West need to look at the traditions that exist elsewhere in the world and reflect on the low incidence of postpartum depression in cultures that give distinct recognition and support to women in the postpartum period.

TO THE WOMEN WHO READ THIS BOOK

For most women, pregnancy and birth are profound events that involve the woman in an emotional and psychological gestation period of defining, testing, and evaluating the possibilities of a redefined self—a self that is now fully a mature female, facing new relationships to the child of whom she is mother, the partner with whom she shares new obligations and an altered dynamic, the parents through whom she is linked to past generations, her circle of social contacts, and society in general. When this period of personal and social growth is compromised by emotional disorder, the contrast between expected joy and fulfillment and the reality of paradoxical feeling and debilitating illness brings particular pain.

Not only is the woman herself particularly vulnerable but so too are those with whom she is linked—the partner whose self has also been engaged in the tasks of redefining himself as a parent, an infant with pressing emotional, physical, and developmental needs, and perhaps older children with their own immediate needs for care and attention. Therapy is complicated by the need for treatment within the context of these relationships, some of them new and fragile.

Pregnancy and motherhood are indisputably challenges in themselves—how much more so, then, for the woman who experiences an emotional disorder at the same time. Anxiety and depression can affect anyone, and these disorders cross all cultural, social, and economic barriers. And what of the woman who is predisposed to mental illness? Research studies show that 8 to 28 percent of women with prior depressive illness will again suffer depressive symptoms in pregnancy or postpartum. These women need more than supportive friends and family; they need the support of professionals to help them through their depressive symptoms. Postpartum symptoms are often dismissed because of the shame associated with emotional problems in this "happy" period of a family's life. Oftentimes, even family, friends, and caregivers will dismiss serious symptoms as a normal adjustment to postpartum, hoping that they will go away. The reality is that the woman is tormented, at times does not get help, and continues alone in her illness.

An emotional disorder in pregnancy is something like a crippling injury to a young child—doubly poignant and frustrating because the illness challenges and undermines what was expected to be a period of growth, development, and increasing fulfillment. Although the incidence of postpartum psychosis is not high—1 to 4 per 100 deliveries—

when it does happen it is truly devastating. The risk of psychotic illness in the first three months postpartum is 15 times the risk in a non-postpartum population. That this is a very vulnerable period should not be underestimated; both the woman herself and those around her must be tuned in to her emotional state from the time she becomes pregnant to the birth to perhaps weeks and months after the baby is born.

Attention to the new mother's emotional well-being is essential if she is to develop a full emotional bond with the new baby as well as to continue to express her love for other family members. If she is not well herself, depression can make her feel very self-centered, and she will find it almost impossible to mother. We, as women, must come forward and nurture each other. We must make it *acceptable* for mothers to "have problems" and to receive help for those problems. The patients whose stories I related are, in a way, extending that sense of encouragement and support through the pages of this book.

TO MY COLLEAGUES IN THE
HEALTH CARE PROFESSIONS

The recognition that emotional disorder can accompany pregnancy and the postpartum period is centuries old. Yet even today, with our increasing knowledge of the etiology of emotional illness, the causes and progression of emotional disorders in pregnancy and the postpartum are regarded as something of a puzzle and viewed differently within the medical profession—with the result that women who suffer these disorders not uncommonly go undiagnosed or receive inappropriate treatment.

In the early 1800s, Dr. J. E. D. Esquirol, a French physician who was one of the first to attempt to analyze postpartum disorders, wrote very sensitively of the loneliness of new mothers who were emotionally troubled. He was convinced that for every woman whose troubled state was recognized, there were many more who *suffered in silence* because they feared the consequences of disclosing their emotional state. In this respect, there is still today a great deal of progress to be made.

Certainly within the medical and caregiving community, we are achieving both a better understanding of emotional disorders in general and more successful approaches to their treatment. We are also beginning to acquire useful clinical data that allow us to relate aspects of the female reproductive cycle to emotional disorders. Most promisingly, we have the benefit of much better drug therapy to alleviate acute symptoms, and we are developing more reliable information about the long-term impact of mothers' drug therapy on the health of their children. In addition, we are gaining more experience in how drug and non-drug therapies can best be used, singly and in combination.

Despite numerous improvements and better education, however, we are still faced with popular misconceptions that discourage women from seeking help. Every caregiver who has taken part in the treatment of a patient with an emotional disorder is aware that sometimes half the battle is fighting the patient's fear of the stigma that all too commonly attaches to seeking help and following treatment. Fortunately, the services of many professional caregivers in both hospital and community settings intersect with the concerns of pregnant and new mothers, and each of us in our own sphere can play a role in making it more acceptable for out patients to seek the help they need.

Each professional has the opportunity to help identify women at risk, to support and encourage women in seeking help, and to participate in an integrated treatment plan. Family practitioners often are the first caregivers to detect emotional or psychiatric problems and can intervene at an early stage. Obstetricians, by virtue of their involvement with difficult pregnancies, can often identify those women at high risk, whereas social workers and community health nurses often have the most frequent contact with postpartum mothers and families in distress. Counselors of all kinds who treat female patients are in a position to participate in pevention, assisting women to prepare before hand for the emotional demands of pregnancy. Each of us has an opportunity to help our patients address the complex emotional, familial, and social factors in pregnancy—to invite discussion around difficult situations, to encourage frank expression of feelings, to make connections between our patients and other professionals who can help them.

I have written this book to share the experience and insights gained in a psychiatric practice almost exclusively concerned with emotional disorders accompanying the female reproductive cycle. The sharing of such experience across disciplines has already helped in the development of a common approach to the treatment of various psychiatric disorders. As we continue to share the knowledge gained in our practices, we will achieve an increased awareness of and greater consistency in approach to the particular emotional disorders of pregnancy—which will surely aid our patients.

WHAT IS NORMAL AND WHAT IS NOT?

Deeply felt emotions and intense emotional highs and lows can be components of normal pregnancies. For this reason, it is easy for both women themselves and for their health practitioners to mistake the reality of an emotional disorder. In our North American society, too, extraordinary levels of stress are increasingly accepted as ordinary accompaniments to the demands of parenting and career building. Both the individual and the surrounding society place extreme expectations on young women to "have it all"—to be perfect mothers, partners, achievers. In this setting, a woman is reluctant to break ranks, to admit loss of control, or to acknowledge real feelings when they are in conflict with those positive feelings she expects and is expected by others to feel.

Psychotherapists and women themselves are beginning to acknowledge the depth of those feelings and to expand our definitions of "normal" and "abnormal." This kind of approach offers a challenge to both women and health care practitioners—for women, to recognize and express feelings openly and to seek help; for practitioners, to provide sensitive and comprehensive support that takes fully into consideration the bio/psycho/social model of care.

HOW TO USE THIS BOOK

The mental picture I have held throughout the writing of this book is that of a woman who may find help as she reads these pages. I imagine the most likely reader is a woman who herself has suffered a psychiatric disorder related to pregnancy or postpartum and is looking for greater understanding of what happened to her and why. Perhaps she is a woman who experienced a past pregnancy during which she felt emotionally troubled but never sought help and feels worried and uncertain as she faces a new pregnancy. My reader might also be a husband or partner—a new father who is baffled by unexpected emotional upheaval in the mother of their new infant. Or my reader might be a sister, a parent, or a friend, looking for some way to help a troubled loved one.

It is natural for any of these readers to look first for specifics—information on a particular kind of disorder, on the phases of pregnancy or postpartum, on the effects of medications. As you read about your specific area of interest, you will often find references to related material in other chapters. I encourage you to pursue these references as well, and to read the more general chapters for a broad understanding of the causes, treatment, and occurrence of emotional disorders in pregnancy and postpartum. In most chapters, I have included a short section entitled "What I Tell My Patients," which summarizes the issues and very general advice I most often find meaningful in particular circumstances. In reading the book, you will also find the stories of many women who are typical of my patients—the very women who formed my mental image of the women who might read my book—and you will find answers to some questions I am typically asked by my patients.

I imagine that, having read this book, my readers might be able to begin a dialogue—with their partner, with their friend, with their family doctor, with their counselor. I hope that the work I describe in this book will contribute to a lasting dialogue between women and health care professionals on the emotional realities of pregnancy and motherhood. I hope that troubled women who read this book will realize that there is no reason to feel stigmatized. I hope that by exchanging feelings, knowledge, and insights, we may someday create such an environment of confidence and trust that no woman will choose to suffer in silence.

PART I

PROBLEMS NEW MOTHERS MIGHT EXPERIENCE

CHAPTER 1

"IT WASN'T SUPPOSED TO BE LIKE THIS"

Psychological Problems in Pregnancy

WHAT I TELL MY PATIENTS

What I would like to tell my patients is that anxiety and mood changes in pregnancy are to be expected and generally do not require any professional help. However, a minority of women experience extreme symptoms of anxiety, obsessive-compulsive disorder, or psychosis, and these women need psychiatric help. When symptoms of anxiety or obsessive-compulsive disorder happen for the first time, the woman is often unable to recognize them for what they are because the whole experience is so new. And when there are emotional complications in pregnancy, it often becomes doubly difficult not only for her to recognize her turmoil but to verbalize her feelings to her partner or her family doctor.

When a pregnant woman is *dramatically* ill, either physically or emotionally, her family will be aware of it and will see that she gets help. But many psychiatric illnesses, although devastating to the woman who is suffering, are not so readily apparent to the family. A woman with a prior history of psychiatric illness may be afraid to acknowledge that she needs care again at this special family time. A woman who suffers psychiatric illness for the first time in pregnancy may be completely shocked by what

---

3

is happening and reluctant to seek help. Furthermore, nobody ever wants to talk about any negative feelings that one might feel during pregnancy. Pregnancy is expected to be a happy event, and therefore it becomes problematic to speak openly about troubling emotions—even to loved ones.

Remember, though, that as the expectant mother, you play a pivotal role in your family. You have to be emotionally well— not only to carry the pregnancy to term, but to have the emotional strength to care for your baby. It is your responsibility to look and ask for appropriate help. However, it is not your fault if you do not recognize that emotionally you are not doing well.

My hope is that women who have disturbing emotions will become aware, through reading this book, that they are not isolated and alone. The problems they are experiencing have been experienced by many other women, and treatment is available. The first step may be the hardest, but it is important to speak openly and frankly with your family physician, community nurse, or other professional counselor about your difficulties. There is plenty of help available—you only need to ask for it— and you may be surprised at how supportive people around you will be.

The basic impetus for this book came from my patients, who said that they needed to understand whether what they were feeling was normal or not and to feel validated in what they were experiencing. In most cases, of course, the symptoms and signs of pregnancy are so new that the woman is not really in a position to differentiate normal symptoms from abnormal, alarming ones. Furthermore, as any woman who has experienced more than one pregnancy knows, each pregnancy has its own particular quality. While it is natural to feel anxious about the new sensations of a first pregnancy, a woman might in fact sail through her first pregnancy—both physically and emotionally—only to experience difficulties in a subsequent pregnancy.

Any pregnancy is a major landmark in a woman's life. The first pregnancy, particularly, is fraught with anxieties, and I shall address these common fears first. In this chapter, my aim is to provide an understanding of emotional distress that might lead a pregnant woman to seek professional help, whether from a psychologist, a psychiatrist, a social worker, or another type of counselor, depending on the type of emotional problems she experiences.

NORMAL UPS AND DOWNS

From the very first time a woman thinks about conception, she does so with a sense of excitement, of anticipation, and also uncertainty about whether or not she will achieve this particular goal she has set, in most cases in agreement with a partner. Not surprisingly, the circumstances surrounding conception are important. Is the baby wanted? Has conception occurred in a relationship that is rocky? These issues are important because they reflect the woman's feelings towards the baby-to-be even before conception takes place.

A woman who has been planning a pregnancy with enthusiastic support of her partner will likely be overjoyed at learning that she is pregnant. On the other hand, a woman who is experiencing difficulty in her relationship might respond to the news of pregnancy in a very different way. For example, Joan, a 35-year-old single woman who came to see me recently, became pregnant by a man she had dated very briefly. The man then disappeared from her life completely. Her dilemma was whether or not to continue the pregnancy. "I've decided to have this baby," Joan said when she first came to see me, "but I am really anxious and worried about even the smallest little change I'm experiencing emotionally and in my body." She is not alone. Today, many women make their own decision to become pregnant or to continue the pregnancy, whether or not they have a partner in their lives. Needless to say, such a pregnancy presents its own difficulties to the mother.

That many emotional changes accompany pregnancy is normal and to be expected. It is almost taken for granted that the prevailing feeling will be, "I am so happy about this!" In reality, however, one does not *always* expect to be happy when pregnancy occurs. Normal emotional response to pregnancy varies according to the kind of symptoms the woman has, how advanced the pregnancy is, and the circumstances and family setting into which the baby will arrive.

Many pregnancies today are planned and anticipated. And in general, they happen amid cultural expectations that pregnancy and family life will be joyful and positive. What's more, the popular media—which seem to have so much to do with women's self-image—

present an idealized picture in which All is Possible for the woman of today. Magazines tell us and television shows us that not only can today's woman savor every moment of childbearing and child rearing, she can do all of this at the same time she enchants her husband, climbs a steep career ladder, and satisfies even the most critical parents or in-laws with her ability to run an organized and attractive home.

It's well for women to be aware of these stereotypes at the outset of pregnancy because our popular culture confronts women with an array of conflicting—and extraordinarily stressful—demands. In the last hundred years, pregnancy has "come out of the closet," but now it's dressed in designer clothes—trappings of role expectations and pressures that can provoke serious emotional conflicts during pregnancy and beyond.

Recently, Louise, a 31-year-old secretary, consulted me. She was determined to climb the corporate ladder and was working during the day, taking evening courses, and trying to be supportive of her husband, who was going to school. She told me, "I didn't realize that the nausea and the vomiting that I'm experiencing with pregnancy would make me run to the bathroom every few minutes. Will I need to run out during my evening class? How will I handle the demands of my working day? If only I'd known this before, if someone had warned me, maybe I'd have been prepared. I'm happy that I'm pregnant, but I've also been worried—how much longer can I carry on like this? I'm so glad you told me that after ten or twelve weeks of pregnancy, I'm likely to get beyond this."

It might be said that at the same time women are "allowed" all kinds of lifestyle options, the very wealth of options and the perception that all of them can be claimed without strain is itself a source of stress. Maureen, a 29-year-old lawyer's wife who had moved to the West Coast, came to me recently, having experienced obstetrical problems in her first trimester. She was the owner of a riding stable, and was also a riding instructor, and now it was mandatory for her to have complete bed rest in order to avoid problems in the pregnancy. Maureen was very much preoccupied with how her business would run without her, especially given the monumental task of finding someone to replace her in this rather specialized field. The source of stress in a situation like this is obvious. Careful planning and the support of her spouse were needed both to handle the practical business problems she faced and to care for her developing baby.

Discussions throughout this book will make it apparent that the *exact* triggers to extremes of disruptive emotions are seldom clear. At different times, different factors have a bearing on emotional states—one's personal and family medical and psychiatric history, hormonal changes in one's body, the strength of one's personal relationships and support systems, and the stress of circumstances and surroundings. Sandra, a 33-year-old woman who became pregnant again when her first child was 18 months of age came to me filled with both joy and trepidation. Sandra and her husband had planned to have a second child, but not so soon. The pregnancy created a set of new problems just as they had moved to a new city. Since she had more job qualifications than her husband, Sandra was the family's primary breadwinner, and they had expected that she could easily find work. Her husband was unemployed and worked in a trade where jobs were unpredictable. Had there been no problems in the pregnancy, their situation might have been handled easily by finding the right day-care situation for their toddler while she started a new job. However, Sandra developed insomnia, which escalated in her first trimester. She was extremely fatigued and felt drained of energy. Unable to concentrate after her sleepless nights, she had difficulty interviewing for jobs. This, along with the demands of looking after her 18-month-old son at the end of the day, added to her stress and contributed to the tension between Sandra and her husband. Finally, the only solution was for Sandra to stay home all day, looking after the child, while her husband actively looked for work.

Sandra's case is an example of how demands of a difficult pregnancy can create stressful changes in family dynamics and relationships. Relatively speaking, these can be small and minor problems of pregnancy. But the woman who has a personal or family history of emotional problems or has received psychiatric care in the past must make sure that her doctor is aware of her history so that she can receive supportive care throughout the pregnancy. And no woman who experiences early pregnancy should underestimate the stress that can be generated by role conflicts and societal expectations or ignore the fact that excessive stress can contribute to serious emotional disturbance.

In the early months of pregnancy, you'll be seeking advice and starting to follow regimens that benefit your baby's health and keep you as healthy and comfortable as possible. At the same time that you're paying careful attention to nutrition and exercise, and perhaps getting special advice on medical conditions you may have, you should also be paying particular attention to your emotional state and well-being. Just as pregnancy has come out of the closet, so too the complex issue of emotional and mental well-being is beginning to be understood and accepted by the public as a medical condition that merits understanding and proper care.

THE NORMAL CONCERNS OF
PREGNANCY AND POSTPARTUM

It's important to recognize that pregnancy and postpartum, as times of real change, are naturally also times of strong emotions—fear, anxiety, and sadness, as well as great happiness. During pregnancy and postpartum, every woman, particularly a first-time mother, experiences change on every conceivable level: in physical appearance and sensation, in emotional concerns, in life status within her family, community, and work environment, in daily routine and level of activities, both physical and intellectual. Questions and concerns, some quite specific to a particular point in the pregnancy and others quite general, are inevitable and quite normal. In addition, as medical science and technology give us more information and form an ever greater part of our daily lives, we find we have more concerns. For instance, now that ultrasound and amniocentesis are widely available, the pregnant woman is prey to the high anxiety that can accompany these tests as well as benefiting from the reassurance their results can provide.

From the time they first contemplate pregnancy, women are concerned about the baby they will carry and give birth to—its health and well-being, its future, and its effect on the rest of the family, mother included. And while pregnancy and postpartum have always been times of some questioning and concern for the prospective mother (and father!), these days, the societal expectation that a woman will be an exemplary mother, an attractive, sexy, caring wife, usually while holding down a successful job outside the home, puts an even greater burden on the pregnant woman.

Given all these changes and concerns, it's no wonder that a new or prospective mother often feels like a bundle of anxiety, or gets a bit blue, or finds herself wondering how she ever got into this situation. This is all perfectly normal. Although no two women will have the exact same experiences while pregnant or after—and while the same woman may have completely different experiences from one pregnancy to the next—all women become anxious, blue, sad at one time or another. And every woman brings her own concerns to this time of her life. If she's been pregnant before and had any complications, she's likely to worry that the same circumstances will prevail again. If a close friend or relative had difficulties of one sort or another, she may fear that she too will have to be put on bed rest, or give herself insulin injections, or spend nights trying to comfort a colicky baby. And if she's had any physical or emotional problems, it's natural for her to be concerned that they may resurface now, to threaten her happiness.

Most women have questions, concerns, and worries as they face pregnancy. And for the most part, these are well within the range of normal and relatively easy to deal with. As we will see, worrying about the results of a test or how your childless friends will relate to you is perfectly normal: it's only when you find it impossible to shake a par-ticular anxiety and your worry upsets your routine, or when one sleep-less night becomes weeks of insomnia, or an occasional crying jag becomes a permanently hopeless mood that the situation has become abnormal and help is called for.

Dozens of books have been written to help women understand what is happening to their bodies and emotions during pregnancy and to help them prepare for childbirth, and it would serve no purpose for me to attempt to duplicate the information found in those books here. However, the questions that follow are typical of the normal concerns of the emotionally healthy pregnant or postpartum woman, and should serve as a guideline for the range of concerns that may be facing you as you journey through pregnancy:

Before conception: Is this the right time for pregnancy? Will I be able to get pregnant? Can we afford to have a baby now? Do I really want a child, or do I just like babies? Will I be a good mother? Will I lose my identity as a person when I become a mother? Will my marriage be as happy as it is now?

In the first trimester: Will I miscarry? Will I have horrible morning sickness? Is the pregnancy progressing properly? Will I be able to stick to a diet that's healthy for my baby? Am I putting on too much weight too quickly? When should I tell my family? Will I have to rethink my career and perhaps put it on hold? In addition to these questions, women in the first trimester find themselves wondering about the signs and symptoms of early pregnancy—the disappearing waistline, the fre-quent urination, the fatigue—and about environmental influences on their developing child. Is it safe to work at a computer terminal? Do we have to get rid of our cat? Is it safe to sleep under an electric blan-ket? What do I do about my allergy medicine, and what about the wine I drank before I knew I was pregnant?

In the second trimester: Why are my gums bleeding? Why don't I feel the baby's movements yet? What will the ultrasound examination show? What about the amniocentesis? Now that I'm starting to lose my figure, will my partner find me less attractive? Is it safe to have sex? What will I do if my placenta previa doesn't migrate up and I have to go on bed rest? Is it normal to be more scared than thrilled at the prospect of twins? Why am I becoming so forgetful? Will I be able to keep working?

In the third trimester: I have a searing pain down the back of my leg—is that normal? Are those Braxton-Hicks contractions, or am I going into premature labor? Will my husband and I be able to go on one last vacation, or is it tempting fate to travel? Will we get the baby's room done before she arrives? What if my doctor isn't available when I go into labor? What will we do if the baby doesn't turn—I don't want to have a C-section! My boss still doesn't seem to realize that I'm going on maternity leave; will my job be here when I get back? Will I lose control when I go into labor?

Postpartum: Is my baby healthy? Why am I so tired? Will I be able to nurse? What if I can't lift the baby after the C-section? What if I can't quiet the baby? Will I drop the baby when I'm bathing him? Will my baby like the baby-sitter better than me if I go back to work? Will I ever feel like having sex again? Will sex ever feel good again? Will I be able to lose all the weight I put on?

Throughout the pregnancy: Is this the right time? Will my baby be healthy? Will my partner still love me? Will my baby be smart? Do we have enough space—and can we afford more if we need it? Will I be able to deal with my first child and the new baby? Will my stretch marks go away? Will I become my mother? Will I be a good mother?

Now let me start to discuss what happens when a woman's concerns and behavior go beyond the normal zone and jeopardize her life or the life of the baby she carries.

In this chapter, I will first discuss the less severe emotional problems associated with pregnancies and then consider the extremes of emotional disturbance that may affect a woman's ability to function normally in the first trimester. It is important to recognize the range of emotional disorders, from less severe to more severe, so that you will know when to seek help. The less severe emotional disorders associated with pregnancy are often part of the normal feelings of pregnancy and do not require professional help. I want to point out the differences between the various emotional disorders and also to provide reassurance that *severe emotional disorders can be treated and alleviated*.

COMMON NAUSEA

Let me first talk about nausea, which is a normal occurrence caused by body changes as the pregnancy advances; associated headache is also common. During the first weeks—or even days—of the first trimester, most women—over 50 percent—will experience changes in their appetite and feel queasiness in their stomach, similar to the motion sickness they might experience on a boat or plane ride. This queasy feeling can make the woman feel that she is going to vomit. Often food does not interest her. She may have a total aversion to certain types of food, and the moment she attempts to eat any food, she might feel nausea again. The nausea is often more pronounced if the woman eats nothing, and so the vicious cycle continues. Many women report that nausea is more common towards the morning, when the stomach is empty, and again towards evening, when additional stresses of attending to other members of the family and preparing the meal are likely. The nausea and vomiting usually begin to abate by the twelfth week, lingering only occasionally into the second trimester.

When a woman first visits her doctor to confirm her suspicions that she is pregnant, she is very likely to be asked, "Do you feel like you're going to throw up?" Nausea in early pregnancy is so characteristic that her doctor checks for this sign. Unfortunately, this natural question often has the effect of setting the stage for anxiety, as the woman, particularly the first-time mother, assumes that pregnancy *means* she is going to be vomiting frequently.

During the first trimester, the woman is often unable to rest properly and fatigue sets in, which can make the nausea and vomiting worse. Very rarely, though, does the nausea and vomiting require any medical support other than reassurance and a briefing on the kinds of food that should be eaten. In most cases, the problem then resolves and vomiting does not become a major emotional, or for that matter, physical problem. Reassurance and affirmation that the symptoms are common often come from a patient's mother, sister, or women friends.

HYPEREMESIS: WHEN NAUSEA AND VOMITING ARE SEVERE

As I have discussed, a moderate amount of nausea and vomiting is part of the expected norm in pregnancy. Often, family stories retold years later include the words, "When I was expecting you, it just seemed that I couldn't keep anything down." However, some women experience *hyperemesis gravidarum*, an extreme degree of nausea with vomiting that is dangerous to both their health and their babies during pregnancy. This results in severe imbalance of electrolytes, significant weight loss, ketosis, acetonuria, and/or damage to the internal organs. Hyperemesis gravidarum is a rare condition, occurring in approximately one in a thousand pregnancies. Whereas the normal nausea and vomiting of pregnancy usually stop sometime early in the second trimester, the severe vomiting of hyperemesis continues throughout the pregnancy. The vomiting and nausea may be so severe that a woman may require repeated hospitalizations so that she can be properly fed through intravenous feedings.

What Causes Hyperemesis?

Specialists hold different views about the causes of hyperemesis. Those who see it as solely a physical condition attribute the severe nausea and vomiting to shifting hormone levels. Those who see it as a psychological condition view hyperemesis as the result of conflict in a woman who would prefer not to be pregnant but has nevertheless opted to continue her pregnancy. The theory is that in these cases, the pregnancy is unwanted or unplanned, and the woman feels trapped or resentful. Fearing that her feelings are abnormal, unacceptable, or incomprehensible, she may be unable to talk about them. The physical act of vomiting, then, becomes her body's way of symbolically rejecting the pregnancy.

My own view is that internal conflicts usually—but not always—have a role to play in hyperemesis. Consequently, hyperemesis is more likely to occur in women who have mixed feelings about the pregnancy and the changes that the responsibility of child care will make in their lives. In these cases, the pregnant woman may unconsciously develop hyperemesis as an "acceptable" way of both getting the reassurance of medical attention and diverting her attention from the real issues that are causing her conflict. On the other hand, I have also known a few cases of hyperemesis in which pregnant women experienced the extreme symptoms of hyperemesis in the complete absence of any detectable psychological or lifestyle conflicts.

What Can Be Done for Hyperemesis?

A pregnant woman's obstetrician or family doctor invariably asks her if she is feeling nauseated or is vomiting, and a woman should be very clear about the frequency and severity of her symptoms when she answers the question. Sometimes, nausea can be relieved by eating smaller, more frequent meals, changing bowel habits to avoid constipation, and getting adequate rest. In addition, the symptoms are sometimes relieved once the woman has discussed them with her doctor and understands that their occurrence in early pregnancy is quite common. Often, less severe nausea and vomiting is discussed in prenatal classes, and advice is given there about diet and food consumption. This can be tremendously helpful. The woman's partner may be able to take over preparation of meals, which is often very helpful to a woman who cannot bear the smells of different foods. Basically, the focus at this time is on helping to reduce the woman's fears and keeping her properly informed. These measures alone can help a woman complete the first trimester as comfortably, and with as little nausea and vomiting, as possible.

True hyperemesis, however, usually requires hospitalization. Once in the hospital, the expectant mother will receive intravenous feeding, supplemented by vitamins and minerals. In these situations, it's recommended that the woman get plenty of bed rest, try to relax, and limit visitors. Her doctor should involve a psychiatrist to help the woman explore issues of conflict. Severe cases might require repeated hospitalizations to ensure that the woman is nourished sufficiently to carry her baby to term.

In one case of hyperemesis, the course of events unfolded as follows.

MARIA'S STORY

Recently, I was asked to see Maria, a 28-year-old graduate student who had been hospitalized for treatment of her symptoms of extreme nausea and vomiting in early pregnancy. Her family physician had referred her to me to help investigate possible underlying causes. Her husband, also a graduate student at the local university, was present throughout the interview and appeared to be very supportive. Despite the physical discomfort she had been experiencing, Maria appeared to be extraordinarily cheerful and tried to convince me that everything was absolutely perfect in their family situation and especially with regard to the expected child.

The next day I received an emergency call from the nurse on the ward, saying that Maria was sobbing uncontrollably. When I talked with Maria, she "confessed" to me that since her husband had insisted on being present at the previous day's interview, she had not been able to speak openly.

Maria told me that although she and her partner had been together for many years, their marriage was quite recent and had taken place as a result of this pregnancy. A highly ambitious woman, Maria had always planned to do well for herself by getting an education. However, she had a student loan debt of more than $10,000, and she felt it unlikely that she would be able to return to graduate school and finish her work after the birth of this baby.

Even before the problems connected to the pregnancy, the relationship between Maria and her husband had been quite rocky. Her husband had physically abused her several times, to the extent that she had needed treatment in the hospital's emergency department. Just prior to the current admission, he had roughly pushed her down the hallway, and Maria had hoped that somehow this trauma would result in a miscarriage.

Her husband had been quite unhappy when Maria's pregnancy had forced them to marry, though his attitude became more positive as the pregnancy continued. Nevertheless, his physical abuse of Maria became more frequent during pregnancy, as happens all too commonly in such situations. In this particular couple, it was obvious that Maria's symptoms of hyperemesis were closely associated with her relationship with her husband. Consequently, the symptoms waxed and waned as the pregnancy went on. She eventually developed a severe case of nausea and vomiting and with this, she was admitted to the hospital.

In talking with Maria, I realized how truly trapped she felt and how much she wanted this pregnancy to end. A Roman Catholic, she did not believe in terminating the pregnancy, and she had realized some days before that she should get some professional help in dealing with her problems. She wasn't certain how to go about being put in touch with a psychiatrist, but in this roundabout way, her emergency admission brought her into my care.

I continued to see Maria throughout her pregnancy and focused supportively on interpersonal conflicts. Eventually she and her husband were also referred to a marital therapy clinic for further treatment. Despite her difficulties with vomiting and hyperemesis throughout the pregnancy, Maria gave birth to a bouncing eight-pound girl. She has decided to wait another few years, she tells me, before she attempts another pregnancy.

Maria's story is one that shows a significant association between psychological and marital conflicts and her extreme physical symptoms. Conflicts like this are not always associated with hyperemesis, however, and each case requires careful investigation so that the right avenues or therapy can be found and followed. It should also be emphasized that a woman who has been incredibly healthy before pregnancy can still have hyperemesis.

A QUESTION YOU MIGHT HAVE
ABOUT EXTREME VOMITING

? *I'm just beginning the second trimester of my first pregnancy and I've been desperately sick for weeks with nausea and vomiting. I haven't wanted to tell anyone just how bad I've been feeling because I've heard that sickness like this means you subconsciously don't want your baby. This baby is coming right on schedule, and I just can't believe that I'm unhappy about it, and neither will my husband.*

What you've heard is a very simplified version of just one of several theories about the cause of extreme nausea and vomiting, or hyperemesis. Hyperemesis tends to occur more commonly in women who are experiencing some kind of conflict or difficulty around the circumstances of their pregnancy. However, hyperemesis *has* occurred in women whose environments are entirely positive and supportive.

Let's take first things first. Your family doctor needs to know about your symptoms. Some first trimesters are rockier than others, and the sickness you're having may still be within "normal" limits and perhaps can be alleviated with changes as simple as getting proper rest, making minor changes in your diet, and so on. On the other hand, if this is truly a case of hyperemesis, you and your baby are going to need nutritional support to see you through this successfully. Don't be surprised if your doctor also suggests referral to a psychiatrist—this is good medical practice for the investigation of hyperemesis.

No matter how positively one anticipates pregnancy, it can nevertheless be a stressful time. Different women are affected differently by the stresses of adjustment to being a mother, such as applying for pregnancy leave, reorganizing the home front, and thinking of child care, even though it's still months away. I'd encourage you not only to seek prompt medical advice, but to speak frankly to your doctor or counselor about your emotions and feelings. It's easy to be bombarded with friends' well-meaning advice and sometimes misinformation. You may be suffering from just an ordinary case of first trimester vomiting and nausea which, in your own view, seems severe and have become even more worried when a friend advises you that severe vomiting is a serious problem. Or you might experience marked vomiting and nausea that you are considering telling your doctor about. Don't let friends or family scare you or deter you from getting the care you and your baby need. The best practice is to keep your doctor well informed about what you are experiencing and let your doctor give you professional, objective advice.

NORMAL RESPONSES TO FOOD AND EATING DURING PREGNANCY

A woman's first clue that she is pregnant is often a distinct new food preference, or "food fetish." Some women seek out foods that are bland, while others may seek out foods that are spicy or pungent in taste. These early indications that a woman is pregnant are part of her body's response to changing hormones, and are entirely normal. The complexity of changing hormones eventually affects all aspects of a woman's functions, including the appetite center in the brain.

The baby developing inside the mother's womb naturally requires additional nourishment to grow. The mother's increased appetite, usually a feature of the second trimester, is the way her body encourages her to take in the additional food now needed. Even in the first trimester, however, the tiny developing embryo requires extra nutrition. Accordingly, many doctors routinely prescribe a vitamin supplement to the woman whose pregnancy has just been diagnosed—not because she is likely to be missing vitamins, but simply to make sure that she and her baby get the proper balance of vitamins and minerals.

Recently, I saw a woman who is a health care professional and whose sister had severe problems with bulimia—excessive eating followed by self-induced vomiting. My patient was in her second trimester and concerned that her increased food consumption was a sign of an eating disorder like her sister's. After talking with her about her eating patterns, I was able to reassure her that she was experiencing the typical and healthy increased appetite of the second trimester.

The natural and necessary weight gain of pregnancy is something that every expectant mother has to come to terms with. Our society places a great emphasis on slimness as a desirable feminine attribute, regardless of a woman's age or body build. Slimness itself has come to be equated with a healthy lifestyle, and many women are extremely alert to their smallest weight gain and exert a great deal of control to maintain their "ideal" weight. Nature has planned a healthy pregnancy according to a different model, however, and medical professionals agree that a reasonable weight gain is an expected and essential component of pregnancy, both for the mother and the fetus. With good prenatal counseling and awareness of the nutritional requirements of pregnancy, most women come to enjoy a new self-image of healthy expectant motherhood.

Nevertheless, many women who are very careful about their diet and make a point of exercising regularly to maintain fitness become anxious when they suddenly begin to crave the ice cream and chocolate that they have seldom allowed themselves to indulge in before. Some women give themselves "permission" to indulge in "forbidden foods," such as desserts and fried foods, on the grounds that this is such a special time in their lives. All this is quite normal!

For most people, their appearance and body image are closely linked to their identity, their sense of self, and thus, their level of self-confidence. Not surprisingly, then, many women are quite shocked by the growth of the abdomen and the widening of the hips that take place as pregnancy progresses. Some women may put off wearing maternity clothes for the longest time, attempting to disguise what they see as a "disgraceful" body. Again, these are quite normal, even expected, responses to pregnancy. It's important to keep in mind that for most people, no change in body image is easy to accept. Changes in body image, whether resulting from surgery, medical treatment, or pregnancy, can alter one's sense of ego. And in addition to the stresses of increasing weight and changing body shape, a young woman may also feel the anxiety associated with the practical need for and expense of maternity clothes.

Having discussed the normal range of issues seen in the pregnant woman's responses to food, eating, and body image, I would now like to introduce the more severe disorders relating to eating and body image during pregnancy. Although these severe psychiatric illnesses are relatively rare, they do exist and treatment should be sought early.

EATING DISORDERS

The stereotypes of popular culture have played many cruel jokes on today's women, and some of them become increasingly dangerous in pregnancy, when not just one, but two lives, are at stake. The female images in television and magazine advertising incessantly show that the "model" woman has the shape and weight of a girl in early adolescence. This is obviously not the shape that nature intended for the mature female of the species—and it is very far from the maternal shape required for a healthy pregnancy and the delivery of a healthy baby.

The eating disorders of *anorexia nervosa* and *bulimia* are tragic "fashion diseases" of the past few decades, and it took medical science some time to recognize that they are indeed physiological as well as psychological disorders. A woman with anorexia is driven by a distorted self-image to starve herself into a dangerously malnourished condition. Even when excessively thin, she sees herself as overweight and is terrified of gaining any weight at all. To reach her elusive goal of being "thin enough," a woman with anorexia must carry on a secretive campaign involving altered eating habits and excuses that will somehow hide from her family the fact that she is starving herself.

As in anorexia, in bulimia a woman has an exaggerated preoccupation with body image. With bulimia, however, the woman "binges,"— eating an enormous amount of food in a short period of time—and then compensates for doing so in a variety of ways: by making herself vomit, by taking laxatives or diuretics, by engaging in fasts or overly strict diets, and/or by exercising excessively. Bulimia is another secretive disorder, and one in which the woman's appearance may offer no clues of ill health to her family. Unlike a woman with the starved appearance of anorexia, the woman with bulimia may be of normal body weight—a weight she maintains through her abnormal eating practices.

At the other extreme, *obesity* is also an eating disorder that can have grave health implications in pregnancy. An obese person is one who seemingly has no control over appetite and food consumption and weighs at least 20 percent more than the normal body weight for his or her age and height. The health consequences of excessive weight were recognized much earlier than those of excessive thinness. Clearly, a pregnant woman with obesity is at extra risk of severe heart and respiratory complications, and while she is eating more than enough, she may not be eating the best diet for her baby's development.

Eating Disorders and Pregnancy

Women with the eating disorders of anorexia and bulimia very often have difficulty becoming pregnant. One of the characteristic symptoms of these disorders is *amenorrhea*—cessation of menstruation. In addition to affecting the woman's overall health, both anorexia and bulimia disturb the normal production and functioning of hormones. Whether or not the woman with either disorder fully ceases having periods, her menstrual cycles may be so disrupted as to interfere with her ability to conceive. In fact, a percentage of infertile women will have an undisclosed history of either bulimia or anorexia, both of which can affect the menstrual cycle.

The majority of eating disorders in pregnancy represent the continuation of preexisting disorders. Very few cases of a woman experiencing an eating disorder for the first time during pregnancy have been reported. There is also some suggestion that women with extreme cases of vomiting or hyperemesis may have had a history of an eating disorder prior to the pregnancy. The natural healthy weight gain of pregnancy is a punishing dilemma for the woman with anorexia or bulimia. And sometimes, the normal stresses of pregnancy, such as coming to terms with motherhood and increased responsibility, may contribute to the uncontrolled food consumption of the obese woman.

It is unclear whether eating disorders occur more frequently during pregnancy. However, what is clear is that both these disorders can affect the ability of a woman to bear a child successfully.

Assuming that a woman with any of the three eating disorders I have described is able to carry out her pregnancy, these disorders affect her health and the long-term health of her unborn child. Even with the most positive attitude towards the pregnancy and expected child, women with eating disorders are seldom able to alter their self-destructive behavior on their own. They need both the sympathetic awareness of and support from their families, and also the professional resources of trained counselors to assist them.

Because women with eating disorders have a distorted view of their body, the health-care giver must have available correct and appropriate information regarding the healthy range of weight gain during pregnancy and what is acceptable versus unacceptable behavior in the context of an eating disorder, for the woman and for her growing baby. It can be confusing to a patient when she receives inconsistent information from health-care professionals, since she will also balance the information against her own sense of the weight at which she feels comfortable and can live with given peer or societal pressures.

What Causes Eating Disorders?

There are various explanations for the appearance of eating disorders. Clearly, powerful popular stereotypes of the ideal feminine body image may contribute to the development of anorexia and bulimia. The question of why some women are plagued by these disorders while other women are not is more complex. Some researchers suggest that by forcing herself to maintain a preadolescent body shape, an anorexic woman may be trying to avoid conflicts over sexual identity or the demands of sexual maturity. Others have suggested that the emotional profiles of one or the other of the woman's parents are factors, and there are even some suggestions that imbalances in the body chemistry may predispose some women to these disorders.

Similarly, a combination of causes is suggested for obesity. Heredity is a major factor, as demonstrated by studies of obesity in families. Other possible factors are the individual's metabolism and the way the individual's nervous system processes messages about appetite.

What Can Be Done for Eating Disorders?

The recognition of eating disorders as behaviors that can be treated is fairly recent, and effective treatment programs are beginning to be developed. The usual first step is supportive psychological counseling, which may continue on a long-term basis until the individual establishes patterns of successful eating behavior. Both individual counseling and group therapy can help the individual recognize inappropriate behavior and then examine and practice alternate behaviors. Treatment of eating disorders involves the patient's adjusting to a new self-image, and she may need supportive care to deal with problems, such as depression or anxiety, which might accompany the new realities she is facing. The dietician also has an important role to play in treatment of eating disorders.

Extreme cases of anorexia usually require hospitalization for both medical and psychiatric treatment, and extreme cases of obesity may also be treated in hospital. In severe cases of eating disorders, antidepressant medications may be recommended. When a woman with eating disorders becomes pregnant, it's especially important for her baby's welfare that she seek treatment. This is how one anorexic woman came to receive care for her eating disorder in her first trimester:

JOANNE'S STORY

Joanne was a 32-year-old dental hygienist of Italian origin, married to a construction worker. In her family, food was accorded a great deal of importance, both in itself and as the social focus of family gatherings. Joanne, however, rebelled against this. Her family and her colleagues found her to be extraordinarily thin, and Joanne always found some excuse or another to explain why she was not hungry at mealtimes. She made a point of not being around the home at dinner time and eventually came to avoid family gatherings.

Joanne and her husband planned her pregnancy, but when she became pregnant, she carried on her eating habits unchanged. Joanne's anorexia was not identified until her family doctor, who had diagnosed her pregnancy, also detected some abnormalities about her eating patterns and referred her to me. I learned that the most important thing in Joanne's thinking was being thin. She regarded her mother, who was just slightly over-weight, as "repulsive," and she was terrified that if she gained even five pounds, her husband would leave her. Joanne was so committed to her thinness that she was a "secret eater," hiding small bits of food, and she scrupulously weighed the small amount that she ate—but basically what she was doing was starving herself.

When she became pregnant, she became obsessed with the fact that she would now gain weight. She checked her appear-ance constantly in the mirror and weighed herself repeatedly. The illness progressed so rapidly in the first trimester that she al-most stopped eating completely. She was admitted to hospital for a week to be fed intravenously so that she could be suffi-ciently nourished to maintain her pregnancy.

In addition to psychiatric care, Joanne received additional supportive therapy from nurses, psychologists, and a dietitian from the hospital's Eating Disorders Clinic. Her weight was main-tained appropriate to her pregnancy, and after about three weeks, she felt she could manage the diet at home. For the balance of her pregnancy, she returned to the hospital for weekly visits to the dietician and a psychologist.

Through counseling, Joanne developed an understanding of the importance of being well and avoiding excessive dieting during pregnancy, and she gave birth to a healthy baby girl. She has had two subsequent pregnancies and suffered from anorexia during neither. In between pregnancies, however, she had inter-vals of struggling again with her eating disorder, but with coun-seling and support, she has for the most part brought her eating disorder under control.

To come to an understanding of this disease, and most importantly, to control it, is a difficult task as we have seen. Joanne is a patient who exemplifies two important messages about eating disorders. First, al-though her disease was diagnosed and treated, she had a few relapses. However, with proper help from professionals—a psychologist, who used techniques of behavior modification therapy, a dietician, who weighed the patient daily, and a supportive counselor—the illness was brought under control during her pregnancies, and she was able to give birth to healthy infants.

A QUESTION YOU MIGHT HAVE
ABOUT EATING DISORDERS

? *I've read about anorexia nervosa, and I'm sure that my sister has this condition. She's been married for a year and says she's planning to get pregnant. Is it possible for women with anorexia nervosa to become pregnant? Would her baby be healthy?*

Women with severe anorexia nervosa stop having periods and, in less severe cases, they usually have irregularities in their menstrual cycles that interfere with fertility. However, it is possible for an anorexic woman to become pregnant and when this happens, a major concern is that the mother receive sufficient nutrition to bring a healthy baby to term. Women who cannot do this on their own may have to be hospitalized in order to be nourished with intravenous feedings.

Evidently, your sister's thinness or eating habits have made you suspect anorexia, and if this is the case, she needs supportive understanding. Anorexics usually develop habits of secrecy to hide their near-starvation from their family, and you might not have much luck tackling the issue with her head-on. Since she and her husband want to have a family, you might explore with her the need for careful nutrition and sensible weight gain in pregnancy and encourage her to speak with her family doctor now about her general health status and eating habits. Her family doctor should be in a position to suggest where behavioral support may be available in your community.

DEPRESSION DURING PREGNANCY

In daily conversation, people often talk about feeling "depressed" when they describe quite normal lows in their range of emotions—disappointment, occasional pessimism, sadness related to a specific event, and so on. In medical terms, however, *depression* refers to a mood disorder in which one's low mood has become so pronounced and continuous that it disrupts normal functioning,

All pregnant women must make some psychological adjustments—

some of them more difficult than others. What many women do not know, and so need to learn from their friends and loved ones, is that the special joy of pride and accomplishment in pregnancy is likely to be accompanied by feelings of insecurity and uncertainty. While their body is obviously affected by the changes of pregnancy, the psyche is, too. Even in the best and easiest pregnancies, it is common for women to experience a kind of "mourning" for the youthful girlhood they are unequivocally leaving behind, as well as for a lifestyle that will be forever changed when the baby arrives.

The woman who has chosen to delay pregnancy in order to get ahead in her career may find herself quite isolated and insecure when the planned pregnancy finally gets underway. Both female and male co-workers and superiors may place unrealistic expectations on her performance, and she may find the interests and concerns of her peers at work quite removed from her own new situation.

Minor Depressions and Mood Changes in the First Trimester

Within the context of the normal range of human emotions, depression—the feelings of a person who is extremely unhappy about a certain situation or circumstances, and then comes out of his mood state when the situation or circumstance has changed—is very common. Rarely, however, is this mood pervasive or long-lasting, and rarely does it interfere with the person's functioning on a daily basis.

By the same token, feeling extraordinarily happy under certain circumstances is also a normal part of the range of human emotions. Consider what typically happens when you have achieved a goal such as getting a new job or passing an examination: you are elated; friends celebrate with you; it is a particularly joyful time. When it is over, you once again feel "normal." Thus, there is usually a balance in a person's life between these two extremes of being happy and unhappy.

Because pregnancy is associated with changes in one's body, in one's life circumstances, and in family dynamics, especially marital relationships, it is common for one to experience mood changes in response. These mood changes can range from being extraordinarily happy and euphoric to being very upset, angry, and depressed over being pregnant, especially if the pregnancy is unplanned. No great deal of attention need be paid to these fluctuations, nor is there any reason for the woman to do anything particular about them except to experience them as part of pregnancy. One would expect that she would receive normal family support when she is feeling down, and one would likewise expect that her euphoria and happiness would also be a shared event.

When pregnancy occurs under trying circumstances, however, the unhappiness may persist, and the woman may want to talk with various health-care professionals about this unhappiness, where it comes from, and what she can do for it. A short-term, supportive, focused therapy may be helpful in treating minor depressions, which usually have their origins in psychosocial factors, for example, loss of employment, a death in the family, or a move to another city. The partner may help by showing understanding and empathy for the pregnant woman. Family members may want to help indirectly and directly by offering such assistance as baby-sitting or cooking. With appropriate help, the woman will then come out of this mood state and continue to lead a life that enables her to adjust to her pregnancy.

Now let us focus on what happens when depressive mood states are extreme and explore the kind of treatment that is available if a woman experiences a major depression.

Major Depression and Pregnancy

Major depression during pregnancy affects only between 4 and 12 percent of women, in contrast to depression in the postpartum period, which strikes some 12 to 28 percent of new mothers. However, when depression does occur early in pregnancy, there is increased likelihood that postpartum depression will also develop. And if conception takes place while a woman is in a depressed state, her symptoms may continue throughout the pregnancy and into the postpartum period. (See Chapter Five for discussion of postpartum depression.)

The symptoms of depression are both physical and emotional. The woman may experience sleeping disturbances, consistently waking in the early morning hours and being unable to fall back asleep easily, which leads to exhaustion. Along with physical exhaustion, she may have an unusual increase or decrease in appetite and usually feels a total loss of sexual energy as well.

Emotionally, a depressed woman may feel out of control, experience unpredictable tearfulness, and have spontaneous crying spells that occur without any obvious cause. She may feel a pervasive sense of sadness or melancholy, a weary anger, or general despair. If you are a newly expectant mother, you should be aware of the symptoms of depression and talk with your doctor or counselor if these trouble you.

Karen's story shows how a very healthy pregnancy and birth experience became possible after a woman decided to speak with a friend about her fears of depression.

KAREN'S STORY

Karen was a 28-year-old occupational therapist who had worked in a hospital since her graduation from university five years before. Her family had a strong history of depression, and after Karen's own birth, her mother experienced postpartum depression. Because of this, Karen had always worried that she would someday suffer from severe depression, and she did not want to become pregnant for this reason.

When Karen confided her fears in a next-door neighbor, she learned that this friend had also experienced postpartum depression. The neighbor's advice was reassuring: she told Karen that depression could be treated and that fear of depression was no reason not to have children. With her neighbor's encouragement, Karen talked with her family doctor and was referred to me.

Karen's husband, who shared her concerns, decided to accompany her. We discussed their concerns, and I reassured them that Karen's family history did not preclude pregnancy. I stressed that should Karen become pregnant, it would be important for her emotional state to be continually monitored during the pregnancy and after the delivery. After a couple of sessions, they decided that they wanted to proceed with plans for a family, and Karen soon became pregnant.

Towards the end of her first trimester, Karen experienced all the classic signs of depressive illness—early morning wakening, loss of appetite, difficulty concentrating, extraordinary fatigue, and extremes of mood, especially one of depression. These symptoms had developed slowly and insidiously, but because Karen had remained under my care, it was not difficult to keep track of her symptoms. Her depression became so severe that I felt I had no choice but to prescribe antidepressant medication; however, I decided that hospitalization was not required. Karen was very concerned about the medication's effect on her baby, and an ultrasound was done to reassure her that the baby was developing normally. Karen stayed on a minimal dose of medication and was able to discontinue the antidepressant towards the end of her second trimester. Fortunately, she remained well and was not depressed for the rest of the pregnancy.

From the time that Karen had first talked with her neighbor, she had felt free of her old fears that she had previously kept secret. She felt confident in having sought treatment, and she saw no reason to hide her experience. In addition to speaking comfortably about her emotions with her husband, her family doctor, and me, she was also able to talk openly in her prenatal class about her illness and concerns. She spoke without feeling any embarrassment or stigma, and she felt that the open discussion that resulted had been a healthy experience for the group of pregnant women and their partners.

Following the birth of her healthy baby, Karen had quite intense postpartum blues, which then progressed to depression. It is common for women who experience depression in pregnancy to experience postpartum depression; thus, in light of Karen's depression in early pregnancy, this was not unexpected. Once again I prescribed antidepressant medication. Her mother had been very supportive of Karen's concerns and came to stay with the family for some weeks after the birth to help out. Karen stayed on the antidepressants for six months and decided not to nurse the baby.

Despite having to take medications, Karen found the overall experience of pregnancy and postpartum fulfilling. She and her husband are thrilled with their little son and have decided that their family is now complete; Karen did not want to go through another experience of being depressed in pregnancy or the postpartum period, despite many reassurances from her doctor and me that if she were to experience the illness again, it would be detected and treated early. She has now returned to work and is successfully balancing her role as a mother with the contribution she makes as an occupational therapist.

Second Trimester Depression

Studies show that mood changes occur much less frequently in the second trimester compared to the first and third trimester. In fact, the second trimester of pregnancy is usually a happy time for the woman, who now begins to experience the movement of the baby for the first time. Also, ultrasound examination is able to show the baby's body parts clearly—an exciting event for both the woman and her partner. If minor mood changes do occur around this time, supportive psycho-therapy is usually adequate.

My own clinical practice indicates that a degree of distress or de-pression related to second trimester has its origin in the women's im-mediate environment, or in reliving the anxieties or events of a past pregnancy. In particular, if a woman has had a second trimester loss, she is reminded of the loss again in her subsequent pregnancies. For this reason, I oftentimes see these women in my practice anywhere from 20th week right up to the middle or end of the third trimester. It must be understood that these mood changes or depressions are not "major depression," but rather mood changes or anxieties related to previous negative events in their pregnancy. In some cases ongoing marital discord may also contribute to second trimester mood changes. In most of these cases, supportive psychotherapy is all that is needed in order to help women deal with and overcome these symptoms. How-ever, one has to always watch out for and differentiate between these minor mood disorders and a major depression.

Third Trimester Depression

As mentioned earlier, depression in pregnancy is less common than in the postpartum period. However, in the third trimester, the pregnant woman experiences physical symptoms quite similar to the physical symptoms of depression. She is physically uncomfortable, often feels excessively bloated, and does not feel hungry. She may experience in-creasing difficulty in sleeping, and she may also feel a sense of exhaus-tion with increasing weight. All of this results in increased irritability, irrational mood swings, and increasing impatience to get on with the birth of the baby. If during this time a major clinical depression sets in, it may be difficult to diagnose simply because the normal symptoms of pregnancy appear to be similar to the symptoms of depression.

It is only when other symptoms—such as continuous sadness, con-stant tearfulness, a sense of hopelessness—appear that the woman may realize that "this is not normal." "Why do I want to end my life when I am about to have a baby?" she may ask herself. Because the woman herself is usually unaware of how ill she is, she may not be able to con-vey her distress to her family doctor. Oftentimes, the woman may hope and pray that her feelings of inadequacy and hopelessness will go away, only to realize as time goes on that a pervading sense of doom and gloom continues to plague her. But delay in seeking help adversely affects the woman, her family, other children if any, and most of all, the unborn baby, since the woman often starts to feel resentful of the pregnancy.

EVE'S STORY

Eve, a 28-year-old evangelical Christian, had been forced to marry when she became pregnant during a relationship with a young man she'd been seeing for only four months. During the first trimester, she had to stop attending school because of excessive vomiting, and she had essentially been confined to her home since. When she was referred to me in her third trimester, Eve was severely depressed. The year before, she had had a previous depression that had required hospitalization. Her grandmother had also suffered severe depressions and had committed suicide.

I admitted Eve to hospital, where she responded very well to small doses of tricyclic antidepressant. After two weeks, she was discharged, and eventually had an uncomplicated delivery and gave birth to a healthy little boy. She continued on antidepressant medication and had no symptoms of depression in the postpartum period.

I continued to see Eve for about nine months, after which time her antidepressant medication was discontinued. Her marital situation was not an easy one, which was not surprising since the relationship had been quite new when the unplanned pregnancy occurred. In addition, both Eve and her husband had large student loans to pay off, and at one point, both had to go on social assistance. Despite their difficulties, however, they decided to seek marital therapy and work on their problems. Eve's mother is now looking after the baby so that Eve can go back to school on a part-time basis. In a few years, she will have her university degree.

There are several things to keep in mind about third trimester mood disorders. First of all, the symptoms themselves will be just the same as those you've read about in the first trimester. However, when emotional disorders develop late in pregnancy, there's a strong possibility that they will carry over or resurface in the postpartum period. In addition, there is a good possibility that the woman will experience similar problems in later pregnancies. For these reasons, women who are emotionally troubled in their third trimester should get advice from their doctor and plan future management. Prompt treatment is essential so the illness does not worsen, as is close contact with the doctor throughout the rest of the pregnancy and into the postpartum period.

QUESTIONS YOU MIGHT HAVE ABOUT DEPRESSION

? *What exactly are the symptoms of depression?*
The symptoms of clinical depression can be both physical and emotional, and individuals tend to experience depressive symptoms in individual ways. In general, however, the following symptoms might indicate depression when they continue on a daily basis over a period of time: difficulty in falling asleep or consistent waking in the early morning hours; difficulty concentrating; loss of appetite; constant sense of fatigue; unusual increase or decrease in appetite; total loss of sexual energy; crying without any reason; general feeling of anger or despair; constant feeling of sadness without an apparent cause.

? *I'm a 30-year-old woman in the third trimester of my fourth pregnancy. After each of my previous pregnancies, I had a severe postpartum depression, and the last time I was hospitalized. I considered not continuing with this pregnancy but decided against this for religious reasons. My husband is very understanding and supportive, but I feel very shaky about the possibility of another depression.*

Your concern about this pregnancy is completely understandable. Someone with a history like yours—three successive pregnancies with a depressive illness following the birth of the baby—puts you at high risk for another episode. Now that you are in your third trimester, you need to keep very careful track of your emotions and the possible return of symptoms. You should discuss any symptoms with your doctor and also consider the possibility of starting antidepressant medication on a prophylactic (preventative) basis.

Many women feel more confident knowing that they have immediate psychiatric treatment available for them if they have any symptoms. It seems most likely that you will need some kind of treatment, and I would suggest you talk to your doctor now and seek referral to a psychiatrist.

? *Although I don't suffer from depression, I have had periods of unhappiness all my life. I'm very happy in my marriage, and I have no family history of depression, but I'm concerned that I'm the kind of person who may become clinically depressed once I get pregnant. I have a close friend at work who has bouts of depression and who had a severe postpartum depression. Will this happen to me?*

With no family history or personal history of depression, you are most likely not "the kind of person" who may become clinically depressed either during pregnancy or in the postpartum period. Remember that depression, as doctors use the term and as I have it in this book, is a disorder in which one's emotional state interferes with the ability to function. It is not at all the same thing as unhappiness.

Although you are unlikely to develop depression, you might want to talk with your doctor—or another counselor to whom you are referred—about the nature of those unhappy periods in your life. Were they related to difficult times, specific disappointments, perhaps a death in your family? These are natural life events to which unhappiness is a normal response. You should also be aware that periods of unhappiness are the normal response to some of the usual events of pregnancy—bodily discomfort, lifestyle adjustment, and so on.

I encourage you to talk with your family doctor about your fears and to clarify your understanding of the symptoms of depression. This will give you the confidence to recognize when your feelings of unhappiness or discouragement are within the range of normal reactions. As your pregnancy progresses, your doctor will want to follow your moods closely, and you should continue to express your feelings to your doctor, your husband, and to the nurse who may be involved with your care after your baby's birth.

ANXIETY

Feelings of *anxiety* have both physical and psychological components. When we anticipate something fearful that may happen to us, our body responds by feeling anxious. For example, it is not uncommon to find your heart beating faster when you are taking part in an event with an uncertain or worrisome outcome—for example, visiting an ill friend or relative in the hospital. Similarly, anxiety is common when one is experiencing a happy occasion, such as attending a wedding. How many brides have felt "butterflies in their stomach" before saying "I do?" Sometimes we experience anxiety in anticipation, even though the event itself—a long trip, or a move to a new location or a new job—may be far in the future. In response to this kind of situation, you might become restless, have an occasional sleepless night, or show intermittent signs of being unable to concentrate. These kinds of bodily or psychological responses are normal.

The foregoing are examples of normal feelings of anxiety that a human being commonly experiences under different circumstances. Most of the time, the anxiety will pass when the event is over or when the sense of fear no longer exists.

Many women experience feelings of anxiety when they want to become pregnant. Commonly, women who are trying to conceive become very anxious and upset each time their period comes. Conversely, when a woman becomes pregnant unexpectedly, she may become anxious about the pregnancy interfering with her career or with family plans such as moving or saving money for a new house. These kinds of reactions are quite normal. With time, the feelings of anxiety usually settle, and the woman will not need any psychological or medical treatment of any kind.

What I will describe next is what happens when the symptoms of anxiety are severe, and the woman is unable to function in her daily life without treatment. This is called *anxiety disorder*, a state which is by no means common during pregnancy. Researchers do not know whether or not pregnancy may trigger an anxiety (or "panic") disorder, but if one does suffer extreme feelings of anxiety during pregnancy or the postpartum period, it is important to seek help.

ANXIETY DISORDER

Some women have their first experience with a disruptive psychiatric condition called *anxiety disorder* during pregnancy and, because they do not understand what is happening, they may be afraid to seek help. The casual conversational use of the terms "anxiety" and "feeling anxious" cannot begin to describe the range and seriousness of symptoms that a woman with anxiety disorder encounters. *Panic attack* and *panic disorder* more accurately describe an acute episode of severe discomfort.

Anxiety disorders tend to involve both physical and emotional symptoms. For this reason, women can suffer terribly before they are diagnosed correctly and begin to receive treatment. The physical symptoms include churning stomach and nausea, palpitations (distinctive and rapid heartbeats), sweatiness, feelings of tingling and numbness, dizziness, shortness of breath (hyperventilation), crushing sensations in the chest, a sense of impending doom, and the fear of dying or going crazy. Typically, a woman will experience some of these symptoms in a sudden attack that may last minutes or hours. Usually, her first thought is that she's having a heart attack and is going to die.

When women seek help for these physical symptoms, they are frequently sent first to heart specialists or chest specialists. When no physical ailment can be pinpointed, they may find themselves in a frightening cycle of repeated visits to the family doctor or even the emergency room—while becoming even more terrified that their obvious problem is going untreated. The costs in health care dollars for these fruitless investigations are significant, but greater still is the anguish of women who endure the fears and frustrations of anxiety disorder that continues undiagnosed.

In the beginning, the woman may have one or two panic attacks a day. These gradually increase in number and, if her symptoms continue undiagnosed and untreated, the woman may eventually experience an almost continual condition of anxiety. She comes to fear the next attack (remaining in a state of *anticipatory anxiety*), and by remembering it, provokes the next one. She might seek to avoid situations where the early attacks occurred—avoiding leaving the house (a condition called *agoraphobia*) if they occurred away from home, avoiding returning home if the first attacks occurred there. This is obviously a crippling situation for the woman and her family.

Anxiety Disorder and Pregnancy

A woman who experiences these symptoms *must* get help. If anxiety disorder arises for the first time in early pregnancy, its course is variable. However, there is a likelihood of recurrence of attacks during the postpartum. The woman who suffers such attacks should be sure to describe her emotional state during and between attacks to her doctor.

When a woman is in a state of panic, it is impossible for her to enjoy her pregnancy. She might also fear that the panic attacks are affecting the way she feels about the pregnancy and the new baby. While it is not clear whether panic attacks can create obstetrical problems, it is clear that continued panic attacks during pregnancy can be a true nightmare for the woman involved.

What happens when a woman previously diagnosed with anxiety disorder becomes pregnant? Strangely enough, in some cases the pregnancy will alleviate the symptoms completely. In a small percentage of women, however, the anxiety disorder may worsen during pregnancy. The third and most common course, however, is one in which episodes of panic come and go throughout pregnancy. In any of these situations, a past history of anxiety disorder may predispose a woman to continuing or re-experiencing anxiety disorder in the postpartum period. (A discussion of postpartum anxiety disorder can be found in Chapter Five.)

What Causes Anxiety Disorder?

While specialists continue research into the causes of anxiety disorders, it is clear that some anxiety disorders are closely related to stress. An individual's critical stress factors are not always easy to pinpoint, and panic episodes may be a combined body and mind response to a general stressful situation involving many factors. Separation or divorce, a death in the family, the loss of a job—all make for a risky environment. Pregnancy itself can be a critical stress factor for a woman who is ambivalent about the experience or her relationship with her partner or fearful of the new obligations that parenthood will bring. Occasionally, a panic attack in a predisposed individual may begin without any apparent stress.

What Can Be Done for Anxiety Disorder?

The treatment for anxiety disorder is a combination of behavioral therapy, supportive psychotherapy, and medication. In pregnant patients, therapies that do not rely on medication are usually engaged first. For example, a behavioral counselor may be called in to help the patient examine sources of stress and develop new coping strategies. If a woman is newly diagnosed with anxiety disorder, she may sometimes find that the very fact that a diagnosis has been made—and the knowledge that a psychiatrist is available to help her if needed—reduces the number of attacks. If behavioral treatment and supportive counseling prove inadequate, drug therapy may be the answer. Chapter Eleven is devoted to a discussion of the uses and impacts of medications in pregnancy.

Nola's story is typical of the many women who suffer in silence because they do not know what panic disorder is or that it can be treated. In some ways, her case is tragic because she suffered an entire first pregnancy and postpartum period marked by panic disorder, alone and unsupported, receiving help only by a lucky coincidence partway through her second troubled pregnancy.

NOLA'S STORY

Nola and her husband manage a retail store that was started by her father-in-law and now employs quite a few members of the large extended family. Nola's in-laws are of German background, and are very stoic and self-contained in public but very close and communicative within the family circle. Nothing was ever kept a secret from family members, to such an extent that Nola at times felt her privacy was threatened. Naturally, the news of her pregnancy was immediately circulated to all the family members, and even to the store's regular customers.

About six weeks into her pregnancy, Nola suddenly woke in the middle of the night experiencing acute shortness of breath, rapid heartbeats, and nausea. She thought these symptoms were related to her pregnancy and eventually fell back asleep. The following night, however, the same thing happened again, and the next week similar episodes occurred almost daily.

Eventually, Nola was experiencing four or five panic attacks a day. She could no longer speak easily with customers in the store, and she began to feel anxious about going to work. Nola knew that something was wrong, but she felt that if she spoke to her husband, his whole family would learn that she was "having emotional problems"—and she knew all too well this stoic family's attitudes about seeking psychiatric help.

She stopped working and began leading a very isolated existence at home. She went to her church more frequently, and this gave her a feeling of support. In her second trimester, the panic disorder eased somewhat but returned again in force in the third trimester. Though Nola was by now rather used to daily panic attacks, which she kept completely to herself, she began dreading the baby's birth—both the actual labor and delivery, and the arrival of the baby with all the changes that would mean. After the baby's birth, the panic attacks worsened—but still she did not seek help.

Since this illness typically follows a fluctuating course, Nola at some point stopped experiencing panic attacks completely and began to lead a nearly normal life. However, she was not the same Nola as before her pregnancy. She returned to work part-time, but she was always worried about making mistakes, and she found it difficult to concentrate. And occasionally, she would have a panic attack.

When Nola became pregnant again, the panic disorder became worse. One day, a customer noticed that Nola was short of breath and gulping for air, and for some reason, Nola found herself telling the woman that the problem had started in her first pregnancy. The customer cheerfully told her not to worry; she knew of a clinic at the local maternity hospital, where problems like Nola's were treated successfully. It was at this point that Nola asked her family doctor to refer her, and she came to see me.

Nola was very reluctant to use any medications, and we decided to start treatment with behavioral therapy. She was seen by a psychologist who showed her a number of relaxation and breathing techniques. Focusing on positive imagery, as well as using techniques of hypnosis, seems to help milder cases of panic disorder, and with these tools, Nola was able to control her panic attacks. Although the problem did not disappear completely, Nola was able to go through the rest of her pregnancy and the postpartum period with the help of behavioral therapy alone. Having learned that her disorder was not uncommon, she felt much less isolated and in command of her situation. Fortunately for Nola, her second pregnancy and successful childbirth did not duplicate the lonely, frightening experience she had had the first time.

A QUESTION YOU MIGHT HAVE
ABOUT ANXIETY DISORDER

I've been receiving medical treatment for panic disorder, and now I've learned I'm pregnant with my second child. I'm quite happy about the pregnancy but concerned about the effects my medication might have on the baby. Are there other treatments for panic disorder?

The most important thing you can do immediately is to be sure that the doctors involved in your care—your family doctor and your obstetrician—are fully aware of your condition and the medications you are taking. Many women with panic disorder feel as you do, and some of them have been successful in doing without medication for the course of their pregnancy. You should not try to "go it alone," however. Your doctor will want to see you frequently to check on your status, and you might ask if this is a good time to be referred to a psychiatrist who can help monitor and advise you. Whether or not you need medication will depend on the severity of your symptoms. The effect on the baby depends on the type of medication you are on. As you will read in Chapter Eleven, though the long-term effects of the medication on the baby are not known, there is no danger to the baby if short-acting benzodiazepines are taken with caution.

You can also make some lifestyle adjustments that are thought to minimize the intensity of panic attacks, and, coincidentally, are healthy choices for pregnant mothers in general. For instance, panic attacks can be brought on by consuming excessive sweets and caffeine, by drinking too much alcohol, and by heavy smoking. Of course, most pregnant women make efforts not to smoke or consume alcohol or excessive amounts of sweets or coffee. For the rest, it is helpful to get adequate rest, avoid cola soft drinks and excessive tea or coffee, and follow a sensible exercise routine. Keeping stress levels down helps control panic attacks. It's a good idea to discuss with your partner the contribution that extraordinary stress makes to panic disorder. While we can rarely control life's major events, we can control many of the minor ones. Remember, pregnancy is not the ideal time to renovate the house!

OBSESSIVE-COMPULSIVE DISORDER

The ideal of "perfection" and aiming to do a certain task in a flawless, methodical way is something that is taught to us by our teachers, parents, and peers. A person who is disorganized suffers in more than one way. In planning a mission to outer space, for instance, one has to be exact in checking that the spacecraft is properly functioning; otherwise, the mission will be a disaster. Similarly, if you are going to sail across an ocean, you want to make sure that the ship is built to standards and you have adequate expertise to do the steering.

The need to be "perfect" is normal under the circumstances I have just described. And applying this concept to our daily lives has some value, since most of us function better when beds are routinely made and clean dishes on hand when it is time to prepare and serve the evening meal. Who does not prefer to sleep on clean sheets and to wear clothes that are clean and tidy? There are human requirements and preferences that fall within the normal category of cleanliness and organization. However, there is a wide range of acceptable human behavior associated with these daily tasks. Some people prefer to change bedsheets once a week; others change them every two weeks. In some kitchens, dishes are put away after every meal, whereas in others the routine is to wait until the day's dishes accumulate and then clean them up all at once. In these matters, there is no absolute right or wrong.

Obviously, our environment, our upbringing, and our own personalities and temperaments play important roles in the way we carry out the normal routine of our lives. In addition, there tend to be different cultural norms that define what is obsessive and what is not. Behavior that might be perceived by some people of a particular cultural background as "obsessional" might be perceived by another group as being completely normal. Similarly, in our Western culture, perfection is considered almost synonymous with success, yet people of other cultures look upon a certain kind of perfectionism as being too severe and inflexible.

Clearly, there is a very wide range of behavior that can be considered normal. Some people tend to be highly meticulous and strive to be perfect in every way. These people are usually not very adaptable and tend to be preoccupied with thoughts of perfection when they carry out their tasks. However, when this drive for perfection becomes too intense, there is cause for concern. A person who carries out a task repetitively, with an overwhelming obsessive drive for perfection, going beyond the normal range of behavior suffers from *obsessive-compulsive disorder* (OCD).

Obsessive-compulsive disorder is a condition characterized by obsessive thoughts and compulsive rituals. An obsessive thought is one that cannot be controlled and comes back again and again in an unwanted and disruptive pattern. Compulsive rituals are habits gone wrong—repetitive behaviors that come to dominate the day's activities and for which there is no reasonable explanation. Often, obsessive-compulsive disorder may occur together with anxiety disorder.

Little is known about how pregnancy affects the course of obsessive-compulsive disorder. New and conflicting research is beginning to emerge on this topic, and the relationship between obsessive-compulsive disorder and pregnancy is just beginning to be understood. Although there are no specific obsessive-compulsive symptoms associated with pregnancy per se, it is possible for a woman to develop obsessive-compulsive disorder for the first time in pregnancy. However, it is more common for obsessive-compulsive disorder in pregnancy to be a continuation of a previous condition. When the woman with this disorder becomes pregnant, her condition may continue unchanged throughout the pregnancy, may worsen, or in some cases, probably related to hormonal changes, may actually improve. If a woman had prepregnancy obsessive-compulsive disorder, then the particular obsessive behaviors may become worse during pregnancy or she may acquire new ones.

Ideally, a woman with obsessive-compulsive disorder who expects to become pregnant should consult her doctor or psychiatrist in advance so that her care can be supervised throughout the pregnancy. If it is necessary for her to continue taking the specific medications that are used to treat obsessive thoughts and compulsive rituals, she should be monitored very closely and her baby should be monitored after its birth. Treatment of obsessive-compulsive disorder involves both behavior therapy and pharmacotherapy in combination. (See Chapter Eleven.)

JILL'S STORY

Jill was a 26-year-old homemaker who had been a "perfect" child. The oldest of three siblings, she had always received A's on her report cards, and throughout her childhood, she had kept her room exceptionally clean and tidy. Her parents were always very proud of how "perfect" their little Jill was.

In high school, she began showing signs of excessive devotion to being perfect. She occasionally cleaned her room three or four times a day, knowing that it was clean but feeling that it might "just have become a bit dusty." Her mother found this a bit unusual at first, but put it down to Jill's being anxious about her exams. Jill graduated from high school and went on to college to get a teaching degree. She met her husband-to-be in college, and they decided to marry and have children right away.

Within 18 months of the marriage, Jill conceived, and she and her husband planned that she would remain at home for several years to care for their child. During the first trimester of her pregnancy, Jill found herself excessively cleaning again. She would make the bed at least ten times in the morning, checking every corner to make sure the bedsheet was perfect and the quilt cover had no creases. While her husband thought this behavior was odd, he was used to the family's idea of the "perfect Jill." One day, however, he came home unannounced, just two hours after leaving for work, and found that Jill was still in the process of remaking the bed—for approximately the 25th time that morning!

Now quite concerned, her husband called his mother-in-law and described Jill's behavior. However, his mother-in-law felt the description she heard was no more than the conscientious housekeeping of her "perfect Jill."

As the pregnancy went on, her compulsive housekeeping activities dominated Jill's day. She began to reorganize the rest of the house, and she dusted and swept all day long. Soon she was completely exhausted; she was unable to make meals and eventually became totally withdrawn. Fortunately, her sister, who was a nurse, realized that "perfect Jill" had a severe problem that needed psychiatric intervention. Her husband was relieved to have his sister-in-law confirm his instincts that Jill's was not normal behavior.

When Jill and her husband came to see me, it was decided that she should be treated with a combination of behavioral therapy, psychotherapy, and medications. I started with behavioral therapy, hoping this would lessen her symptoms, but this was not to be the case. Her obsessive-compulsive symptoms and rituals became so pronounced that she required an antidepressant medication to bring the illness under control.

Jill gave birth to a healthy infant and continued to see me for a year after she gave birth. During the postpartum period, she again began to show obsessive-compulsive symptoms—an occurrence to be expected in a woman who had shown obsessive-compulsive symptoms in the pregnancy. Since these symptoms were recognized immediately and treatment was started, they did not become nearly as severe as they had been early in her pregnancy.

Jill has since joined a support group for people with obsessive-compulsive disorder; in meeting with other women and men who have the same problem, she receives support that has helped in her continuing recovery.

Women with OCD have been found to follow various patterns in pregnancy. The following case shows the importance of advance planning when there has been a previous psychiatric history.

MARILYN'S STORY

Marilyn was a 31-year-old woman who had experienced two miscarriages and was very anxious to become pregnant again and deliver her first child. At 32 weeks in her third pregnancy, she began to experience obsessive thoughts about the safety of her home and also developed compulsive rituals of handwashing.

Throughout the day, she constantly checked and rechecked the doors of her house, making sure that they were locked. Soon Marilyn was unable to leave the house for any reason because she could never convince herself that the house was secure and had to keep checking and rechecking the locks. She also began washing her hands repeatedly, and by the time she was referred to me, she was washing her hands about fifty times a day. She had become completely dysfunctional—glued to her home, where the entire day was a round of checking locks and washing her hands.

Marilyn was admitted to hospital and given a course of tricyclic antidepressant medication. When she went into labor, the baby was monitored during and after birth. Just after the baby's birth, Marilyn's symptoms of OCD became worse. I increased Marilyn's medication dosage over the course of a few weeks, and she subsequently became symptom-free. She continued to see me on a regular basis so that I could review her emotional state and assess the need for continued medication.

About a year later, Marilyn told me that she and her husband planned another pregnancy. We talked about the possibility of her symptoms occurring again and the need for her to be in close touch with me. I discontinued her medication before conception took place.

In this second successful pregnancy, Marilyn had the "best case scenario"—that is, her emotional condition was very stable, with no recurrence of symptoms of OCD or depression. After the birth, however, she relapsed. She was prescribed tricyclic antidepressants again, and her postpartum period took the same course as before. Her condition stabilized before long, and she continued to see me periodically throughout the next year.

Marilyn and her husband are aware that OCD is an illness with a fluctuating course and that her emotional state must be monitored, with professional support when needed.

QUESTIONS YOU MIGHT HAVE ABOUT OBSESSIVE-COMPULSIVE DISORDER IN PREGNANCY

? *I am a married woman who is contemplating becoming pregnant. Both my 50-year-old mother and my 29-year-old sister have suffered from obsessive-compulsive disorder for several years. They are both under psychiatric care, take antidepres-*

sants, and attend support groups for obsessive-compulsive behavior. Will I also develop obsessive-compulsive disorder once
I've become pregnant?

Since two members of your family suffer from this disorder,
your anxiety is quite legitimate and you are wise to seek advice.
Doctors don't know the exact role of heredity in obsessive-
compulsive disorder; therefore, it's not possible to predict the
chances that this disorder will affect you, although your risk of
developing OCD is higher than someone whose relatives do not
suffer from it. Although the question of whether you'll develop
this condition in your lifetime remains open, we can say with
some confidence that your risk of developing this disorder *for
the first time during pregnancy* is not very high. Your family history is no reason to choose against pregnancy.

It would be a good idea for you and your husband to arrange
a meeting to discuss your family history and concerns with your
family doctor. Before pregnancy, it's always wise to be sure that
those close to you and those involved in your medical care have
a full picture of any possible risks. Should some problem develop, your doctor will have all the information to make the
right diagnosis quickly. You might also want to request that you
and your husband be referred for a consultation with a psychiatrist, who can clarify the symptoms of obsessive-compulsive disorder, reassure you as to your small chance of developing the
problem during pregnancy, and then see you again during your
pregnancy if this seems called for.

? *I am a patient who suffers from obsessive-compulsive disorder. For the past ten years, I have been taking medications for this regularly, under the care of a psychiatrist. I am
married now and my husband and I would like to have a child.
What advice would you give me about the possibility of continuing to take medications during the pregnancy, the effects on
the baby, and the course of my illness during pregnancy?*

The course of obsessive-compulsive disorder in pregnancy is
unpredictable. Some women feel well during pregnancy and are
completely asymptomatic, while others continue to have the illness irrespective of the pregnancy, and still others may become
worse. You should be monitored as you go along in your preg-

nancy. In terms of medications and their effects on the fetus, we know of no medication that is completely safe for the developing baby. Sometimes one has to weigh the risks versus the benefits of continuing the medications during pregnancy—in other words, the risk for you if you stop taking the medications, versus the risk of giving you the medications to keep your illness under control while monitoring you very carefully with the help of ultrasound all through pregnancy.

These questions can only be answered by the doctor who knows your condition best. However, I initially advise all my patients to try to go off their medications or taper off them before attempting to get pregnant. No woman should elect to become pregnant while on medications if at all possible. However, the decision to continue medications must be made in consultation with your doctor; in some cases, the illness may relapse once medications are discontinued. If you still want to become pregnant while on medications, I suggest that you consult with a psychiatrist who is an expert in this area to explore which antidepressant is most suitable.

PSYCHOSIS IN PREGNANCY

Expectant mothers should be reassured that *psychosis*—a loss of contact with reality—is extremely uncommon and that it is virtually unknown for a woman to develop psychosis (schizophrenia or manic-depressive disorder) as a first-time event in early pregnancy. In fact, in my fifteen years of practice, I have seen only two cases of new psychosis during pregnancy in women with no prior history of psychotic illness. In the unusual cases where psychosis does develop—usually in the postpartum period—there is virtually always a personal or family history of this severe disorder. Unfortunately, women with an existing chronic history of psychosis usually continue to be psychotic throughout the pregnancy.

Too often, the schizophrenic woman who is pregnant must also deal with unemployment, poverty, and sometimes nonexistent social support. There also is a high incidence of substance abuse among schizophrenics and many of their pregnancies are unplanned. Not surprisingly, I do not often see women from this patient population in my practice since they are women who "slip through the cracks" of our social network all too easily. Many of them do not receive adequate prenatal or postpartum care. Many of them live in "halfway houses" and are unable to look after themselves well. Because infants left alone with schizophrenic mothers, especially those with no social support and in a delusional state, are at high risk, it is important that women with such psychiatric histories receive ongoing medical care. (See Chapter Five for more information on postpartum psychosis.)

A pregnant woman who has a blood relative with schizophrenic or manic-depressive disorders should be sure that her doctor is aware of this family history early in the pregnancy. Once aware of this background, her doctor can pay special attention to her emotional state in the postpartum period.

Melissa's story illustrates how a woman with a long-standing history of schizophrenia coped with her illness in the first trimester.

MELISSA'S STORY

Melissa was a 26-year-old woman who had a history of schizophrenia going back to age 18. A single woman, living on social assistance in a residential home for the mentally ill, she did not practice birth control and became pregnant by another resident of the same halfway house. She had discontinued taking her medications and was quite psychotic. She did not attend any prenatal classes and did not really take care of her emotional or physical needs at all.

Melissa had little contact with her family, though her mother occasionally visited her. When her mother came to visit after an interval of two months, she saw that Melissa was quite obviously pregnant and, as well, quite out of touch with reality. Melissa, on the other hand, was not aware of her pregnancy or of the need for proper prenatal care. Her mother insisted on bringing her daughter to the clinic at the hospital where I worked, and in this way, Melissa was referred to me for continuing psychiatric care.

Throughout the eight-year history of her illness, Melissa had not been a compliant patient in terms of taking care of herself and continuing with medications. She had been prescribed injectable neuroleptics (antipsychosis drugs), but on many occasions, she had missed her injections and become psychotic. At the time she was referred to me, she was experiencing hallucinations and delusions and did not understand the implications of pregnancy. She was placed on medications immediately, and she had to be hospitalized for a few weeks until her symptoms resolved enough for her to go back into the community again. She was followed regularly then by a health care team in the community so that a team of health care givers could attend to her care on a regular basis.

Thanks possibly to the balance of hormones achieved in the second trimester, it is uncommon for psychiatric disorders to develop as new signs during this phase of pregnancy. As we have seen, the few women who develop anxiety disorder or depression for the first time in the second trimester usually have a personal or family history of these problems. The same is true of new psychosis. Nevertheless, when this disorder occurs, it is a likely indicator that the problem will surface again in the postpartum period, so it is important that the woman's family and caregivers recognize that continued monitoring is essential.

RENATA'S STORY

Renata was a 39-year-old chartered accountant who was pregnant for the first time. In the second trimester, she began having sleepless nights, and, after a period in which her daytime behaviour seemed very "hyper," she began to express unusual thoughts. Both her husband and her co-workers felt that sometimes Renata's reactions to events showed she was completely out of touch with reality. After her husband had accompanied her to an appointment with her family physician, Renata was referred to me and I made the diagnosis of *manic depressive* or *bipolar illness*—an illness with two extremes, depression and hyperactivity.

It was obvious that Renata needed to be hospitalized and closely followed. Her husband was very supportive, accepting of and encouraging her hospitalization. She was placed on quite a low dose of antipsychotic medication and remained an inpatient for about two months, until her symptoms had cleared. As Renata's situation stabilized, and I was able to explore her history in some detail, it became apparent that in her early adulthood she had gone through several periods of "feeling low" that had not required any therapy. She was also aware that her mother's younger sister, who had died when Renata was a child, had apparently suffered psychiatric illness.

When Renata was readmitted to hospital for the birth of her baby—a normal, healthy little girl—she again developed acute manic symptoms within days after childbirth. Medication was once again prescribed, and it was necessary for her to remain in hospital for some months under psychiatric care.

It is extremely unusual for severe illness of this kind to occur for the first time in pregnancy, particularly in the calm of the second trimester. When it does occur, however, there is invariably a previous psychiatric history in the individual or her family. The reason I decided to share Renata's story with you is to illustrate that even with psychotic episodes in pregnancy and postpartum, a successful outcome is quite possible with proper treatment.

Advice for Patients with a History of Prior Psychosis

If you have had a history of prior psychosis either in the postpartum period or at any other time in your life, several things can help you prepare for pregnancy. First of all, you need to know your diagnosis. Perhaps you have a schizophrenic illness, perhaps a bipolar or manic depressive illness. If you have had a bipolar illness, you may or may not be taking lithium, depending on the number of episodes you have had. Ideally, I aim to take my bipolar patients off lithium to see if a pregnancy can occur without the first trimester exposure to lithium. If this is impossible—for example, if the woman relapses several times in the process of becoming pregnant—then it might be inevitable that she will have to continue with her pregnancy in spite of being medicated. The optimum case scenario, however, is for the woman to be taken off lithium before trying to become pregnant and for the doctor to observe her progress closely throughout the pregnancy. If symptoms do appear, the psychotropic medications that have kept the patient well in the past can then be reintroduced, since there is less concern about exposure to this kind of medication during the second and third trimesters.

For a woman with a history of schizophrenic illness, too, the optimum case scenario would be to take her off the psychotropic medications if possible, depending on the type and severity of her schizophrenic illness. If it proves impossible, then she will have to continue to try for a pregnancy, being aware of the risk versus benefits of the medication. Before endeavoring to become pregnant, the patient should meet all of the health care professionals who are involved in her care—her family doctor, her psychiatrist, the obstetrician—and "plan a pregnancy." This planned approach ensures that all through the pregnancy she will have supervision regarding her medications and receive expert advice regarding the exposure to medication of the growing fetus. (See Chapter Eleven for more information on medication during pregnancy.)

When a patient has a history of psychiatric illness, the support of her family, especially her partner, is invaluable. When extended family is not available, it might be possible to pay for extra assistance in the home. Planning extra support, from whatever source, can help achieve the goal of successful pregnancy and motherhood in spite of dealing with challenging and difficult symptoms of a manic-depressive illness or schizophrenic illness.

A QUESTION YOU MIGHT HAVE ABOUT
PSYCHOSIS IN PREGNANCY

? *I am a 32-year-old woman contemplating my first pregnancy. I have a sister who has been treated for schizophrenic illness for the past ten years. I am afraid that I might develop a severe problem such as hers during pregnancy or the postpartum period. What is your advice?*

Because your sister has a schizophrenic illness, your risk of having a psychotic episode in the postpartum period is high. The exact incidence of schizophrenic illness during the postpartum period is not known, but in general, about one in 1,000 women will become psychotic in the postpartum.

I would encourage you not to worry overly about this, but to educate yourself about the illness and to assure that you have proper professional attention in this regard after your baby is born. Your doctor can be of help with this and should be able to refer you to a specialist who will be involved in your care and monitoring your condition after the birth of your baby.

UNUSUAL DESIRE FOR PREGNANCY

The desire to become pregnant is not abnormal. The extent and intensity of the desire to become pregnant varies from woman to woman and couple to couple and also depends on the situation they are in. For example, in a stable married couple who has tried unsuccessfully for a pregnancy for a number of years, the intensity of wanting to have a child usually increases steadily. I have seen many infertile women in my practice, and have observed that the intensity of the desire to become pregnant in women who have repeatedly failed to conceive is surpassed by few other feelings.

Such women usually feel a tremendous sense of failure for being "barren," unable to procreate, unable to carry on the family's name, and so on. This becomes a major issue in the woman's life, and she wants to become pregnant almost at any cost. If the woman fails to become pregnant month after month, this emotional distress may take different forms. Some women will actually feign pregnancy or tell their partners that they have become pregnant in order to receive attention. Then, later, they may announce that they have had a miscarriage. Other women will have a strong unshakable sense that they are pregnant when their periods are merely delayed a week or two.

The desire to become pregnant can affect a woman in various ways. When the preoccupation with pregnancy reaches an extreme degree, it can take on a form of what is called *conversion reaction*. This means that psychological symptoms are converted into physical symptoms. A woman's obsession with becoming pregnant can result in marital problems; likewise, her emotional distress may reach such proportions that she becomes delusional and thinks that she is pregnant in the absence of any real signs and symptoms.

KARLA'S STORY

Karla was a 28-year-old woman who had been trying to get pregnant ever since her marriage at the age of 18. In talking with her, I understood that being married and having children were the sole sources of her identity. Both Karla and her husband had had fertility workups, and no reasons could be identified for her inability to conceive.

Slowly and surely, she had become preoccupied with the desire to become pregnant. She repeatedly went to her family doctor, requesting pregnancy tests. After a while, her doctor referred her to me for possible treatment of depression or other help. When I met with her, I found that this pleasant young woman was very intent on becoming pregnant.

We met for several sessions, and eventually it became clear to her that above and beyond her own wish to have a family, Karla also wanted to become pregnant and have a baby to please her mother. She was an only child and had missed having brothers or sisters. She felt that the family she had grown up in had been "incomplete," and from an early age, she had vowed to have lots of children.

However, she realized that feigning pregnancies month after month—with the resulting attention and then pity and sympathy, especially from her mother—was getting her nowhere. Karla and I decided that she would see a psychologist to work through her ongoing childhood-related issues. I did not hear anything about Karla for about two years, since she was no longer under my care. Then one day I was surprised by a telephone call from her, announcing the birth of her baby boy at BC Women's Hospital. I had the opportunity to visit Karla and her son, and she told me that the therapy had helped her a great deal in coming to terms with her desire to be a mother.

I see many women who are anxious to become pregnant, though few of them are as preoccupied with this single goal as Karla was. Most of them consider womanhood a very important aspect of their being and, of course, wish to have a child as part of a woman's life expression. In very extreme cases, as will be described in the following section, there is need for hospitalization to treat an obsession so complete that the woman takes on the physical signs of pregnancy.

PSEUDOCYESIS

Pseudocyesis, or false pregnancy, is an extremely unusual condition that demonstrates the very powerful link between mind, body, and emotions. In this rare syndrome, a woman believes that she is pregnant and develops convincing signs and symptoms of pregnancy—even though she is not pregnant! Women with pseudocyesis are totally preoccupied with the thought of being pregnant, sometimes to the degree of being delusional. Firmly believing that they are pregnant, they function normally in the world, and their bodies agree by developing the contours and signs of pregnancy. Because the thought of being pregnant is so fixed in the woman's mind, some physicians refer to it as a "mono-symptomatic delusion."

These false signs of pregnancy can be extremely pronounced and realistic. The woman stops menstruating, her hormone levels mimic a pregnant state and are measurably higher than normal, her cervix may dilate, and her breasts and abdomen become enlarged. Before the days of ultrasound, even the woman's doctor could be baffled when an apparently pregnant woman arrived for examination, and no fetus could be detected.

Although pseudocyesis happens very rarely, some theories have been suggested as to its cause. Women with pseudocyesis may have "borderline" or histrionic personality disorders and display characteristics of being extremely emotional, intense, overly dramatic, and unpredictable. Very often, the woman's sense of maternal identity is tied to her self-image and the way she is perceived by people significant to her. She might have feelings of insecurity or inadequacy and feel that she will not be respected in the world unless she becomes pregnant and assumes the role of a mother. In some cases of pseudocyesis, the woman is infertile and cannot conceive; or she may be having marital problems and sees pregnancy as a way to save the marriage.

A prominent woman of the nineteenth century, England's Queen Victoria, was found to be repeatedly suffering from pseudocyesis. Her personal values and her official reign were characterized by an almost religious emphasis on the family unit and the importance of the mother as the center of the home. It is interesting to speculate on how the personality of this powerful woman, who gave birth successfully to nine children, apparently translated itself into a need to be seen as pregnant, even when she was not.

MELANIE'S STORY

Melanie was a 35-year-old woman on social assistance who came to the emergency room insisting that her waters had broken and that she was in labor. As it happened, the doctor on duty had seen her previously when she had made several visits to emergency within a short period of time. Each time, she had complained of abdominal pain connected to her pregnancy.

No signs of pregnancy had been evident in these earlier visits to emergency and the doctor on duty had counseled her to visit her family doctor. Again, on this occasion, there was no fetal movement, and except for a pronounced swelling of the abdomen, there were no other findings of pregnancy. Melanie nevertheless refused to accept that she was not pregnant, and I was called to see her. Hers was one of only two cases of pseudocyesis I have seen in my years of practice.

Melanie was admitted to the psychiatric ward and was placed on neuroleptic medication. The nurses there were supportive and kind to her. She was eventually prepared for the idea that she would be given an ultrasound examination to confirm that there was no pregnancy. When the ultrasound was done, she could see clearly that there was no fetus, and although she accepted the fact that she was not pregnant, she obviously needed some continuing psychiatric care to deal with various issues in her background.

She remained in hospital for a brief time and continued to see me as an outpatient. She had been married ten years before to a lawyer who abandoned her after the birth of her second child. One day after running errands, Melanie came home to an empty house. Everything was gone—furniture, clothes, and the two children, aged two years and six months.

She had experienced an episode of postpartum psychosis after the birth of her first child. This was treated and she had no symptoms after the birth of the second child. She and her husband then began to experience marital problems, and her husband, who was familiar with the legal profession, found an easy way to get rid of her—to leave the country and disappear.

One can only imagine the plight of this poor woman whose world changed dramatically overnight. In the next four years, her obsession to have a child reached a delusional quality to the point of presenting it as pseudocyesis.

Unfortunately, I lost touch with Melanie when she decided to leave Vancouver and move to the rural north.

As we have seen, a woman's mental state can have a major effect on her life during pregnancy and the postpartum period. Often, however, a pregnant woman's mental state is influenced by her physical state—as I shall explore in the next chapter.

CHAPTER 2

"WHY IS THIS HAPPENING?"

Medical and Obstetrical Complications

F ortunately in today's modern world, the majority of women who experience pregnancy do so within the normal range of expected emotions. Most North American women who choose to be pregnant are aware that good prenatal care and nutrition are important factors in the baby's health, and most of these women have access to good medical advice. As I will discuss in Chapter 3, modern technology allows most abnormalities to be diagnosed early in the pregnancy, and if families choose to terminate these pregnancies, they have access to medically safe procedures. When actual or potential medical complications are identified, women can be carefully monitored throughout the pregnancy, and, with a relatively high degree of success, be brought to term and deliver healthy babies. Nevertheless, unexpected problems do arise and the outcomes can be tragic even when women have good continuing prenatal care.

Despite "high-tech" medicine and the most conscientious medical care, a few types of serious problems can occur any time during pregnancy or at birth. Some of these problems can neither be predicted nor prevented, and they will likely continue to be present in a small percentage of pregnancies. And some irregularities in the developing fetus will be undetectable, even with the use of careful monitoring. Accordingly, the family may have only a brief time to face the idea that the infant is in serious difficulty, or they may be confronted with an emergency situation that comes as a complete surprise. In either case, the depth of legitimate feelings of confusion, disbelief, and losses is not always recognized, and the woman may feel quite alone as she endures a major emotional trauma.

This chapter will focus on psychological consequences related to medical and obstetrical complications in pregnancy. I will also discuss the emotional issues related to prolonged hospitalization and explore ways to cope with Caesarean section.

DIAGNOSIS OF MEDICAL COMPLICATIONS

Changes in the Mother's Health

Medical complications of pregnancy, such as high blood pressure and gestational diabetes, may show up in the first, second, or third trimester. They can sometimes result in extreme physical and emotional distress. This is particularly likely in some cases of diabetes, when the woman's blood sugar cannot be controlled by diet and exercise and she must therefore be admitted to hospital for management of her illness.

Up to 10 percent of pregnant women develop *gestational diabetes*—that is, they develop diabetes mellitus during pregnancy in the absence of any prepregnancy problems with blood sugar levels. Usually at high risk for developing gestational diabetes are women who are overweight and have a prior history of gestational diabetes, women with family history of diabetes, and women carrying twins or triplets. While symptoms vary, the woman with gestational diabetes usually experiences frequent urination—a symptom sometimes difficult to differentiate from the frequent urination associated with normal pregnancy. However, the woman will herself be able to identify that the frequency of her urination has increased dramatically. She may also gain an unusual amount of weight and will usually experience frequent thirst, dryness of mouth, and unusual appetite.

When abnormal blood sugar levels are first diagnosed, the doctor may ask the pregnant patient and her spouse to go to a special clinic at the local hospital where they can receive information about the general treatment of diabetes. Usually, a visit to a diabetic clinic will include the showing of educational videotapes and meetings with counselors who give advice about special diet and exercise regimes that will help control the diabetes during pregnancy. If undertaking these measures does not stabilize the blood sugar level, insulin will be prescribed, and the amount of insulin each diabetic requires can vary considerably. It's often necessary to admit diabetic patients to hospital for a matter of weeks while their individual insulin requirements are determined, which involves daily insulin injections and constant monitoring of the blood and urine sugar level with laboratory tests.

The development of this medical complication can be quite distressing for a pregnant woman, and a psychiatrist or other counselor may become involved in helping her cope with the new restrictions in her lifestyle. The last thing a pregnant woman generally expects, as her pregnancy progresses, is to be confined to hospital and constantly poked with needles. Her partner and any children in the family are left in the difficult situation of having to reorganize family responsibilities around her absence. On top of the lifestyle alterations she is already making in dealing with pregnancy, she must now adjust to a special diet in addition—one that does not permit giving in to the food cravings of pregnancy, and she must resign herself to the prospect of giving herself regular insulin doses.

Some women react to the hospital confinement by becoming excessively irritable, angry, and uncooperative with the medical staff. They're resentful of this intrusion into their family life and plans, and they may "act out" their resentments in various ways on the hospital ward. Although such acting out is neither an extreme medical emergency nor an extreme emotional state, women who are confined to hospital during pregnancy may benefit from short-term counseling. At the very least, the counselor is a neutral party—not someone administering the poking needles!—and can listen empathetically to the woman's concerns and anger.

Rarely is it necessary for a professional counselor to provide more than the initial discussion during the time of crisis. However, in some cases, where a woman is extremely uncooperative, is fighting treatment, or is having a great deal of difficulty conforming to the requirements of the hospital stay, deeper issues are involved. She may have unresolved psychological problems that have resurfaced under these restrictions. For example, a woman with deep-seated problems around the issues of power and authority may act out a power struggle with doctors and nurses.

More often, however, the hospitalized woman simply needs some short-term reassurance and sympathy from an objective counselor, and in addition some practical advice on managing her predicament. For this, many hospitals have diabetic clinics to which patients can return on an outpatient basis. The staffs at these clinics are especially attuned to the adjustment problems that may be experienced by patients, particularly women who are coping with both a pregnancy and a new diagnosis of diabetes.

BARB'S STORY

Barb was a 22-year-old single mother admitted to the local maternity hospital in her second trimester with a moderate to severe case of gestational diabetes. I was asked to see her because she was not being cooperative in her treatment.

Barb was a pleasant young woman whose parents had split up when she was only four. Her father was a heavy drinker, and her mother was a diabetic who had taken insulin injections for as long as Barb could remember. This was something she certainly did not want for herself, and she had not realized that as the daughter of a diabetic, she was at risk of developing diabetes in pregnancy.

Due to contraceptive failure, Barb had become pregnant in a relationship that was stormy. The baby's father withdrew from the situation, and although Barb could not quite see herself raising a child on her own, she felt she should carry the baby to term. She tried not to think about the baby she was carrying and tried in every way possible to avoid becoming attached to it. She told me later that when she was diagnosed with diabetes, she thought that not taking the prescribed insulin would somehow result in a loss of pregnancy. Consequently, she thought, she would not have to worry about future decisions about raising the baby. Her ambivalence about the pregnancy was obvious.

After seeing her for a few visits, I realized how complicated this young woman's life was and that she would need continuing help to establish a consistent diabetic regime, take proper medications, and carry out the pregnancy. At the time, she was involved in a cycle of self-punishment, punishing both herself and the baby she carried for the situation she was in. In the course of her therapy, Barb came to realize that some of her acting out behavior had to do with the distress associated with the diagnosis of gestational diabetes, as well as many issues between her parents and herself that had remained unresolved since childhood. In addition to talk therapy, I also referred Barb to a health care team that included a social worker who could see her regularly, visit her home, and help her deal with some practical arrangements. With this support, she was able to continue to attend the diabetic clinic and maintain her health during the pregnancy.

Barb gave birth to a healthy baby boy. She is now making an adjustment to single parenthood and raising her little son on her own.

QUESTIONS YOU MIGHT HAVE ABOUT GESTATIONAL DIABETES

During my first pregnancy, I developed diabetes mellitus and had to adjust to a routine of insulin injections for the course of my pregnancy. I'm expecting my second child and wondering about my chances of becoming diabetic again.

It would be a good idea for you to talk with your doctor about being referred to a specialist in diabetes, who would be an appropriate person to monitor your symptoms as your pregnancy progresses. The fact that you've been able to keep your blood sugar under control since the birth of your first child is a good sign. However, it wouldn't be at all surprising if you were to develop gestational diabetes again, and the specialist will probably alert you to the need for maintaining a careful diet and exercise program even before the symptoms develop. Your anxiety is understandable given your first experience, and the best way to address this anxiety is to get expert advice before any symptoms develop.

With my first pregnancy I was hospitalized in my third trimester for six weeks with the diagnosis of gestational diabetes. I remember going through a very difficult time with the hospitalization, and I am really not mentally prepared for another episode of diabetes in pregnancy. I would like to become pregnant again, but I am hesitating because of the high possibility of gestational diabetes. What advice can you give me about it? My child is now four years old, and I have been well and in good health since my first pregnancy.

The fact that you have been free of diabetes in the last four years indicates the illness is under control. All your good habits of careful dietary control and exercise will be helpful to you in your next pregnancy. However, I would suggest that you see a diabetic specialist who will be able to discuss this fully with you. The hospitalization you experienced understandably worries you more than the diabetic condition itself. Though this is difficult, you need to prepare yourself mentally for the possibility of another hospital stay so that you can cope with it in a less traumatic manner if it is required. You might also benefit from counseling sessions to explore your previous experience with trauma and help you go into a second pregnancy better prepared, whether or not you need repeat hospitalization.

OBSTETRICAL COMPLICATIONS

Another unexpected and serious medical complication of pregnancy is premature rupture of the uterine membranes. Sometimes this can occur in the first trimester but may resolve without any treatment; with bed rest alone, the leakage of the amniotic fluid may spontaneously stop as membranes close again. But in some percentage of women, the leakage continues. The typical patient for premature rupture is a woman in her 21st or 22nd week of pregnancy who reports that her waters have broken. Her doctor will immediately admit her to the hospital, where she will be confined to bed rest. This situation is marked with considerable uncertainty about the final outcome. The main question is whether the membranes will continue to leak, sending the woman into labor, or whether—with continued bed rest—the mother will be able to be maintained in the same condition until the pregnancy is advanced enough for labor to be induced and the baby safely delivered.

Rupture of the membranes in any trimester is always dangerous, and the earlier in the pregnancy, the more dangerous it is. The chances of an early second trimester baby surviving are small, and much depends on the baby's weight. The situation is particularly difficult if rupture of the membranes occurs around the 25th to 26th week since the baby's lungs may or may not be mature enough for him to survive, even in the intensive care unit. Indeed, the outcome is never a certainty, and sometimes these tiny babies of almost-adequate birth weight survive briefly in intensive care, only to die within hours or days.

A woman who is hospitalized with ruptured membranes and faces this scenario is in an agonizing state. Not surprisingly, as she lies in her hospital bed, wondering each day whether her membranes will hold or whether she will go into labor, she is usually plagued with extreme anxiety and all the self-doubts and guilt that surround any negative developments in pregnancy. Worst of all she is almost invariably faced with the impending loss of a loved baby who has become an increasingly real person to her as it has begun to kick and move inside her.

Second trimester births as the result of ruptured membranes are a grim study in contrasts, and the experience of these mothers in labor and delivery is terribly poignant. What should have been the long-awaited triumph, the happy new beginning, is instead a time of great anxiety and, all too often, of painful tragedy. What heartache when the baby is born and lives just a few minutes—and yet is a whole person, perfectly formed.

The consequences for the mother and her partner are just as serious as for those families who lose a full-term baby at birth, and the range of emotions they experience is just as wide and traumatic. These mothers have many emotions to work through—feelings of anger, of being cheated, and often, too, of being isolated now in a strange way from friends who are still pregnant and happily awaiting childbirth.

Is it important that family members and caregivers not underestimate the depth of the loss and time needed for healing to take place. Vera's story shows how individual counseling may be needed in addition to family support systems.

VERA'S STORY

Vera, a pleasant, extroverted woman, had lost her first baby at 21 weeks of pregnancy. At that time, she was diagnosed as having an incompetent cervix, and a cervical suture was put in, with the hope that this would prevent premature rupture of the membranes in her next pregnancy.

Vera had decided to seek counseling to help her in the grieving period, and after a time she felt ready for a second pregnancy. She was very confident that the cervical suture would enable her to go to full term, and in the second trimester of this second pregnancy, she was busily organizing the baby's bedroom and knitting baby sweaters and socks. Her mother had applied for a leave of absence from her job in order to be with Vera after the baby was born.

Unfortunately, rupture of membranes occurred again in the 22nd week of pregnancy. Vera was admitted to hospital and gave premature birth to a baby whose weight was low and whose lungs were not developed enough to allow him to survive. To lose her first baby and then to see her second baby born alive, only to die within hours, was an extraordinary and horrifying experience that she could barely grasp. Vera remained in the hospital a few days and realized that she was going to need help in coming to terms with her loss, and it was then that she was referred to me.

In seeing Vera over a period of time, I learned that her own mother had had similar experiences, and Vera was the only live birth in the six pregnancies her mother had had. Vera had grown up with this fear that she, too, would lose her babies. Despite her positive approach to the second pregnancy, the loss of the second baby was too much, and the fear she had always carried became larger than life. She became depressed to the point that she was practically immobilized and couldn't carry out ordinary day-to-day functions.

Vera's mother, having expected to care for her first grandchild, took her leave of absence and came to stay with her daughter. Seeing them together, I fully realized how the mother's own losses had affected the daughter and just how this history Vera had lived with from childhood had become a reality in her own life. Nevertheless, the mother's kind and sympathetic support was very helpful. In addition, Vera's husband was involved with her in therapy from time to time and was able to put his own disappointments in the background and help her through her anguish.

Vera visited me regularly and was able to explore her fears and choices. After about six months, her serious depression had resolved and she had recovered her usual positive outlook. Her obstetrician felt that a successful pregnancy was not out of the question, and Vera and her husband decided that eventually they would try again.

PROLONGED HOSPITALIZATION

Prolonged hospitalization in pregnancy occurs most often as the result of maternal medical complications like diagnosis of diabetes mellitus or hypertension. In the third trimester, prolonged hospitalization can be even more distressing because it can be associated with obstetrical complications. Prolonged hospitalization at any stage in the pregnancy can create a crisis for the family, who must cope with practicalities in the mother's absence. The woman's partner may have to become more active in household organization, arranging child care and getting the children to and from school and after-school activities. Weekends, which formerly offered a break from work, now are taken up with extra duties of cleaning and grocery shopping. Weekday mornings bring the extra chore of preparing the children's lunches, and the end of the workday brings dinner preparation for the whole family. Suddenly, what were once shared household responsibilities fall entirely on the partner's shoulders. These are some of the concrete ways in which the family will have to come together and help each other when the mother is hospitalized. The task is not an easy one; patience and understanding are necessary in successful response to a crisis of this nature.

At the advanced stage of the third trimester, however, the overwhelming issue is the real and daily fear that the pregnancy may fail and the infant's health may be threatened. Third trimester hospitalization may be necessary for a number of reasons. The woman's physician might advise that she be closely monitored in the hospital because of her high blood pressure or diabetes or because of concerns about the status of twins or triplets. More frightening for the mother are cases in which hospitalization is required for premature labor or sudden bleeding that occurs as the result of placenta previa or abruptio placenta.

Placenta previa is a condition in which the placenta becomes implanted in the lower segment of the uterus, covering or partially covering the mouth of the uterus. As the uterus grows and stretches, a usually painless vaginal bleeding begins to take place. A change like this occurs for no apparent reason and the woman, who may even be quietly resting when it takes place, is truly shocked and frightened at this unexpected sign. Bleeding can also signal *abruptio placenta*, in which a change that normally occurs close to the time of delivery instead happens too early. In abruptio placenta, the placenta starts separating from the wall of the uterus, and if a great deal of bleeding takes place, the fetus can be in real danger.

In both cases, the mother must be hospitalized immediately. An ultrasound is taken to monitor the baby's condition, and the mother is then confined to bed rest either in the hospital or at home. The goal of this treatment is to keep the placenta in a stable condition and allow the pregnancy to progress to full term or to the point where a Caesarean section can be safely performed without compromising the infant's health.

Coping with Prolonged Hospitalization

The unexpected complication of prolonged hospitalization of the pregnant woman is a real challenge for busy modern families, and it would be naive to overlook the difficulties and emotions that surround this event. Most pregnant women who work outside the home fully expect to continue at their jobs virtually up to their due date. An unexpected hospitalization is truly a major lifestyle interruption, with a range of possible consequences—boredom, financial worries, conflicts over changes in the couple's normal roles, worry about the emotional needs of other children, and very real practical demands of maintaining the home and family—all in addition to concern about the woman's health and the pregnancy.

In the Western world, few nuclear families have an extended family unit on call to come to their rescue. In other cultures and other times, the female members of the family were likely to be on hand, in the home, to look after the children of the family and see that the household ran smoothly. Today, however, families are usually smaller and are often geographically separated. Even when female members of the extended family live nearby, they're often involved in busy careers outside their own homes and simply can't drop what they're doing to help out.

Most often, the father in the family is left to make adjustment in his working life and the family's home life. The practical organizational challenges in our mobile society can be truly complex when two parents' duties suddenly fall onto one parent. This harassed and worried father may find himself making mental maps on the best route from the grocery store in one direction, to his son's preschool in another direction, while including a visit to his wife in the hospital, 45 minutes away on the expressway.

The hospitalized mother fully realizes that things are not easy at home, and she easily falls prey to guilt that she's not at home, resentment at her own boredom and restlessness, and unending worry and fear at this new element of risk in her pregnancy. The woman confined to bed rest at home is no less frustrated. She sees and is frustrated by the chaos around her; she chafes at being fully dependent on someone else for her needs, and she is resentful as she looks around her at all the normal activity in which she cannot participate. After all, pregnancy isn't an illness, it isn't a disease; but pregnancy wasn't meant to be like this, either!

Most families make their adjustments and get through this time, often with a successful birth as the result. Family members and care-givers, though, need to be sensitive to the woman's emotional state and to be aware that additional counseling support can be arranged when needed.

DIANE'S STORY

Diane, a 39-year-old social worker, was admitted to hospital for acute bleeding (placenta previa) at 29 weeks of pregnancy. She was the mother of two little boys, the first of whom had been conceived after many years of difficulty. Two years after his birth, she had experienced a tubal pregnancy, which was terminated and left her with only one Fallopian tube. Luckily, after two more years, she was able to conceive again, and a second healthy son was born. She was determined to continue trying for a third child, and although it took an additional two years for her to con-ceive, everything appeared to be going well in this pregnancy.

For Diane, the diagnosis of placenta previa understandably exacerbated her continuing fears that she might not be able to successfully carry another baby to term. She was confined to hospital for bed rest, and her world began to close in on her. Her husband was a busy and successful businessman with a number of major new projects underway. She herself had a de-manding but rewarding career as a social worker employed by the government and had hired a nanny to help with the little boys and the housekeeping. She had been working on several complicated cases, and now these had to be turned over to a colleague. In addition, she had dozens of caseloads to prepare reports on, and she was determined to do her part to make the transition as smooth as possible for her co-workers and clients.

I was asked to see Diane because she had talked with one of the nurses about her failed pregnancies and frustrations, and she expressed an interest in seeing a psychiatrist. When I came to see her, I found Diane working furiously, juggling papers and a dictaphone. Her files were methodically lined up by her bed-side, and a laptop computer was nearby.

As Diane and I talked about her fears and past pregnancies, I learned that she was a woman with remarkable determination and a positive attitude towards all of life's circumstances. As the oldest of three children, she had set and achieved goals throughout her life. Now, from her hospital bed, she was as much in command of events as possible. The nanny was fully organized to handle all aspects of the little boys' care. Though Diane's husband was able to visit her only erratically because of his business commitments, she seemed fully understanding and tolerant of the other demands on his time. Meanwhile, she worked as industriously on her own projects as if she were still at work full-time.

She seemed very willing to take a break to discuss the situation with me, indicating that it helped her collect her thoughts. We both agreed that she would call me if she wanted to talk again, but I left her feeling that she was a woman with an unusually positive outlook and no obvious need for the support I could provide. Diane did ask to see me once again as the weeks progressed, but once she had talked through some of her frustrations, she felt much better.

Diane's pregnancy was brought successfully close to term and she delivered another baby boy by Caesarean section. I continue to hear from Diane from time to time when she refers a client to me and volunteers an update on her three young sons. Once when we spoke, she told me that our talks in the hospital had been very important to her in helping her catch her breath, as it were, and continue a steady course. As important as the talks, she told me, was the immense reassurance she had in knowing that if ever she needed it, this kind of help was available to her.

Diane's story illustrated how prolonged hospitalization during pregnancy can give a woman a new way of coping with life. She was a woman who had been very active and involved all her life and suddenly found herself completely bedridden. But even while spending months in hospital for obstetrical problems, she was able to find coping strategies. There is no question that most women feel stress when "trapped" within the four walls of a hospital, unable to pursue their regular family routines and responsibilities, separated from their families except for visits from their partner and perhaps young children. Diane's story, however, illustrates that the experience can also be a source of challenge and self-development.

A QUESTION YOU MIGHT HAVE ABOUT PROLONGED HOSPITALIZATION

In the third trimester of my first pregnancy, I began to bleed and was diagnosed as having placenta previa. I was hospitalized for bed rest until the birth of my son. I felt quite depressed and hopeless all through the pregnancy, and I remember the hospitalization as the worst time in my life. I have a healthy three-year-old now, and my husband and I had planned on having two children. I'm worried that a second pregnancy would be the same, and I can't face the thought of another extended confinement.

Placenta previa is a rare medical complication, affecting only a small percentage of pregnancies. Even if a woman has this complication in one pregnancy, she will not necessarily have it ever again. It's understandable that you would feel apprehensive, especially in the third trimester of your next pregnancy. It's important that you talk with your doctor about the risks of placenta previa and then focus on maintaining a positive attitude. Three years of interaction with your healthy little boy should give you many positive thoughts and memories to help you face another pregnancy with enthusiasm and anticipation.

JUDY'S STORY

Judy, a 29-year-old woman, married to a doctor and the mother of a four-year-old daughter, had been my patient following her first pregnancy, when she became depressed in the postpartum period. When their little girl was ready to start preschool the couple decided the time was right for a second child. As planned, Judy became pregnant just as her husband finished medical school and began to set up his busy medical practice in a small rural community.

At 30 weeks in her pregnancy, as Judy was driving Katie to preschool, she had an acute, painful bleeding spell. At the medical clinic, she was diagnosed as having abruptio placenta. Because her husband was a doctor and because their town was a long commute from the maternity hospital, it was decided that she could take bed rest at home. Her mother lived some distance away, but was able to come and help out.

In spite of her mother's presence, Judy felt terribly alone and isolated during this period. Her mother was of course busy with the household and Katie's routines—Judy's own normal duties, in fact! Her husband was easily accessible, fully understood the medical need for her bed rest, and was very supportive. His time and thoughts were occupied with his new practice, though, and Judy was cautious about putting extra emotional demands on him. Despite her mother's help, she felt that the situation was terribly bleak, and with ample time on her hands, she began to brood about the postpartum depression she'd experienced before.

Judy made a long-distance call to me and talked about her hopelessness and despair. Despite the earlier postpartum depression, her first pregnancy had been uneventful and joyful; this time she felt that life was passing her by. She remembered the earlier depression, and said that, as grim as it had been, she had always had the feeling that help was available and had had confidence that her illness would end and she would be healthy again. This time, she couldn't see the ending. She viewed the ten weeks ahead of her as bleakly as if they were like an indefinite prison term.

We arranged a three-way phone conversation when her husband was present. Together, we decided that while Judy was not clinically depressed, she needed extra support to help her through the difficult weeks. In these circumstances we agreed on a somewhat unusual approach. Since Judy had been my patient before and since personal visits were impossible at this distance, we made an arrangement for Judy to phone me at a specific time each week. This kind of telephone consultation is not something that I had envisioned as a part of my practice, but in this special case it was possible and helpful. Judy's depression was mild, there was no other psychiatric support available in her community, and her husband had the medical awareness of the issues.

For the next few weeks, Judy called me at the designated time, and we talked for a half-hour or so about her thoughts and feelings. As the summer went on, she couldn't escape her feelings of being kept prisoner from the outside world. Until the diagnosis of abruptio placenta, she'd been enjoying her new home and had started a new garden along with her new pregnancy. "If only I could go out and smell the roses," she said to me one week. My advice to her was to enjoy the roses she so loved by reading books and catalogs, studying the different types, and planning the roses she would add to her garden next year. Since Judy was also devoted to opera music, I suggested that this was a wonderful time to absorb herself in the histories and personalities of the great composers and tenors who were her favorites—all without leaving her bedroom, through reading books and listening to tapes. In the course of her busy life, she had never had a chance to explore these byways, and I urged her to look on this as a "once-in-a-lifetime chance" rather than as a "prison sentence."

At 38 weeks, Judy was admitted to her local hospital and gave birth by C-section to a healthy baby daughter. She then came to my office for regular visits, but sailed through the postpartum period without depression. She was delighted to be at home and in good health, able to function fully as the wife and mother in this young family. She also said that just talking to me once a week, having someone outside the family listen to whatever she had to say, had in her words, "helped her see the light at the end of the tunnel."

Bed Rest and Home Monitoring

It is exceedingly difficult to have to rest at home and be subject to monitoring. There is no doubt that it can be lonely and isolating, and that one can feel "shut out" from the world, but with some obstetrical complications, the woman has no choice. On the other hand, bed rest may prove to be a welcome change for a woman any time during her pregnancy, especially if fatigue and insomnia become bothersome. However, nobody plans for prolonged bed rest.

Anxiety associated with bed rest takes many forms. The woman may become easily irritable, tearful, sometimes difficult to live with. She feels she is helpless and that the situation is beyond her control. In fact it is! Many of my patients have told me they felt "victimized." What keeps women hopeful in these circumstances is thoughts of the much-awaited baby. Anything endured seems worth it.

Once the woman gets over and deals with her initial anger and shock at having been "imprisoned," she will begin to adjust. Fortunately, in some localities, there are telephone support services (such as "The Confinement Line"), designed especially for expectant mothers confined to bed rest.

Surprisingy enough, one can be very busy in spite of being bedridden. One can be creative in many ways, and modern technological advances—fax machines, computers, and of course, the telephone—can make almost anything accessible. For a pregnant woman who must take bed rest, there is at least a definite end to the situation—in fact, a prize: the long-awaited baby for whom she is willing to undergo incredible hardship. So often, a patient whose "sentence" has ended with a successful delivery will tell me with joy, "It was worth all those weeks of lying in my room—look, I have my reward!"

COPING WITH DECISIONS ABOUT CAESAREAN SECTIONS

The good news about high-risk pregnancies is that with the help of modern technologies, problems can be identified at an early stage, and careful monitoring immensely increases the chances of a successful birth of a healthy baby. Accompanying this approach, though, is the possibility that the baby must be delivered by Caesarean section, or "C-section." C-section is a surgical procedure in which the baby is removed through its mother's abdomen rather than being delivered vaginally.

In emergencies, there may be no room for choice, and the only safe delivery for the baby is by Caesarean, such as is the case, for example, in some severe cases of abruptio placenta. In other cases, though, the mother's condition remains stable with bed rest, and there comes a point when it's a judgment call as to whether to deliver by Caesarean or to continue bed rest to full term. In these cases, the family should participate with the doctor in weighing the pros and cons and reaching a decision.

If Caesarean delivery is a possibility in your case, you are encouraged to do two things. First of all, have a full discussion with your partner and your doctor about exactly why the procedure is being considered in your case, exactly how it will be performed, and what the risks are. It is important that when this possibility is actually before you, you take time to get complete information and talk with your doctor about what you've read in books, learned in your prenatal class, or discussed with your friends.

Secondly, you and your partner should take a frank, objective look at your feelings about the birth experience. The advent of choice about pregnancy has made birth an arena in which many choices can be made. This relatively new outlook on pregnancy and childbirth is wholesome and healthy. Fathers play a greater role than in past times, and the couple together may participate deeply and meaningfully in every phase of pregnancy and delivery. However, when a couple is faced with choices in pregnancy and birth, it is important that they be able to adapt to a "non-choice" imposed on them by outside influences. If they have attended prenatal classes together, practiced breathing, and anticipated the drama and partnership of labor and childbirth, it may be difficult to even consider the possibility of a C-section. If an emergency C-section is required, they may resent having been unable to control events and feel deeply cheated of the birth experience.

In these circumstances, couples must try to look beyond the picture of how they would have enjoyed a normal delivery to the family's most important goals—the mother's health, the baby's health, the love and well-being of the family unit. If you are having trouble deciding what to do, or if you and your partner have very different ideas, you should be aware that a counselor can help support you in the process and guide you in reaching a decision that is truly your own.

BIRTH OF A PREMATURE BABY

A baby arriving early often ushers in a difficult period for the whole family. Not uncommonly, the baby is born with immature lungs and as a result must be kept on a respirator in a special care or intensive care nursery at the hospital. Provided there are no other risks or complications, most premature infants are able to go home once they reach a certain weight and adequate development—usually after a few weeks. For the parents, this relatively short period in between the birth and the homecoming may be marked by numerous conflicts in addition to sheer physical and mental exhaustion and anxiety about the baby.

Mothers are usually discharged from hospital after two to three days.

In addition to her constant worry about the newborn, the mother of the premature baby faces many practical demands. If she has other children at home, she now faces the dilemma of trying to care for the older children while spending as much time as possible at the hospital with the newborn. She desperately wants to touch the baby, to hold and comfort it, to nurse it, and unfortunately, the baby is "unreachable" in its respirator unit.

If the mother chooses to nurse, she must organize her routines around pumping her breast milk and delivering it to the hospital up to three times a day—a significant source of stress in itself. She eventually may find herself in a state of chronic fatigue. For her, there is no time to rest or recuperate in the postpartum period—no respite!

Charlene's story gives us some insight into the difficulties families may face with a premature birth. The mother, especially, may be faced with extraordinary new burdens. Supportive family members, friends, and in general, access to a "helping hand" will lessen the anxiety that surrounds this challenging time.

CHARLENE'S STORY

Charlene, a 28-year-old homemaker with a daughter aged 3, had lost her second pregnancy at 21 weeks due to premature rupture of membranes. I saw her in therapy for six weeks and helped her deal with this pregnancy loss. A year later, she conceived again and came to see me a few times around 18 to 20 weeks of pregnancy for reassurance and help in coping with feelings of anxiety. Her anxiety was normal, given her earlier pregnancy loss around this same time.

Charlene delivered a healthy baby boy six weeks before her due date. The baby was approximately four pounds at birth and had to be put into the special care nursery immediately.

When visiting little Joseph, Charlene would come by and see me twice a week and update me on his progress. She experienced a myriad of emotions as he lay there quietly, day after day, under the close supervision of a nurse. She constantly asked questions like, "What if he stops growing?" "What if he stopped breathing?"

Charlene's husband visited the baby whenever he could and also took on a greater role in the care of their little girl. Charlene herself spent endless hours in the hospital. It was a wonderful milestone when Joey came off the respirator and then intravenous feeding, and Charlene began to feel relieved and hopeful.

She came in to see me on the day it was decided her baby could go home. To this day, I remember her beaming, radiant face as she announced, "I finally won my trophy!"

A QUESTION YOU MIGHT HAVE ABOUT OBSTETRICAL COMPLICATIONS

? *My sister had third trimester bleeding that eventually led to a C-section although she was very much opposed to this. I was going to be a labor coach for my sister, and the whole family shared her disappointment at this outcome. She decided she would not become pregnant again. Now it's my turn, and I'm also afraid of the possibility of a C-section. I would like some advice about the safety of this procedure in case I need it, and I wonder what the chances are that this will happen to me, too.*

Your sister's disappointment has been shared by many women who have prepared themselves during pregnancy for a natural vaginal delivery and suddenly find this is not possible. However, a C-section delivery is sometimes a necessity and may in fact save the life of the infant, which seems to have been the case with your sister. Every woman's pregnancy develops differently, and the circumstances that call for a C-section may also vary. In your particular case, your anxiety and fear is completely understandable; however, your relationship does not automatically make you a candidate for a C-section.

I suggest that you discuss this matter with your obstetrician and ask him or her what percentage of women in your community have C-sections and for what reasons. This will help you realize that you will not have a C-section unless it is absolutely necessary to save the infant's life. Women like your sister, who experience disappointment because of a Caesarean delivery, can often benefit from some postpartum counseling to examine their feelings of loss.

WHAT I TELL MY PATIENTS

For every woman, whether or not she is self-observant and analytical by nature, pregnancy is a life event during which personal attitudes are examined and personality traits are scrutinized. A woman can't help but reflect on her values, her personal characteristics, and her behavior as she dreams and speculates about the future of the child within her. She might not actually put the question into words, but every pregnant woman asks herself, "What kind of mother will I be?"

This private reflection is bolstered by messages from others. Her partner might gently tease her—"Well, if it's a girl, I hope she doesn't have your temper!" But this very interest and support, the very fact of the progressing pregnancy, confirms that she is a mother already and is being a good mother in bringing the pregnancy to happy completion.

No wonder, then, that when complications arise the woman can be deeply wounded in how she views herself. For the pregnant woman, the interruption of pregnancy, prolonged hospitalization, or the need to have a C-section—for whatever reasons these might occur—can translate to, "I'm not a good mother," and this sad equation can become worse as she concludes, "There's something wrong with me. I've somehow deserved this." These feelings of wounded motherhood and wounded self can make it doubly difficult for a woman to seek and accept the support, counseling, or psychiatric help that may be needed.

The situation is not helped when family or friends say things that suggest some kind of personality weakness is at the heart of the problem. Think for a minute about the comments some people so thoughtlessly make about others with emotional problems: "She's just got to get over this" or "He's got to pull himself together." These are quite common attitudes, and they suggest that the person who is emotionally troubled need just exert a little will power to "get their act together" or that they are showing some kind of weakness by "not being able to get over it." Very often, psychiatrists and counselors must spend a lot of time helping women get beyond the damage these kinds of remarks inflict before they can begin to help them cope with the issues that are troubling them. Women who are professional caregivers themselves—doctors, nurses, psychologists, social workers—have sometimes learned their most important lessons about emotional distress by experiencing their own pregnancies.

When I counsel women with medical or obstetrical complications that confine them to bed rest or other difficult regimens, I encourage them to see the new restrictions as a commitment to their babies' welfare, which is of course tied up with their own welfare. Motherhood, after all, is a responsibility that begins with pregnancy, not with birth.

Medical and obstetrical complications of pregnancy are something that no woman ever wants to think about, even when she goes to prenatal classes. C-sections and abnormal births are discussed, but the actual implications of these are usually not covered. When a woman, then, finds that she must take bed rest in hospital or at home, it is important to address her ability to cope with the situation. Not all women can "pull up their socks" by responding in the way society expects—that is, without any negative feelings. In fact, it is quite unrealistic to expect a woman in such a situation to effortlessly readjust her pace, feel no qualms about what her family is going through at home, and handle the whole situation with good cheer. Once a woman understands this, she generally has an easier time.

CHAPTER 3

"HOW COULD THIS BE
HAPPENING TO ME?"

Miscarriage, Fetal Abnormalities, and Congenital Defects

In this chapter, I will discuss some of the most difficult and painful events of pregnancy—loss of a developing fetus to whom the mother has closely bonded, decisions around termination of pregnancy, and coping with abnormalities in the infant. These events can be crushing to parents and can sometimes be devastating to a marriage; they call for the utmost love and generosity on the part of the two partners and great compassion and patience on the part of family members and caregivers.

When mothers, when parents, face these same issues, their reactions almost always have some element of guilt and of blame for both themselves and their partner. Insofar as these feelings occur commonly, they are normal—but they can be horribly destructive, affecting personalities adversely and destroying relationships.

The most important thing I tell my patients is that the tragedy is not their fault and not their partner's fault—their body has not failed them; there is not something they should have done differently. The fact that they have a particular genetic makeup or developed a medical complication is not a matter for blame and guilt. Pregnancy and birth are so miraculous—from two cells that meet and multiply, a new human being is formed. It is a complex process, this everyday event, and at any stage, things can go wrong. The fact that most of the time everything goes perfectly is in itself amazing.

As painful as the event is, the mother and father need to share the labor and delivery of a child who is incompatible with life just as closely as they had planned to share a joyous birth. In olden days, when babies were born dead or died just at birth, mothers were discouraged from even seeing the baby. Now we realize what a cruel thing this is—not to see this tiny loved one who has been inside you, been a part of you, for so long. No matter how tiny the baby, it is important that the mother and father be able to see it; this is an essential step in coming to terms with the loss.

Both partners need to support and to accept support from each other. For some couples, the loss of an infant or the birth of a child with abnormalities can bring the marriage to a crisis stage, and the couple may need help not only in confronting their grief but in dealing with issues in their marriage that have surfaced with their loss.

As I will discuss in this chapter, the needs of other children in the family must also be considered, and the parents, especially the mothers, need the time to grieve their loss before considering another pregnancy.

PSYCHOLOGICAL RESPONSE TO MISCARRIAGE

Although societal encouragement and family participation contribute to the enjoyable features of pregnancy, not as much support is offered to the woman who experiences a miscarriage, particularly in the first trimester. Well-meaning friends often gloss over the event with the reassurance that "It happened for the best." Even the woman's partner, who must deal with his own disappointment, may be awkward or uncertain about how to be supportive.

The bonding women feel with an unborn child can be very intense, and the grief and loss they may feel about an early-stage miscarriage are legitimate. There is no reason for a woman to deny that she has sustained a painful loss, and talking in these terms with the family may be helpful. In recent years, the medical profession has realized—because women have insisted on this awareness—that grief for the loss of an unborn child can be very difficult and terribly lonely. At the same time, we have learned more about the stages of the grieving process and how to help people work through the stages at a normal pace. If you are frank with your doctor or counselor, he or she should readily recognize your grief and be able to help you understand the feelings you're experiencing. Obstetricians and gynecologists usually have very busy practices, and you are most likely to find support and help from a counselor specially trained in dealing with grief. Your family doctor should be able to advise you about the resources available in your community.

Women may feel a range of troubling emotions both at the onset of miscarriage and after the event. Even though a woman is frightened by severe cramping or bleeding, she may try to deny that anything is wrong and avoid treatment. Once the miscarriage is confirmed, the woman's sense of losing control of her pregnancy may produce a feeling of helplessness, or, in reaction to helplessness, an attempt to take control again by refusing to accept the diagnosis and follow medical advice.

After a miscarriage, it is very easy for a woman to feel guilty and to believe that if she had done some small thing differently, her baby would be all right. It's also easy to look for someone else to blame—the two likeliest candidates are the woman's doctor and her husband. A woman's blame of and anger at her partner might take the form of rage; she might also become cool and withdraw affection and attention.

As is discussed in greater detail in Chapter Eight, the husband or partner, too, must make his own adjustments to this unexpected turn of events. Miscarriage may present to the first-time father all his worst fears about the realities of pregnancy—a complex, nearly incomprehensible event for which he has had little preparation has suddenly gone badly wrong. Like his partner, he may feel troubled by this confirmation that events are beyond his control. And although men experience pregnancy as individuals, it's safe to say that the father will experience the event quite differently than does his partner. Typically, men in our culture tend to be more "future-oriented," and the man may find his words of intended reassurance ("Don't worry—we'll have another one") are exactly the wrong thing to say. The very difference in the man's and woman's feelings might make for conflicts between them. The disappointments of miscarriage can thus create a distance and discord in the marriage just when both partners are in need of each other's understanding.

I describe this range of feelings so that readers will have a sense of what many bereaved parents feel and experience. There is a normal time for grieving, for readjusting, for being ready to set new goals, and this time varies among individuals. No one can determine that time for you, but you should be able to sense for yourself whether healing is taking place. I would encourage you to seek help from a counselor if, after some time, you can't seem to move beyond preoccupation with your loss, if your behavior and feelings towards others change in unusual ways, or if the circumstances around your marriage relate to marital problems.

Sandra's story was such a case.

SANDRA'S STORY

Sandra was a 29-year-old graduate student of European descent who had caused a family controversy by marrying an African-American. She and her husband deliberately put off having a baby for several years because Sandra continued to hope her parents would come to accept her husband. This was not the case, however, for her parents were quite conservative and their feelings were deeply ingrained. Eventually, the couple decided to proceed with their plans to have children nonetheless. Although her parents were antagonistic to the prospect of a grandchild of mixed race, Sandra and her husband were elated when Sandra's pregnancy was confirmed.

When Sandra suffered a miscarriage in the tenth week, she and her husband were both disappointed. Some weeks later, though, she realized that she also felt relief, since the miscarriage allowed her to avoid additional problems with her parents. She then became troubled at her "abnormal" feelings, criticizing herself harshly for feeling relief rather than grief. She found she could no longer concentrate at work, and she began having crying spells. Sandra's family doctor referred her to me.

When I began seeing Sandra, I learned that her husband was very understanding about her concern for her parents but could not change his own feelings about wanting to have children. Thus it became important to help Sandra explore these issues from her own point of view. In the course of several sessions, Sandra became clear about her own choices. She became less conflicted and, having confirmed for herself her desire to have children in this relationship, she went on to become pregnant again.

Even more difficult is the experience of women who have repeated miscarriages. In these women, grief is quite intense and prolonged, and professional help is often required. Different women have different ways of handling the grief of miscarriage, and the same is true of their partners, whose reactions are also variable.

DAPHNE'S STORY

Daphne was a 42-year-old professional woman who had had four miscarriages. In each pregnancy, she lost her baby at seven to eight weeks. When this happened for the third time, she consulted a specialist in difficult pregnancies. The doctor discovered that Daphne has an unusual condition that does not allow her to carry the pregnancy past eight or nine weeks. Research into this particular condition continues, and there have been attempts to maintain the pregnancy by giving the woman injections of gamma-globulin. However, this therapy is still in the early stages of investigation.

When Daphne had miscarried for the second time, her family doctor asked me to see her, and she has been my patient for the past year, occasionally bringing her husband as well. She is still exploring the possibility of pregnancy and thinks she might go to a particular medical center that specializes in treating this type of miscarriage. However, there are other issues she has to deal with—for example, her advancing maternal age, her repeated experience of grief, and her apprehension about carrying a baby to term at her age.

Because Daphne came to me after her second miscarriage, I have seen her through both her third and fourth miscarriages. There are no obvious issues from her past that are relevant to our present discussion; instead, our focus is how she feels about herself and how she deals with her sense of failure in achieving motherhood.

A QUESTION YOU MIGHT HAVE ABOUT MISCARRIAGE

[?] *I am a 35-year-old woman, and I have lost four pregnancies, all in my first trimester. My doctor is unable to understand why I have not carried the pregnancies into the second trimester, and she's sent me to several specialists who have assured me that there's "nothing wrong physically." However, I have*

not been able to conceive again, and I still worry about the lost
pregnancies. What should be my approach to pregnancy now?

Your experience of recurrent pregnancy loss leaves you understandably apprehensive and fearful. More and more, researchers believe that a woman's state of mind and emotional well-being are just as important to conception as the healthy functioning of her ovaries, tubes, and uterus. Even if you are functioning perfectly physically, it is important that you are also ready to conceive psychologically. That is one of the reasons many doctors advise that a woman should wait three to six months before attempting pregnancy again after a miscarriage. What this means is that the woman should deal with her grief about the miscarriage before considering herself emotionally ready to become pregnant again.

Naturally, you are anxious about your ability to maintain a successful pregnancy and you may be worried that your "biological clock" is ticking away. I suggest that just as you've taken steps to check on your physical health, you take a number of steps to get yourself into the best possible emotional health. First, talk with your doctor about your preoccupation with your past pregnancies, and ask that you be referred to a therapist who can help you explore your feelings about those losses.

Then, start on your own campaign of emotional fitness by developing a full and absorbing daily routine. Follow your own talents and inclinations and develop other points of interest and activity in your life, in addition to your work and your absorption in having a family. Your aim is to replace anxiety with enthusiasm and contentment and to develop a sustaining identity and interest in life beyond the role of "mother" on which you have been counting. There is no easy answer, but I hope you will find yourself among those women who are able to conceive—once they've stopped worrying about becoming pregnant.

Your partner faces the loss along with you, though perhaps not so intensely. Reconnecting with him rather than withdrawing will help your healing. Becoming pregnant again involves both partners. The recovery process, also, involves the two of you together.

SECOND TRIMESTER LOSS

The second trimester of pregnancy is normally a joyous time of physical well-being and positive emotions of an intensity not experienced outside of pregnancy. Many women, wanting to be sure they are beyond the time where spontaneous miscarriages are common before making any announcements, choose to keep their pregnancies private during the first trimester. But once into the second trimester, they have a new confidence that their babies will be brought successfully to term and are quite happy to receive congratulations on their condition.

Many women savor the special status they experience and the attention and interest of people around them, who often treat them differently and delicately. It is a time to share news and to make plans, ranging from what clothes to wear to how to decorate the baby's room. There's a special excitement in shopping for maternity clothes and browsing among infants' wear, dreaming and planning for extra-special toys and clothing for the baby. Even assembling the normal day-to-day wardrobe and supplies for a new infant has a special satisfaction.

But the greatest joy of the second trimester is the first feeling of the baby's movement. At those first kicks of the living baby inside her, a woman experiences feelings unlike any she has felt before—a profound delight and awe at this unfolding miracle, a feeling she will never forget, and never fail to be thrilled by in each of her pregnancies. The woman's internal experience is then confirmed by medical examination. Not so long ago, her doctor's stethoscope detecting the heartbeat was a confirmation which she could share by listening. But now, with ultrasound examination, the woman can see the baby's heart beating as early as six to seven weeks into the pregnancy. Whether it is the first ultrasound or a later one, a woman feels tremendous excitement and joyful accomplishment at the sight of the new life, no matter how tiny, floating in its amniotic sac.

In a sense, it is this experience of specialness and confidence, the feeling that after some uncertainty in the first trimester, everything is now on track, that causes particular devastation when something unexpected goes wrong in the second trimester. Yet at the same time, because the pregnancy is not "fully developed," the acute anguish and pain of women who must face this difficult reality at this point is often not fully appreciated by those near to them, even including some health professionals.

I will now talk about problems that may occur in the second

trimester and explore how these problems can be worked through with appropriate support and empathy.

DIAGNOSIS OF ABNORMAL PREGNANCY

When Diagnostic Tests Are Called For

No matter how well her pregnancy is progressing and how positively the expectant mother adapts to its pleasures and challenges, she is never far from the question every woman asks herself throughout her pregnancy: "Will my baby be normal?" This question takes on a sense of dread when the woman's doctor advises that special tests are called for to further assess the health of the fetus.

Abnormalities in the fetus have several causes, and not all of these are fully understood. They can develop during the pregnancy—for example, if the mother is exposed to an illness like rubella (German measles) while she is pregnant. Fetal abnormalities can also be the result of factors present at conception, such as the combined gene patterns of the two parents. Some prenatal testing is commonly performed if the mother is over 35, if there has been a previous fetal abnormality, or if there are medical conditions in the family that are known to have a hereditary component. In Canada and in some parts of the United States, some of these medical investigations are routinely offered in every pregnancy. In addition, modern diagnostic tests may be carried out when factors in the parents' family history or findings in the mother's routine checkups suggest that the health of the fetus should be assessed.

Few mothers choose not to avail themselves of these tests, and few people would choose to turn back the clock to earlier times, when these diagnostic tests were not available. The anguish of mothers throughout history who unknowingly carried to term babies who were doomed to die at birth is nearly unimaginable. Today, we see a different kind of anguish in families who discover in the second trimester that their baby's condition is incompatible with life or that the baby will be born with a serious and uncorrectable defect. Although the medical situation may be clear-cut, the emotional situation now becomes even more complicated. Health care professionals and the parents themselves need to be aware that the emotional strain at such times can be immense, and unconditional emotional support is essential as sophisticated medical techniques reveal the likely outcome of the pregnancy.

When You Have a Test for Fetal Abnormalities

Most tests that detect abnormalities are performed early in the pregnancy, when the fetus is sufficiently developed for abnormalities to be detected but still small enough for the termination of pregnancy if indicated. Having the test, waiting for results, and worrying about the outcome are all sources of anxiety for a pregnant woman. Some of this anxiety can be partly relieved by acquiring as much information as possible while you are undergoing various tests. You should be sure that your doctor explains clearly why tests are being done in your case and how long it will take to get results. In some situations, the tests may be quite routine for all mothers at your stage of pregnancy—at some stages of pregnancy having a blood test or getting an ultrasound is to be expected. Whether or not this is the case, it's a good idea for you and your partner together to meet with your doctor to discuss the different procedures that you may undergo. Sometimes, the result of a particular test may not be clear-cut and an additional ultrasound might be required. At other times, tests may show the infant's condition to be safe and healthy, and the test may be repeated later in the pregnancy.

It is common for women to worry that a given test itself may harm the infant or cause a miscarriage, particularly with amniocentesis or chorionic villus sampling (CVS), which I will describe shortly. The risks of prenatal testing continue to be measured in research studies. When prenatal tests are performed by experienced specialists—as they always should be—the risks are very low. However, your doctor should speak with you about the risks of the specific test you are having so that you can be involved in deciding the risk versus the benefit.

Another common question is how painful the tests will be to the mother herself. Ultrasound and blood tests are virtually painless, except for the slight prick of a needle for a laboratory blood test. The procedures for amniocentesis and CVS have a low level of pain and perhaps some discomfort for several hours afterwards.

Following are the common prenatal tests you might encounter:

Ultrasound, perhaps the most commonly known test, is used quite routinely in the various stages of pregnancy to confirm the age of the fetus and to screen for the possibility of multiple pregnancy. Ultrasound examination can also detect growth retardation, as well as abnormalities in the formation and structure of the heart, kidneys, gastrointestinal system, and musculoskeletal system.

Ultrasound testing is based on the principle that different types of organic structures reflect ultrasonic waves differently. Having an ultrasound test is somewhat like having an X ray in that it is administered externally and is painless. An instrument that sends out and interprets these waves is held against the woman's belly, and the pattern produced by the fetus can be seen immediately on a video screen. One type of ultrasound reveals the structural forms of the fetus, and a second type shows fetal movements, such as the baby's heartbeat. Under normal circumstances, seeing the form and movement of the developing infant is one of the great thrills of modern pregnancy.

Maternal serum alpha-fetoprotein testing is a screening test for the possibility of certain kinds of abnormalities, such as neural tube defects and Down syndrome. Alpha-fetoprotein is a protein substance normally found in the developing fetus; after about seven weeks of pregnancy, it begins to appear in the mother's bloodstream. The amount of maternal alpha-fetoprotein can be tested by a simple laboratory blood test using a small amount of blood drawn from the woman's arm. When high levels of alpha-fetoprotein are found in the mother's blood, there is a possibility that abnormalities such as neural tube defect and other congenital malformations may be present in the fetus. Before a firm diagnosis is made, additional tests such as ultrasound and amniocentesis will be administered to get more information.

Amniocentesis is the testing of fluid from the amniotic sac in which the baby floats. To obtain a sample, the doctor uses ultrasound to determine the position of the fetus, inserts a needle into the amniotic sac through the mother's abdomen, and withdraws a small amount of amniotic fluid. Tests on the fluid can show whether certain irregularities in the infant's chromosome structure or genetic factors are present. This test is performed at approximately 16 weeks of pregnancy, and the results are usually available three to four weeks later—usually before 20 weeks gestation. The risk of any fetal injury due to amniocentesis is very small. Since the risk of retardation in the fetus rises once a woman is over age 35, amniocentesis is commonly used to detect abnormalities during pregnancy. As mentioned before, younger women with past history of any genetic abnormality also commonly undergo amniocentesis.

Chorionic villus sampling (CVS) is a test that analyzes the genetic make-up of the infant's cells. In this test, too, the doctor uses an ultrasound to pinpoint the infant's position and then either inserts a catheter through the mother's cervix or inserts a needle through the mother's abdomen. A sample of tissue from the placenta is drawn up through the needle or catheter for testing. This particular test also is fairly safe when performed by an experienced clinician and is performed between the eighth and twelfth weeks. Results are usually available within a matter of days.

When an Abnormality Is Diagnosed

When second trimester tests are performed as a matter of routine and the health of the baby is confirmed, it is joyful news for the family. The good news is cause for celebration, and the prenatal test may be regarded as just one more hurdle passed on the nine-month adventure of pregnancy. When tests identify an abnormality, however, the devastating news can create real chaos for the woman who has been experiencing the sense of wholeness and well-being of the second trimester. Even a woman who has known that her age may place her at risk for abnormal pregnancy may be genuinely shocked and unable to grasp the situation that now confronts her.

There are two distinct possibilities with the diagnosis of abnormality, and each situation carries its own particular anguish: The infant's abnormality is either compatible or not compatible with life. The most familiar example of the first possibility is the diagnosis of Down syndrome; the family is confronted with the fact that the child to be born will suffer from mental retardation as well as the facial and physical characteristics of this particular defect. With the second possibility, the fetus may be found to be lacking kidneys, or a brain, or any of a number of vital organs that allow it to sustain life. In this case, the parents will be told by the physician that the infant may not live to term or will survive perhaps only minutes or a few hours after birth. Each of these possible scenarios is tragic and fraught with excruciating mental pain and anguish.

Either situation places extreme demands on the family, and it is rare for a woman to be able to endure the findings of abnormal pregnancy without an acute emotional response. After recovering from the initial shock, the mother is often overwhelmed with guilt and rage. One day, she was feeling so well, so buoyantly confident, and now her whole world is in shambles. How could this happen? There can be many scapegoats for her pain and anger, and the first, most accessible target is herself. She might view herself as "defective," or accuse herself of making mistakes in her actions and choices. What did she do to make this happen? Had she always eaten the right foods? Had she had enough milk to drink? Maybe if she'd taken extra vitamins and minerals? Where did she go wrong? What is wrong with her body? She barrages herself with endless questions and may be unable to make a decision about the choice that confronts her.

The self-inflicted torment a women in these crisis situations endures is heartrending; no word of sympathy appeases her, and the loving reassurances of family members may be almost meaningless. Yet experience has shown that support and guidance from caring professionals can help these women and their partners traverse this difficult stage of guilt and self-blame and eventually reach a decision with which they can live. Each family, each person, is unique, and no one answer will suffice. As an outsider to the family unit, the psychiatrist or counselor can in an objective way help the woman realize her strengths, find some firm ground beneath her, and enable her to stand with her decision.

When Abnormalities Are Compatible with Life

When they learn that the child to be born has a severe abnormality compatible with life, the woman and her partner are faced not only with the grave shock of the findings but also with the need to make a decision about whether or not to continue the pregnancy—and fairly quickly. This decision has not only short-term consequences for the life of the fetus but also long-term consequences for the life and future of the family. Although the diagnosis of abnormality can now be made easily with modern medical techniques, the choice this presents—to terminate the pregnancy or to carry it to term and live with an infant whose lifelong abnormality must be coped with—is far from easy.

A woman and her partner must make this choice together, and it is a choice that will strain their perceptions of themselves as parents and human beings and touch on their deepest beliefs about life itself. Not surprisingly, there are many opportunities, in this short period of time, for much pain and much lasting regret. It's not uncommon for a couple to discover that they have entirely different views about whether or not to terminate the pregnancy and whether or not they can face a future in which a child with abnormalities is a factor. They must confront their beliefs surrounding family life—are they willing to be parents to a child with these problems? What of the considerations of other children in the family? And there are practical considerations of family finances and the lifelong physical and emotional demands of raising such a child. When couples have different viewpoints—and no assumptions can be made about either the father's or mother's view—marital conflicts that seem almost unresolvable can result.

Even when couples agree on a course of action, their decision is not necessarily a "free choice"—their families may have their viewpoint; their religion may have a viewpoint; they may feel the pressures of societal viewpoints. When individuals feel strongly that life must not be terminated by abortion, or when they belong to a religion with definite views against abortion, the couple may feel that they have no choice—that the woman must carry the pregnancy to term, even though they cannot reconcile themselves to the situation this presents. And even when a choice has been made and the couple agrees that it is the right choice, the mother especially may still look back on the decision with mixed feelings, not sure that this was the choice she would make if she had it to do all over again.

A woman who feels forced to continue her pregnancy against her will, who feels that others' views won out—either her family's or her church's—can come to feel resentful, angry, outraged, and ultimately, victimized. When the woman feels this way, future problems are almost inevitable, since she is unlikely to bond with a baby she does not feel she bargained for.

On the other hand, when the couple decides to terminate the pregnancy because they cannot face the lifelong burden of raising a child with these particular abnormalities, the woman may have tremendous feelings of guilt about taking steps to kill the fetus inside her. No matter where she turns, she faces a dark corner.

Since termination of pregnancy is usually done only until the 20th week of pregnancy, a family may have only a matter of a week or two in which to make the decisions. Although women typically tell me prior to the amniocentesis that they have discussed the options and their feelings in the event that amniocentesis brings them the news that, for example, they had conceived a baby with Down syndrome, they still report being "totally shocked" when this actually happens. Unfortunately, they do not have too many days to think about what to do once they are facing the harsh reality. Therefore, I recommend that when the diagnosis of fetal abnormality is made, the woman and her partner be offered support and given appropriate guidance as soon as possible.

How Supportive Therapy Can Help

There is no pattern to the emotional responses of a couple who have just received the news that their awaited infant has an abnormality like Down syndrome. Every individual is different, and every family has its own responses. Whether the reaction is apparent calm, burning anger, or unrestrained grief, no one should underestimate the trials this couple faces or the turmoil they suffer.

Family members can help by recognizing that this is indeed a situation of emotional crisis and that the couple needs emotional and practical support—and at the same time, respect and privacy in coming to their decision. This is not a time for caring family members to make automatic assumptions about what the couple will decide, to say, "Well, of course, they will terminate the pregnancy," or "They certainly won't consider an abortion." It is also well to remember that, while modern medicine has made an early diagnosis possible and has made termination of pregnancy medically safe, the couple's decision—whatever it is—has long-term consequences, and long-term appropriate support will make a big difference.

Professional caregivers can offer several avenues of help, and this help must be made available quickly, starting with the moment the diagnosis is communicated. Both the woman and her partner need an objective person to help them through the range of emotions that will be experienced—personal emotions of anger, shock, grief, and devastating feelings of blame that can potentially destroy the relationship just at the time they most need each other's support and involvement. Many women have said that this kind of support—empathetic listening from a counselor who is an objective person, outside one's family and one's circumstances—was a safety valve that got them through the immediate crisis of the first reaction. Often women also benefit from continued therapy over several weeks and months while they are coming to terms with the inevitable.

The second support that a professional counselor may give, once the immediate shock and disbelief has been endured, is to assist in putting the woman and thus the couple in a position where they can *make their own decision* about the pregnancy. In part, this is a matter of helping the woman and her partner recognize that this is their decision to make, and then helping them explore how the two of them will make it together if their long-term relationship is to prosper. What helps them make this decision together is knowledge of the facts about the conception—such as whether the fetus is viable at all or how long the baby is likely to live if they were to continue the pregnancy. In addition, the counselor may discuss with them the extra added responsibility the couple may have to take on if they go ahead with the pregnancy when the diagnosis is, for example, Down syndrome. Learning the facts about the outcome of this kind of pregnancy will help them deal with their guilt and minimize mutual blaming and a sense of resentment. The couple may receive additional support by speaking with the professionals who participated in the diagnosis—for example, a genetic specialist. An additional important aid for a couple is peer support groups, where they can ventilate, sharing their feelings with couples facing similar dilemmas.

Unfortunately, support groups of this kind are not always available, especially in less populated areas. However, with the growing awareness of the value of support groups, professionals can often arrange at least informal contact with others who have gone through the same experience. I strongly recommend that the couple talk to other parents who have confronted the same decision—couples who have terminated an abnormal pregnancy, those who have chosen to raise a child with a severe congenital abnormality, and if possible, couples who have chosen to give the child up for adoption. The latter is an equally difficult decision and one with its own emotional turmoil.

After an initial consultation with a therapist, the woman who has chosen to maintain the pregnancy should consider continuing to see a counselor regularly throughout the pregnancy and for some time after the birth. She may need support in exploring issues around her ability to raise such a baby, the desirability of doing so, the emotional consequences for her of placing the baby for adoption if she chooses, and whether there are external factors in her decision making. This is by no means a clear-cut situation, and irrespective of the choices made, there are long-term emotional consequences for the family and the woman. The role of the therapist is to be nonjudgmental and offer support during this turbulent time.

MARTHA'S STORY

Martha, a 35-year-old schoolteacher who lived in a small suburban community, chose not to have an amniocentesis early in her pregnancy despite her age because she felt it would make no difference in her decision to maintain her pregnancy. She was fully confident of delivering a healthy baby because she and her husband had an almost fanatically healthy lifestyle and no family history of any genetic problems.

She and her husband Dan were completely shocked when she gave birth to a baby with Down syndrome. I was asked to see them because, in the midst of their grief and surprise, they were engaged in a mental and emotional struggle about their course of action. Martha wanted to release the baby for adoption, while Dan wanted to keep their little son and see the situation through.

I saw Martha and Dan together and individually for several visits; theirs was an interesting picture of a marriage in which their individual personality differences had not until this point endured such an acid test. Martha was a woman who liked control and strove to maintain a perfectly controlled environment around her. She enjoyed her role as a schoolteacher, and her third-grade students adored her because the class environment was so perfectly directed and organized. In therapy, it became clear that Martha fulfilled this same role in her marriage and was the key decision maker.

Dan was an easy-going, laid-back man who was quite aware that Martha called the shots and usually was very comfortable with her decisions. This had been the case when Martha decided against an amniocentesis. Dan saw no reason to disagree with her; in fact, their relationship was such that he had never felt there was anything to be gained in disagreeing with her on anything. He told me, though, that he had felt some uneasiness about that particular decision because the wife of one of his close friends had given birth to an infant who was not compatible with life. Dan had seen the grief caused by this situation, and he had originally taken it for granted that Martha, in her perfect way, would have all the necessary tests done to avoid this kind of tragedy. When their Down child was born, he was inwardly furious with Martha, and though he kept the words to himself, the thing he most wanted to say to Martha was, "I told you so."

In addition to seeing the two of them initially, I referred them to a marital therapist, who began to help them deal with some of the basic issues in their relationship of control, assertiveness, and submissiveness. Meanwhile, they took the baby home from the hospital, with the question still open in Martha's mind as to whether they would place the child for adoption. After about two months, Martha decided that she was in agreement with Dan's view that they should keep their baby.

About a year later, Martha became pregnant again and gave birth to a healthy baby girl. She is now raising the two children and has come to realize that not everything in life can be perfectly under control. She has also realized that raising a child with Down syndrome is one of the biggest challenges she's undertaken. She and Dan continued to have some marital problems even after the birth of their second child, and they have continued in marital therapy. The couple has tried to work on most of their major problems, and their roles have been redefined somewhat as they face together the demands and decisions of their family life.

When Abnormalities Are Incompatible with Life

A different and no less intense trauma faces the couple when prenatal testing reveals that the baby has an abnormality with which it cannot survive long after birth. The type of abnormality can in itself be a source of shock—as, for example, in the statistically small number of cases of anencephaly, where the fetus may be found not to have a head. On the other hand, the baby may be "perfect"—except that it lacks an organ vital for life, such as the kidneys. In either case, this is an infant who may live only as long as a few minutes after birth. We do not yet have a full explanation for why some of these abnormalities occur—why some genes may mutate, why something "goes wrong" in the formation of the fetus—and this uncertainty can make even more difficult the issues of blame and guilt which the mother almost inevitably experiences.

But once the diagnosis has been made, the major emotional issue the mother must face is that the child developing inside her is doomed to die at or just after birth. Many women have described their experience of receiving this diagnosis as being told that their baby received a death sentence. Tragically, too, the death sentence is a lingering one. The couple must choose—within a matter of weeks—whether to maintain or terminate the pregnancy. For those who choose to terminate pregnancy, the situation is not considered a medical emergency and often the woman ends up waiting for days for admission to a maternity hospital. The grief of their situation is compounded by the contrasts and delays that surround the event. The equilibrium of the second trimester, the happiness of all their plans, is shattered overnight, and now a grim, slow-motion nightmare takes its place. In some hospitals, bureaucratic red tape may cause delay in the actual admission of the woman to hospital. Many hospitals in the United States and Canada have individual rules regarding the termination of pregnancy; and some though not all hospitals have "ethics committees" in place that decide the fate of the pregnancy. The following of these maddening rules, senseless as they seem at one level, may be legally necessary in order to acquire the permission to abort the fetus under medical supervision. This can lead to a terribly grim time of isolation and paralysis, and if a marriage is not in stable condition, the continuing stress of the situation can cause further damage.

The consequences of this kind of diagnosis are very serious for the long-term emotional health of the woman and naturally can affect the marriage. The usual reactions are disbelief, anger, and shock. During this time, mutual support is very important, and the couple should be advised not to fight or blame each other, and to be supportive. Often, it is helpful for a counselor to see each of the couple separately. It is especially important not to overlook the male partner, who may feel especially isolated. In my practice, I often end up seeing my patients' partners, who are very relieved to get support themselves under these circumstances.

The Role of Therapy

While abnormal pregnancies are an age-old problem, in today's world there is a new recognition that the emotional support offered to women who receive this diagnosis must be as sophisticated as their medical care. One can only wonder at the profound grief of women in past times who, unprepared, gave birth to infants who would die within hours. Ironically, the facts that an early diagnosis can be made and intervention is possible do not mean that the woman is any better prepared for what takes place.

Women in this crisis situation need a tremendous amount of understanding and support, and professional counselors can help with both individual attention and conjoint therapy to the couple in crisis. Many times, women have a raging anger at the medical system and the doctors who made the diagnosis. On the one hand, this is a normal and necessary way of expressing their deep grief and sorrow. And unfortunately, it is sometimes a justified anger at the insensitivity of professionals who have not taken time to announce the diagnosis with the gentleness and empathy that the situation deserves.

In the early days of therapy much time is spent in helping women express this anger and address their sorrow. Both the woman and her partner must be able to work through their initial sense of grief before they are in a position to make decisions about the pregnancy. Often, a woman may be truly unable to concentrate on what has happened and what her options are. She may be so shocked that, even after having had the procedures explained to her, she will ask again and again what has happened and what is going to be done about it.

When the decision to terminate pregnancy is made, the emotional turmoil is truly painful. Labor is induced and the woman goes through the delivery just as she had been preparing herself to do—but with the certain knowledge that the baby she delivers will die. This is a horrible reality and one that deserves much compassion and empathy from family members and caregivers. Continued support over a period of time may well be a necessity for this woman and her partner. At no time should this support be misconstrued as a "crutch" or sign of weakness.

Sometimes, even well-meaning people say things that are hurtful and insensitive. What should *not* be said to the woman or the couple are statements like, "You'll soon forget all of this," or "Once you're pregnant again, you'll put this all behind you," or "I'm so relieved for you that you won't have to raise an abnormal child." Instead, friends and family should acknowledge the grief and pain of the couple who has lost a longed-for child. The couple needs to be supported in their very legitimate feeling that no matter how many successful pregnancies that may follow, no matter how many other healthy children they have or have had, the child who has been lost cannot be replaced. It is never easy for anyone, even professionals who witness grief routinely, to find the "right" words to say. But sympathy, patience, and willingness to help by listening will be much more helpful and respectful of the parents' feelings than brisk, practical advice about focusing on another pregnancy.

A YOUNG COUPLE'S STORY

Recently, a young woman was referred to me following the second trimester termination of her pregnancy. She and her husband, a doctor, had had a particularly distressing experience, first with the diagnosis itself and then with the hospital's rules that an ethics committee had to agree that the pregnancy could be terminated. This couple responded to their pain with great maturity and courage, and they decided to document their experience in a letter to the hospital, with the hope that other expectant parents would be spared similar anguish in the future. They sent me a copy of their letter and wanted me to include it in this book:

> We are writing to you to express our feelings of indignity and despair regarding the inaction of your ethics committee. At twenty and one-half weeks of T's pregnancy, we were faced with one of the most difficult decisions of either of our lives, to terminate our precious baby's life because of the overwhelming likelihood of his eventual death. After making this decision, we were forced to wait from Thursday, October 21st, to Monday, October 25th, before the ethics committee could make a decision regarding our request to terminate our pregnancy.
>
> We were shocked that not only did we have to wait all this time to have our life-altering decision accepted or nullified, but also that there is no policy in place regarding the amount of time the ethics committee has to make decisions that have far-reaching consequences for not only our family but our extended families as well. Further consequences of the committee's inaction in our case included a further deterioration in T's health which necessitated that the termination be started on Sunday, October 24th, requiring critical care monitoring. Additionally, T's postpartum recovery is complicated by the physical and emotional consequences of the additional wait to terminate our pregnancy.
>
> We would like . . . to passionately recommend that there be a policy in place that ensures that a decision will be made within twenty-four hours of a request to terminate a pregnancy. We were told that the committee could not be assembled until four days after we had reached our decision to terminate our pregnancy. There must be authorities available on a daily basis seven days a week who have

the power to make these decisions. The feelings we experienced over this time are indescribable, and we feel could have been lessened with quicker action from the ethics committee. If we can prevent one more family from experiencing what we went through in waiting, then this letter will have served its purpose and in some small way our devastating loss will have some positive outcome.

JANET'S STORY

The experience of Janet and Doug still touches me very deeply because they were one of the first couples with this kind of problem I saw in the early days of my practice. Even though they faced their situation with great courage and unity, the range of their emotions and the depth of their pain taught me something I have never forgotten: the impact of a diagnosis of abnormality in the second trimester.

They came to my office literally within hours of having learned from a genetic specialist that the fetus Janet was carrying had no kidneys and would be unable to survive once she gave birth. They had both lost complete control at the news and although they responded to the idea that they be referred to me, Janet could only sob uncontrollably throughout most interviews. At one session, she held a little green woolen hat and clutched the tiny booties of her dead infant. She didn't need to say anything; her grief was heartrending!

I saw them three or four times before the pregnancy was terminated. They felt extraordinarily angry and cheated. They had married early and worked to establish their careers, but they had decided not to delay having children beyond Janet's early thirties specifically because they wanted to avoid any kinds of problems associated with the mother's age. Their plan was extremely well thought-out and organized. Janet was to continue her career as a writer even with a small baby at home.

The ultrasound findings were completely unexpected, and the shock was overwhelming. When the baby was born, it lived only for a few minutes. Except that it lacked kidneys, it was a perfectly formed, completely normal-looking infant. Their outrage and sense of injustice was painful to witness.

I continued to see Janet for several months in individual therapy to help support her through her grief. The couple were Jew-
ish, and they spoke often to their rabbi, who was also a great
source of support. It was heartening to see that although this
couple both reacted extremely emotionally to the event, they
dealt with the issues that confronted them as a unit. This was an
obvious indication of the solidity of their marriage. Neither
blamed the other one, nor did they displace their anger onto
each other or onto the medical profession. They were able to
cope individually and together with the immediate experience
and then move on to viewing it more philosophically.

A year later, they felt ready to undertake another pregnancy.
Although the chance was very small that this rare condition
would occur again, Janet had all the necessary tests which they
faced with considerable apprehension. She gave birth to a perfectly healthy baby daughter, and they have decided to limit
their family to this one healthy child.

Some patients in my practice who have had an extremely difficult experience of this kind decide not to undertake another
pregnancy. Others choose to add to their family and go on to
have more children successfully. The couple's choice in this
matter is highly individualistic.

CHOOSING THE NEXT PREGNANCY

The couple who has faced one pregnancy in which severe abnormalities are diagnosed will relive this experience, in one way or another,
with pregnancies that may follow. Whatever the situation has been,
they have experienced the acute loss of the healthy child that might
have been. Their loss is easily recognized when the woman gives birth
to a baby who dies, but there is loss, too, in termination of pregnancy,
in a decision to place a child with special needs for adoption, and in
giving birth to a child and deciding to raise a child with congenital abnormalities.

Both partners need to support each other and to accept support
from one another. As in other cases of problems in pregnancy, the loss
of an infant or the birth of a child with abnormalities can bring the
marriage to a crisis stage, and the couple may need help not only in
confronting their grief but dealing with issues in their marriage that
have surfaced with their loss.

Many avenues for support exist, and the more help a woman gets, the quicker is her healing process. Peer support groups can provide an atmosphere that allows people with the same experience to talk easily without fear of being criticized. The support of religious counselors, too, can be of particular comfort at this time, whether in one-on-one counseling or in support groups sponsored by the church or temple. It's important to be open to the idea of counseling and to seek out help when it's needed.

Parents, mothers especially, need time to grieve their loss before considering another pregnancy. However, many people do not know how to talk about the experience, and family members, friends, and even the woman's partner may be eager to put it all in the past and uncertain how to offer support. Some women try to "erase" the events from their experience and proceed immediately with a new pregnancy as if the first one had not happened. But if she has not dealt with the events of the first pregnancy, recognizing the fears and conflicts, and working through the grief, a woman will struggle with anguish and fears in the next pregnancy, and even in subsequent pregnancies.

If there are older siblings in the family, their needs must be considered, too, for they have also experienced a change and loss, and depending on their age, they may harbor confusion and guilt of their own. Even a very young child may feel responsibility for what has happened to the expected baby and for the turmoil in the family. Sometimes, too, a bereaved mother may feel an exaggerated sense of either indulgence or resentment towards healthy older children, or she may find herself unable for a time to give her customary nurturing and support to them.

It is essential that the family acknowledge that a diagnosis of abnormal pregnancy affects them all in some way. Difficult as it is, they need to be aware of each other's needs and take time to support each other. The couple should be open for the support of friends and family members and seek the support of professionals who can assist them. Most of all, they need to allow themselves "permission" and time to grieve and to heal.

The woman and her partner are in a better position to proceed healthfully if they wait a good six to eight months before the woman becomes pregnant again. Most women go through months of sadness, as they seek to incorporate and deal with the feeling of loss before moving ahead with plans for another child. During this time, many women find it difficult to hear about others' babies or pregnancies, to see birth announcements in the paper, or to watch any movie or television show that focuses on pregnancy or children. These are not abnormal feelings, but obviously they would interfere with a positive attitude toward a new pregnancy, and women deserve support and assistance in getting beyond this stage. Professional counselors can be a great help in advising the woman how she can talk with family members, which is something she needs to do. Families may gain support from talking to their religious advisor and attending their church or temple regularly. Peer support groups can be especially helpful, since they offer an environment in which a woman can truly feel that those she meets with do understand exactly what she has experienced.

SOME QUESTIONS YOU MIGHT HAVE ABOUT ABNORMAL PREGNANCY

My first baby was born with spina bifida, and my husband and I decided to give the baby up for adoption. I have never really forgotten these events, and I think the memories will be with me for the rest of my life. I am considering trying to get pregnant again, and I can't forget the shock and disappointment of that first pregnancy. What are the chances that I will have to go through this again?

You have indeed had a painful time, and you and your husband have obviously faced a great deal together. Placing a baby for adoption is never an easy decision, and very often, parents carry feelings of guilt and remorse for a long time. There's a difference, though, in the placing for adoption of a healthy child versus a child who was very much wanted but needs extraordinary care.

You need to have an expert pre-conception consultation about the chance of this rare abnormality occurring in your second pregnancy. You will also need to be seen by a genetic specialist who can arrange all the proper tests to detect any possibility of spina bifida, and you need to be carefully monitored throughout your pregnancy. You and your husband should both attend all your meetings with the specialists, and you should both be given all the information available on your condition, on the possibilities of a recurrence, and—depending on the outlook—on your ability to see the pregnancy through. If there are decisions to be made, the two of you must be involved in making them together.

Even if your next baby is completely healthy, you and your husband might well have feelings of anxiety as the pregnancy progresses. You might find it helpful to talk with your doctor about your feelings, and determine what counseling resources might be of help to you.

TRAGEDY IN THE THIRD TRIMESTER

The loss of a baby late in pregnancy or at birth is an event for which a family can never be truly prepared. When the whole process of development and birth turns suddenly to a process of termination and death, all our human feelings are outraged. This is not what was meant to be. Instead of a joyous beginning, the family faces a tragic ending, a death before birth, which we almost cannot grasp emotionally or psychologically. When we see the anguish of parents facing this upheaval, we want to cry out, "No one should have to go through this. It is too terrible."

When there is an intrauterine death in the third trimester, the fact that the baby will not be born alive creates an unreal quality to the events and aftermath. The parents' preparations were not quite complete for this new baby, and now those preparations are interrupted and rendered meaningless. A whole new set of preparations must be made—for telling bad news instead of good news, for consoling rather than celebrating, for going home to a silent nursery rather than to the excitement of a new baby's sounds.

Everyone has trouble with this reversal in events. In spite of their best efforts, even obstetricians and maternity ward staff are often at a loss when things go terribly wrong and a baby dies. Close friends and family members may not know quite how to offer comfort. For the mother and father, the infant who died is a very real person. But for those around them, there might be an awkwardness or uncertainty about how even to talk about "who" or "what" has been lost. Was this a baby or simply a "fetus"? Was this a death or a "complication"?

For the parents, there is no question that this is a dearly loved person who has died. Some couples are keeping an active list of possible names by the third trimester; others have had the child named from Day One: "If it's a girl, she's 'Maria' after my grandmother, and if it's a boy, he's 'David.'" What is more, "Maria" or "David" has been shaping up physically and measurably for almost nine months and in the imagination of the parents, perhaps for years. The parents are right—they have lost a person, a member of their family—and their reality deserves to be supported by caregivers, family, and community. If they are not offered this support, the initial nightmare can become a long painful process of being unable to grasp what happened and what it all meant.

What Causes Third Trimester Loss?

The most common reasons for late pregnancy loss are obstetrical developments—abruptio placenta, placenta previa, premature labor. Other causes are irregularities in the structure of the mother's cervix, malformations in the infant related to chromosomal disorders, problems in the development of multiple infants (twins or triplets), or unpredictable events related to infections or to unusual activities of the mother's metabolic or glandular systems.

There are differences in the timing between diagnosis and loss with different conditions; and there may be variations between individual pregnancies. With some conditions, the mother may be hospitalized for bed rest, have her condition stabilize for several days or weeks, and then go into a pre-term delivery from which the baby cannot survive. With other conditions, a completely unexpected emergency delivery takes place and the infant does not survive. A third possibility is that the mother recognizes the infant has stopped moving and is admitted to the hospital, where the intrauterine death is confirmed; she then must be induced into labor to give birth to a dead child. Each of these possibilities is heartbreaking. The pain and confusion that women experience often can be expressed by them only weeks or months later, after the initial shock wears off, when continuing emotional stress brings them to the care of a counselor.

How Mothers Face a Diagnosis of Fetal Death

The emotional upheaval of third trimester loss is similar to that of mothers whose babies die at or near birth. I will discuss here the situation that women and their partners confront when, in the third trimester or near birth, they are told that the baby has died.

The nightmare of the diagnosis of fetal death is recognized by most medical professionals, and every attempt is made to induce the woman's labor as soon as possible so that delivery of the nonviable baby can take place quickly. Unfortunately, though, "as soon as possible" may mean up to a week in cases where the woman must wait for a nonemergency admission to the hospital. There is no advantage to this waiting game, and every minute the woman must confront the fact that she is carrying a dead baby. Women who have gone through this experience have said that this is a bizarre realization, and they cannot quite describe its impact on them. While they wait for admission to hospital, many women experience sleepless nights or toss and turn with nightmares featuring a distorted baby's body inside them. Their waking moments are preoccupied with fears about what the baby might look like at birth and whether they want to or will be able to look at and hold this long-awaited newborn who is not alive.

At the same time, the couple must face an array of practical details and this process, too, takes on a nightmarish quality. If the woman is already in hospital, the details for funeral arrangements may fall entirely to her husband. Well-meaning friends and family members may arrive to help out only to find that the woman cannot bear to talk about any of this. When religious counselors are involved, the priest, minister, or rabbi may visit to offer comfort and to add one more voice to the discussion on the funeral of a baby still inside the woman's body. Women who recall these events later have described their behavior and those around them as "robotic."

The shock and isolation of this lonely period can have long-term effects on the mother's emotional state, the relationship of the partners, and the prospects and experience of later pregnancies. Family members and caregivers need to realize that recovery from these losses will take months and in many cases needs the help of professional counseling. Even after grieving takes place, these experiences are literally unforgettable for the mother who has endured them.

JODY'S STORY

Jody was a 29-year-old woman whose first pregnancy had ended tragically in the third trimester. She had had some slight bleeding weeks before, but on examination, her doctor told her everything was fine and there was nothing to worry about. She carried on confidently until the 34th week of pregnancy, when all fetal movement stopped and she knew that her baby had died.

Two years later, she was pregnant again and became terrified as she approached the time when the slight bleeding had occurred in the first pregnancy. She was being very closely monitored by her obstetrician, and there were no problems at all with this pregnancy. She was so anxious and fearful, however, that her doctor referred her to me.

Jody saw me once a week throughout the balance of her pregnancy. She had come to take it for granted that this second pregnancy would also terminate tragically, and she felt that she was going to "lose control completely," as she expressed it. We found that supportive counseling was enough in Jody's case to help her get by week to week. Her husband was very supportive, but he was himself uncertain and fearful. The two of them visited me together on several occasions, especially as the 34th week—the time of the previous stillbirth—approached.

Medically, Jody's second pregnancy was uneventful and she gave birth to a healthy nine-pound daughter. She continued to see me for almost half a year after the baby's birth because the experience of the first loss still haunted her. She had come to believe that she didn't quite deserve to have a healthy baby, and for months, she was terrified that the new baby could die at any moment—feelings that we continued to explore in therapy. Eventually, after several sessions, she felt that she could begin to look ahead and enjoy her new baby without any guilt.

Mothers who have come through the death of a child in the third trimester and then give birth to a healthy child often check their babies' breathing frequently at night to see that the infant is alive. Some new mothers need a lot of reassurance about bathing the baby because they are overly concerned about not doing it right. Similarly they may need extra reassurance in regard to the baby's colic or just what to do to calm the baby when it cries. They are so afraid of doing anything wrong in even the smallest way that they may need counseling to learn just what it means to be a new mother and what to expect in the routines of caring for their infant.

WHAT I TELL MY PATIENTS

Recurrent pregnancy loss in the first trimester makes a woman feel angry, helpless, frustrated, and outraged. There seems no logic in why she loses her pregnancy each time she conceives;

she may perceive her loss as the symbol of ultimate failure as a woman.

The impact of second trimester loss on a woman is illustrated in the letter written by my patient and her husband and quoted in this chapter. If the woman becomes apprehensive and anxious in subsequent pregnancies, then support, sympathy, and understanding provide a "safe atmosphere" for the patient in which the pregnancy can continue.

The grief of women who have lost a baby in the third trimester is very intense, and they need a great deal of support and understanding. I've found that it may take six months to a year before these mothers can view their life with some balance and proceed to make plans for the future. Sometimes, individual counseling is needed, but I often find that women benefit most from peer support groups, where they meet with other women who have faced these losses.

As an objective party in a therapist's role, I have to agree with many of the patients I have seen who describe the events they have lived through as "bizarre." Living one day as a happily expectant mother and finding the next day that one is being consulted about funeral arrangements is a grueling trip into unreality. Obviously, these events have to be lived through, and sadly, there are few meaningful supports to help mothers and couples. Blows can be sustained even in the context of a religious support system. Some religions, for example, do not recognize the pre-term birth and do not accord it the same funeral rites as a baby who dies at birth. I have known of circumstances where a funeral home would not go along with the parents' plans for normal funeral arrangements and where the members of a couple's church did not feel that a funeral was called for.

Societal norms and regulations can be truly maddening at such a time, and it is no wonder that the healing process can be difficult and traumatic. If the community—one's church, one's friends—denies that a 38-week-old baby is a person, if the community will not acknowledge the baby's death with funeral rites, what does this say to the mother? This is a very powerful message of negation, severely at odds with the mother's experience and reality. When others cannot see the depth of the loss, when others cannot acknowledge that a person has died, the recovery for the mother, for the parents, is doubly painful.

Occasionally, I have been asked to see women who are in hospital, waiting to have labor induced after having received the diagnosis that their baby is dead. When I become involved at this stage, I am often doing two things—helping the woman express and accept her emotional reactions and also supporting the couple in *making their own decisions* about how the death of their baby will be acknowledged.

My role as a psychiatrist is to be understanding, available, and patient. Time is a great healer!

CHAPTER 4

"I NEVER WANT TO
EXPERIENCE THIS,
EVER"

Death and Disappointment at
Birth or Soon After

Childbirth is a profound experience on many levels and in many
dimensions. At the simplest level, childbirth is the outcome of
a sequence of biological events—the uniting and dividing of
cells that grow in number and complexity to become a new biological
unit that can live independently. This truly miraculous process leads to
the formation and finally to the birth of an infant.

The miracle of childbirth is of course much more than a biological
event. The birth of a child, the external beginning of a unique new
human being, touches all our deepest beliefs about the mysteries of life
and the reasons for existence. What is more, the birth of a child veri-
fies the transformation and adjustment that has taken place over nine
months in the parents and the family into which the child will be
born. The death of a child at birth brings to an abrupt end not only
the child's biological development, but also a whole range of psychological, spiritual, and emotional developments that have taken place
in the expectant parents.

EMOTIONAL REACTIONS AT BIRTH

As pregnancy progresses, the parents-to-be begin to examine what the
arrival of the new baby will mean to their lives. Some of this examina-

tion takes place in a planned manner as they discuss together almost every aspect of their lifestyle: Is their house or apartment big enough? Will their budget need adjusting? Will the mother continue her work outside the home?

Self-examination also happens, privately and sometimes almost unconsciously. Both partners begin to sort out what it means to be a parent, both as an individual and as a member of society. The expectant mother finds herself reflecting on her relationship with her own mother, while her partner thinks along the same lines as he looks at his relationship with his father. The growing awareness that they themselves will fill these parental roles makes changes in the way they relate as a couple and the way they see their position in society. At a deeper level, they can't help but be touched by feelings that they have come fully into adulthood. Now it is their turn to create a new generation, and their pride at procreating is deeply satisfying and at times almost intoxicating.

The parents' adjustment to this new view of themselves is not always effortless or painless. But normally, when pregnancies are planned and happily anticipated, the individuals are eager to accomplish the changes that parenthood will bring in their lives and attitudes. By the time the child's birth is near, they have already become somewhat different individuals than they were nine months before. The birth of a healthy child confirms the positive new views of themselves they have developed and instills confidence as they prepare to continue with their new responsibilities.

WHEN A BABY DIES AT BIRTH

The death of a child at birth alters all this. Bereaved mothers and fathers may feel deeply injured in their individual views of themselves, and if there are underlying problems in their relationship, the marriage may be seriously at risk. The blow to the mother, whose body has nurtured this baby from conception, is particularly wounding. Her whole identity has been focused on her maternal "duty" of producing a healthy baby, and now she feels that her body has failed. She may be deeply ashamed of being a "poor mother," and she may fear that her "failure" has disappointed her partner and the waiting grandparents. The father, too, may have a deeply personal feeling of inadequacy and guilt. After all, he was a partner in the creation of this child, and he shares in the blame and disappointment. Just as his wife feels a blow to her identity as an adult female, he may feel the loss as judgment on his masculinity. The couple together experiences not only the loss of their baby but everything the baby symbolized about their future life as a family and their roles as adult members of society.

The loss of a child is one of the most stressful events in a family's life and the life of a marriage. For some couples, the experience of facing the loss together adds strength and a new depth to their relationship. For other couples, the individuals' reaction to the trauma can lead to distance and blame between the partners and conflicts that threaten the future of the marriage.

It is well-recognized that women and men tend to express their feelings and grief differently, and these differences may lead to misunderstandings and lack of communication between the couple. Sometimes, the father is understandably focused on the health of his partner. Once her health is assured, his relief that she is out of danger may be more evident than his grief at the baby's loss. The mother may be more emotional in her reactions to the baby's death and may want to talk again and again about what has happened, while the father may feel that the painful events need to be left behind, that "there's no point in talking about it." She may judge him to be unfeeling toward the infant or uncaring toward her. He may be resentful that she cannot accept the support he tries to offer and look ahead to the future. These differences in emotional responses and expression can set the stage for conflict even in a very stable marriage.

Later in this chapter, I will discuss the experience of grief and the idea that knowing what to expect can help both partners face their tragedy. For the present, it is important to acknowledge that the death of a child at birth is a personal and family tragedy with deep psychological effects, particularly for mothers. Families who endure this kind of loss need great courage and love to move beyond their loss constructively. Everyone involved should be sensitive to the mother's and the couple's need for support and should not let them feel diminished in their loss.

Joanna's case had a particularly difficult outcome, and her story shows the intense and complicated feelings that are tied up with childbirth and loss.

JOANNA'S STORY

Joanna, a 35-year-old homemaker, was married to a university professor. Her husband's career was established, they were the parents of three young children, and they felt permanently and

comfortably settled in their community. Joanna's fourth pregnancy progressed normally, and she was admitted to hospital after going into labor right on schedule.

The baby was "blue" at birth, and his Apgar score was low. A pediatrician was called immediately and found that the baby's heart was just one of several body organs that could not function properly. The baby died within hours.

In addition to suffering the shock and trauma of the baby's death, Joanna subsequently developed her own medical problems. She had continued to bleed after going home from the hospital, and when this continued for several weeks, her obstetrician decided to perform a D & C. This procedure did not stop the bleeding, and Joanna became anemic from the loss of blood. She was referred to another specialist for a second opinion, and it was determined that she must have a hysterectomy.

Joanna and her husband had always planned on having four children, and despite their recent tragedy, this plan had not altered in her mind. With the removal of her uterus, the knowledge that they would not have a fourth child hit home. Joanna began to think of herself as "barren," and to doubt her sexuality. Gradually, her interest in sex disappeared. At this point, she was referred to me. Joanna saw me for therapy for almost a year and eventually was able to alter her harsh judgment of herself as being "less than a woman."

Joanna's strong reaction to being unable to reproduce shows us how the tightly knit concepts of pregnancy, labor, birth, and motherhood can work negatively against a woman when things go wrong. An event meant to enhance her life, to bring added happiness, to confirm her joys of womanhood, instead became an all-embracing tragedy when one pregnancy failed.

Women who react in this way to the loss of reproductive capability usually benefit from individual counseling to help them deal with these deep challenges to their identity and self-esteem.

WHEN THE BABY DIES BEFORE BIRTH

Perinatal loss refers to the loss of an infant around the time of birth or in the early stages of infancy. *Stillbirth*, the delivery of a baby which has died, is another type of perinatal loss. In Chapter Three I outlined some

of the causes of third trimester loss, some of which have to do with problems within the uterus that cause early labor and delivery. Neonatal and perinatal deaths are generally due to chromosomal and genetic disorders, malformation of vital organs, unpredictable events in the birth process, and complications of multiple birth. Good prenatal care, modern screening techniques, and education of expectant mothers have reduced the risk of most of these possibilities.

In Chapter Three, I also discussed the ways in which women may respond to the diagnosis that the baby they are carrying has died. Women who lose full-term babies at or just prior to birth face the same intensity of shock and anguish, complicated in a different way by the fact that the baby is fully developed and the pregnancy has gone through its natural course. Until the events of the delivery room, these mothers typically have no preparation at all for the idea that there is any threat to their babies. They face the same grueling tasks of coming to terms with a complete and unexpected reversal of fortune. These mothers, too, have often described the whole experience as "unreal" or "bizarre." What is happening is so tragically far removed from what has been anticipated for nine months that they can scarcely grasp it.

No wonder that the experience can have far-reaching impacts, as it did in Louise's case.

LOUISE'S STORY

Louise was a 26-year-old woman who was joyfully pregnant with her first child. She had been trying to conceive for five years and had almost been thought to be infertile. She and her husband had a healthy, athletic lifestyle, and they approached her pregnancy with enthusiasm and great care. Louise followed all the advice of her doctor and with her husband enrolled in Lamaze classes. She never missed a class or appointment, and the couple planned a "natural" childbirth in which he would play a full supporting role. There was never a thought that anything would go less than perfectly.

At 39 weeks, Louise began feeling pains and got up in the night to find that her waters had broken. They called her doctor, who told them the time had come to head for the hospital. On the half-hour ride to the hospital, she felt that the baby had stopped kicking. She told me later that she had immediately been certain that the baby was no longer alive. She calmly

stated to her husband that there was no point in continuing to the hospital because the baby had died. He was shocked and outraged that she would say such a thing, but she had spoken so calmly and definitely that he was terrified that something had indeed gone wrong.

When they reached the hospital, Louise immediately went into labor and gave birth to a beautiful eight-pound baby boy— who was dead. They had to leave the hospital the next day. The baby's body was taken away for autopsy, and her doctor said it might be months before they knew what had gone wrong.

Louise couldn't eat, couldn't sleep, couldn't concentrate. She could only talk about the baby who had died. Before this event, she had had no interest in religion and in fact had described herself as an atheist. Now, she became extraordinarily devout and started going to a nearby church three or four times a week. This new preoccupation bothered her husband both because he didn't feel it was in keeping with her real beliefs and because it came to occupy so much of Louise's time.

Her condition became worse over the months. She began to visit the cemetery daily, taking fresh flowers and spending hours at the graveside. Members of the congregation of the church had become concerned that this young woman spoke incessantly of her dead child, and the minister visited her husband. Her husband, the church members, and Louise's mother all feared she would "go insane" if she did not get some help, and eventually she was referred to my care.

When this sad young woman came to my office, she presented herself as completely distanced from the rest of the world. She seemed to be entirely in a world of her own, comprised only of herself and the baby, Bill. Over the course of some months, Louise was able to talk about the events in her early life that had led to this exaggerated grief.

She told me that when she realized the baby was not moving, she had known with a certainty he was dead because she had never in her life been able to complete anything she had started. Her father had been very critical of her, and it seemed that since her childhood, he had constantly talked about what a "bad girl" she was. Louise hadn't finished high school and had barely managed to keep a job. Meeting her husband had been the saving grace in her life, she felt. She was very happy in her marriage and felt she had left some of the old, sad feelings of her childhood behind. When she became pregnant, she had the feeling that she would now be able to show her father how wrong he had been. The moment she realized the baby had stopped moving, she felt that of course he must be dead because such a "bad girl" could not bring anything to a successful conclusion.

Louise's past had nothing to do with causing the stillbirth—this was due to a medical complication, as she was later able to understand. The tragedy, however, had uncovered old wounds and emotions that she hid beneath her greatly exaggerated preoccupation with the infant's death. It took Louise some time to recognize and face these issues in therapy. Her husband was very supportive. Louise went back to school to finish her high school diploma, and she is now pursuing a career in the arts.

Of course, not everyone has issues from the past such as Louise had, and not everyone who has the unfortunate experience of stillbirth needs to be in therapy. It is only when a person finds it difficult or impossible to cope with these crises that professional help is needed. It took Louise longer to come to terms with the stillbirth because of her complicated past. The doctors were eager to find out the cause of the stillbirth, and this made her feel even more guilty. In many cases, it is impossible to find out why the baby dies before birth. Usually, knowing the cause of the baby's death helps the woman's grieving process by removing her feeling of helplessness.

Another big issue that a couple has to face when such a catastrophe happens is deciding whether or when to attempt the next pregnancy. Couples who have experienced a miscarriage or second trimester loss face the same decision, but when a baby has been carried almost to term, the mother and father may both need additional time to grieve and come to terms with their loss. Most doctors recommend the couple consider postponing pregnancy for three to six months or even up to a year. Subsequent pregnancies will quite likely be marked by intense feelings and anxieties about whether this pregnancy, too, will result in a late-term loss.

Much thought and planning need to go into a subsequent pregnancy. The woman needs to feel ready both psychologically and physically to handle another pregnancy. The woman, her partner, and their doctor should be aware that the extra support of counseling might be helpful as the couple embark on a subsequent pregnancy.

WHEN THE BABY DIES AFTER BIRTH

In this chapter, I use the term "perinatal loss" to describe the death of a baby following a normal delivery and normal birth. These tragedies truly shock the mother, who feels she is home free after having had no problems in the delivery of an apparently healthy infant and must watch as her child develops acute life-threatening complications within a day or two and then dies. There can be no hierarchy to establish which kind of loss is the most anguishing; each event produces emotional stress of a particular type. Certainly, one can empathize with the extraordinary grief and trauma of a mother who loses one or more infants just after birth. But no less haunting is the loss of a child to sudden infant death syndrome (SIDS). With SIDS, there is no advance warning, no indication at all that the baby may die, and the actual cause of these deaths is still unknown. The tragedy is more poignant because the parents have had the experience of bringing a healthy infant home from the hospital and bonding with it over a period of weeks or months.

With all types of perinatal loss I will be describing, the impact on parents is enormous. Parents who have lost a baby, either at birth or to SIDS, almost inevitably experience severe emotional reactions of shock, blame, guilt—and perhaps extreme anxiety about a subsequent pregnancy and childbirth.

Complex Feelings About Loss with Twins and Triplets

Perinatal loss is always a possibility in the multiple births of twins or triplets. There are distinctive risks and potential complications associated with multiple conception, some of which may be identified early in the pregnancy. One or both of the pair or threesome may have abnormalities; in some cases, one baby thrives at the expense of the other(s). In these cases, decisions may have to be faced about the termination of one pregnancy, in order to allow one healthy infant to continue to term.

This type of decision is, of course, very distressing and can be especially so in the case of women who have conceived after taking fertility medications. Some women who have spent years trying to conceive may be able to approach the pregnancy with a view that the birth of just one healthy baby is, for her, an acceptable trade-off to the risks and uncertainties of the pregnancy. This attitude should not be taken for granted, however, and mothers of multiple infants can be expected to have very intense emotions about all the infants they are carrying. When twins occur naturally as a family pattern, the commitment to the pair is especially strong.

Twins and triplets are of special interest to the world at large, and the mother carrying multiple infants is the subject of special attention from friends and families. The normal dreams and fantasies of expectant parents are literally multiplied, for now their parenthood takes on a whole extra dimension. The mother of twins cannot help but feel an additional pride in the unique developments going on inside her. Where twins run in the family, there are extra cross-generational feelings about the importance of these babies' birth in the family identity and history.

Personal and family attitudes towards twins and triplets create extremely complex emotional problems when one or more of the infants is at risk. Parents sometimes have warning late in pregnancy that one of the infants will not survive at birth. In other cases, complications may set in at birth, and one or more of the babies dies within a short time. It's almost impossible to grasp the depth and breadth of the parents' reaction to the loss of any of the expected infants at birth. The survival of only one baby in a twinship or triplet bond can create emotional reactions that are difficult to reconcile with the reality of this extraordinary and tragic event.

When a woman learns that one of the twins she carries may not survive, her emotions may focus exclusively on this child who is not going to live. She might decide definitely on its name, begin to refer to it as a more "real" entity than the healthy baby, and have imaginary dialogues with this child she will never be able to know. In addition to feeling guilty about her "failure," she may develop—even before birth—a kind of love-hate relationship with the surviving twin, holding it somehow responsible for the other's death. Her complicated emotional reactions may be unrecognized or, if recognized, incomprehensible to those around her. In addition to her grief at the loss of her child, she may be faced with raising another child with whom she is initially unable to bond.

SONJA'S STORY

Sonja, a 28-year-old woman, had, not surprisingly, conceived twins in her first pregnancy. In both her family and her husband's, there had been three generations of twin births, and the entire family assumed that Sonja and Phil could carry on the tradition as a matter of course.

Both psychologically and practically, they had made all the arrangements to become parents of twins. Plenty of family experts advised them on the care and treatment of twins, though Sonja and Phil had already decided on their own approach. Each of the two little girls (their sex was known from amniocentesis) would have her own room, and Sonja and Phil spent hours decorating and furnishing the twin nurseries.

Sonja had a smooth pregnancy and delivery, but the second twin died within minutes of birth. Instead of taking home twins, she and her husband went home with only one baby. Everything about the family life they had envisioned seemed only half there. Sonja was overwhelmed with guilt and could not bear to open the door of the bedroom that would have been the second twin's. She began to resent the surviving twin for being there— an incomplete half of the twosome she had expected.

When she mentioned some of this to her doctor, Sonja was referred to me. As we talked, it became obvious that all her thoughts were centered on finding a reason for what happened. Her questions went back and forth from "What did I do wrong that my little girl died?" to "Did the one who lived take something from the one who died?" She could focus only on the twin who had died and the twinship that no longer existed. She rarely spoke of the healthy new infant alone, without raising the other issues.

Sonja couldn't forget how beautiful the two babies had looked together. She had a photo of her daughters taken just after birth; they were together, only one was living and the other was dead. She had wanted to hold the baby that died longer, but she felt it had been snatched away from her. She said she'd wanted to take more pictures of the second twin but hadn't been allowed the time.

Her husband told me that at least twenty pictures had been taken of the twin that died. Sonja talked incessantly, he told me, of the daughter they'd lost, and it didn't seem that she was bonding at all with their surviving daughter. At night, if the baby cried, she had to force herself to get up and attend to the little one who needed her now. In her mind, it seemed that if she was not needed by two, she was not needed by anyone at all.

Sonja's story was a very sad one. Luckily, her husband was supportive and saw her through this crisis with endless endurance and patience. Her relationship with her infant daughter gradually became established. When the child was four years old, Sonja decided to become pregnant again. Although she again gave birth to a single baby girl, she had finally resolved her conflicts about having twins and came to terms with having two little baby girls—though they were four years apart in age. She felt that her family was then complete and felt a renewed sense of joy and happiness.

ABNORMALITY AT BIRTH

In Chapter Three I talked about the possible consequences of a diagnosis of abnormality. The first crucial question is always, "Is the infant's condition compatible with life?" If the answer is no, a sequence of events unfolds around the fact that, once delivered, the baby will die. If the answer is yes, a different but no less difficult sequence of events begins. Either chain of events becomes even more traumatic when there is no warning that what has been a normal pregnancy and normal delivery will produce an infant with abnormalities. Christine's story illustrates both the shock and grief that parents can experience over the short term and the enormously difficult and complex decisions they are called upon to make over the long term.

CHRISTINE'S STORY

Christine, a 29-year-old accountant, was married to Steve, a business manager in his thirties. This couple had devoted the early years of their marriage to establishing their careers, acquiring a comfortable townhouse, and enjoying a very prosperous and socially active lifestyle.

Their backgrounds were quite different. Christine had been one of six children in a large loving family with very traditional views about home life and a great emphasis on self-sacrifice and giving. The family belonged to a strict religious sect that does not believe in hospital care, but Christine had left these beliefs behind when she married Steve. However, she was still closely attached to her parents and siblings, and in fact, it had been quite a surprise for them when Christine chose Steve. The lifestyle of this young couple was very different from that of Christine's family as she was growing up.

Steve had grown up in a family with just one brother, Rob, who was a year older. Throughout childhood and adolescence, the two boys had been fiercely competitive, in sports and in school. When Rob developed a severe form of multiple sclerosis during his adult years, Steve's competitiveness changed to a deep pity and then to aversion. As Rob's disease progressed and he became completely dependent on others, the parents brought him home and were actively involved in all the details of his personal care. Steve couldn't stand either the sight of his brother's disability or the idea that Rob was now completely dependent, and he began to avoid going to his parents' home entirely.

After a few years Christine and Steve decided that the time had come to start a family, and Christine had a healthy, uneventful pregnancy. Steve hoped for a son who would, of course, enjoy sports as much as Steve did.

Christine gave birth to a son, who was found at birth to have spina bifida, which is a developmental defect occurring in the vertebrae and usually causes some paralysis and loss of bowel function, and possible mental retardation. There had been no warning for this, and it was a complete shock. When Steve first saw the baby, he drew away in terror—I learned later that he could think only of Rob's helplessness and dependency. The doctors told Christine and Steve that the baby would live but it wasn't known yet what his physical and mental condition would be. The parents began arguing right there in the delivery room. Steve wanted absolutely nothing to do with this child, and he walked away from Christine and took refuge in drinking with his friends. There was no good news to share, and he was extraordinarily resentful and upset.

Meanwhile, little Derek was taken off to the intensive care unit to be monitored and cared for until his condition stabilized and it was safe for him to be discharged. Christine was sent back to her room on the maternity ward, where she sat completely alone until her parents arrived.

Steve refused to visit Christine and did not want the baby to come home. He wanted to release the baby for adoption immediately, an attitude that outraged Christine and her parents. Without any question, Christine's parents were prepared to stand by the couple and help raise Derek, whatever his condition was.

Christine and Steve were referred to me about two weeks after the birth. The baby was still in the hospital and they were still undecided about the adoption. They obviously had conflicting values, and their differences became more pronounced with this challenge. I felt that they needed marital therapy if they were to begin to resolve this immediate issue. The couple saw a marital therapist for a few sessions, and I later learned that they had split up after the baby was given up for adoption. Christine did not return for further therapy.

This sad family story is another study in conflicts and reversals. Birth, which was meant to be a joyous event, became instead a battleground. An event that should unite a couple did the opposite. The fresh new beginning of life became, for Derek, the start of a tough journey of dependency, medical problems, rejection by his biological father, and finally, adoption.

Another family in my practice, however, faced exactly the same situation as Steve and Christine—but approached things in an entirely different way.

DEIRDRE'S STORY

After several years of marriage, Deirdre and her husband John were looking forward to the birth of their first child. They had shared in all the joys and plans of an effortless pregnancy, and there was no indication that their baby daughter would be born with spina bifida.

I was asked to talk with them both in the hours following the delivery. Deirdre was virtually stunned, and John struggled through his own shock to comfort her. Almost immediately, it was apparent to me that they were a couple who acted as a unit. They were both grappling with an unknown reality, but there was no anger and no reproach. They simply needed time to adjust to their shock and the information they were given about what lay ahead.

I suggested that they might want to talk with another couple who had been my patients for a brief time a few years before. This couple, Maxine and Paul, were the parents of a three-year-old boy who had been born with spina bifida. They were quite active in a support group for parents of children with spina bifida, and they had urged me to call on them if they could be of help to other parents in their situation.

As I was making these arrangements, Deirdre's family doctor had begun to talk with the two of them about the medical aspects of spina bifida, offering the information they needed on the immediate and long-term care of their little girl. Maxine and Paul were as good as their word and they spent many hours with Deirdre and John, helping them through their feelings and their probable future from the perspective of people who could truly say, "We know how you feel."

Deirdre and John never gave a thought to placing baby Kristin for adoption. They were certainly apprehensive about ensuring that she had the right kind of care, and they recognized that their family life would need to adjust to unexpected responsibilities. They experienced shock and sorrow that the pregnancy had not had the healthy outcome they expected, but throughout their crisis they were focused on each other's feelings and needs. As partners, they began to develop a care plan for their little daughter. They looked forward to continuing with the support group that Maxine and Paul introduced them to.

I had reason to see Deirdre again early in her second pregnancy. Her family doctor had suggested that she again "touch base" with me although she had remarkably positive feelings about the prospects for this second baby. She told me that she and John both felt their marriage was even closer than before Kristin's birth. "It hasn't been easy," she said, "but we're a family.

Kristin is a joy to us. She's a real fighter, and she'll be a big sister our new baby can be proud of."

Deirdre told me that she often remembered the early days after Kristin's birth, when it had helped just to be able to talk about her feelings with me and with Paul and Maxine. She and John had continued to take part in the parents' support group, and she told me that she and John, too, would always be ready to extend advice and understanding to other couples who faced the same challenge.

I told Deirdre that I would continue to be available to her, but I feel confident this young woman and her husband, with their positive view of life and the rewards of a family, have already established a very strong mutual support system for whatever life unfolds.

When a couple faces something like the birth of a child with medical problems, the event itself and any therapy that follows will help them focus on what their partnership means. They have come together from different backgrounds to form their own family unit. How does this new unit respond to events, whether it is a happy occasion or a crisis? Most people bring into their marriage or partnership what they have grown up with—their own temperaments, their own personalities, their own coping devices. No two people are alike, and no two people think or feel alike. When a couple faces the issue of bringing up a child who will require lifelong care, they must deal with feelings of anxiety, of guilt, of anger. Until they move beyond these feelings, they cannot make a commitment to raising a child.

The journey of raising a child is itself a long and challenging one, but for most parents it is rewarding. When the journey takes the unexpected route—with the birth of a child who will need particular medical and psychological attention—conflict between the parents may be unavoidable. In therapy, the focus is on mutual respect, mutual love, and a mutual bond to carry on with their new responsibilities.

HOW FAMILIES COPE WITH LOSS

Dealing with the Immediate Reality

When a newborn dies, the immediate emotional problem for parents, especially for mothers, is understanding what has happened. When there is no preparation, the shock is so great that women are sometimes truly unable to grasp what is happening. The details of the baby's medical condition, the possible reasons for the death, can all be explored later. But when the mother hears the news in the delivery room or maternity ward, she may be unable to comprehend the basic information—that despite all apparent signs of health in her pregnancy, her full-term baby has now died.

She may need to hear basic information such as what has happened and what will happen next again and again. Particularly if she is sedated, she may later remember the whole experience exactly as she would a terrible nightmare—full of unexplained events and incomplete information. This inability to grasp events may be very difficult for her partner, who has perhaps been able to take in a fuller explanation and upon whom she calls repeatedly for an explanation of what has gone wrong. Doctors and nurses, too, need to recognize this functional amnesia as a normal response and to spend ample time, even over a period of days, in helping the mother reconstruct what has happened.

This shocked state of mind may predict the way the mother will respond to her loss over time. Painful as it seems, it is only possible to heal after one has recognized the loss that has taken place. The better a woman can grasp the sad reality, the sooner she can begin to heal.

The confusion of events can make it difficult for a mother to express her natural impulses and needs at this time. Some mothers may want to see and hold their dead baby and to spend private time with their baby and partner. It used to be that women were discouraged from seeing their dead infants; women who asked were often told that this was "against the rules." However, the medical profession has more recently come to realize that the mother's wishes are natural and "normal," and that she should in fact be encouraged to make that emotional contact with the dead infant to facilitate the grieving process.

This is especially true if an infant is malformed in some way. If the mother is not permitted to see the baby, her imagination will inevitably produce an unrealistic and upsetting fantasy that she will always have with her. Doctors and nurses are becoming more aware that sometimes mothers are either too confused or perhaps too frightened to express their wish to see and hold the infant, and so are likely to make the suggestion themselves. Partners and family members can help by encouraging the mother to follow her instincts and to connect in this way with the child she has borne.

There is nothing strange about wanting to take photographs of this new baby. Just as healthy births are commemorated with photos of the newborn just after birth, so too photographs of the infant who has died have an important place forming in the family's memories. Photographs are an important way for us to remember events and to later reflect on those special moments in our lives. Parents should be encouraged to take and cherish these photos of the baby they will see so fleetingly. Other mementos such as the baby's identification bracelet or a lock of hair should also be cherished. These can be an important link to the concrete experience and a way to acknowledge that, yes, this pregnancy was real, this person was real, and will not be forgotten.

If it is not too painful for her, the mother should play as active a role as possible in decisions about the baby's funeral. Making decisions like this is one of the brief opportunities the mother and father have to carry out their responsibilities for this baby who has died. It's also a way of participating actively in an event that otherwise may have a disturbing dream-like quality later on. The extended family, friends, and the religious community need to support the couple's grief by according the same recognition to this dead child as they would to a dead adult.

Recently, I treated a woman who had been told that her baby had a condition incompatible with life. She was in her 24th week of pregnancy and would go through a normal labor. I saw her just before she went into the labor room in the knowledge that she would give birth to an infant who would not survive. We discussed all the options that I have outlined in this chapter and talked about how she might come to eventual terms with her grief. She and her husband had made a mutual decision about not wanting to see or hold the baby or involve themselves in any of the rituals that we have described.

There are couples, and particularly mothers, who may not want to "participate" in any way when they know the newborn will not survive. This is also a wish that caregivers must respect. The parents must make their own decision, and no one else's wishes or views should be forced on them. This is a very sensitive area, and a therapist must be very neutral, no matter what the woman or couple decides to do. The therapist's role is to help explore alternatives, to be impartial as the couple makes a decision, and to assure them that, no matter what their decision, the therapist will be 100 percent behind them.

It is important to understand that there is no *requirement* to deal with grief in a particular way. Since most likely the parents have never faced such a situation before, it is vital to help them discover and express their feelings and inclinations. They might wish to take photographs, for instance, and yet worry that this would be considered "abnormal." On the other hand, once they have looked at all the alternatives, they may choose not to become involved. Research and many parents' experience have shown, however, that seeing and holding the dead infant and observing the mourning rituals that would ordinarily be carried out can be very helpful in the parents' coming to terms with their loss over time.

Dealing with Grief Over Time

Grief is a timeless, universal emotion that has been recognized and studied as a distinct psychological event since the middle of this century. Two principles are helpful to keep in mind: First, there is a general pattern and sequence to the responses of grief and, second, as with every human emotion, every individual responds differently. Being aware of the pattern of grief can give people "permission" to express what are perfectly normal feelings. Recognizing a pattern in grief responses is also helpful in determining whether progress is being made in moving ahead into the future.

Individual counselors and support groups make use of knowledge about patterns of grief to offer support to those confronting a variety of losses. After all, grief can be the response not only to death but to other kinds of loss. Job loss and divorce are two major events that typically provoke a grief response. In the last few chapters, I have discussed various losses that are related to both the normal and abnormal events of pregnancy and childbirth. Loss of the previous lifestyle, loss of the dream of the healthy child, loss of a child to adoption may all precipitate or complicate the responses of grief.

In general, the pattern emerges in three stages. Individuals vary greatly, and they do not necessarily proceed through all the emotions of each stage in a fixed order. Reaching the end of a normal grieving process, however, may be expected to take one to two years, rather than a few months. The first stage is one of *protest*, in which the person fights against accepting that a change has taken place or that an end has occurred. Some of the emotions of this stage may be shock, denial, disbelief, or anger. Feelings like anger may surface and then resurface for a time, but the person must accept before long that a loss has occurred.

The second stage is one of *disorganization*, in which the emotions gradually respond to the fact that an end has come. This stage, which can last for months, is characterized by deep sadness, loneliness, isolation from and a lack of warmth towards others, a sense of meaningless-ness in life, and a longing for the life that one had or would have had with the person who died. People in this stage of grief may share some of the emotions and behaviors of people with clinical depression, and in fact they may become clinically depressed or anxious. They may be careless about their personal appearance, suffer sleepless nights and de-creased appetite, and be subject to overwhelmingly intrusive thoughts of the loved one who was lost. They may be restless and have trouble concentrating. This is obviously a difficult period for the grieving per-son and presents challenges for those around her. She greatly needs their patience, love, and support in the form of a loving listener who can let her ventilate her feelings, let her cry when she feels like it. At this stage, feelings resurface unexpectedly, and loved ones need to let the grieving person "have her own space" and avoid encroaching on her too much. It may be helpful for relatives to make sure that not too much is expected of her for a time in terms of additional household or family responsibilities. Love and nurturing can also take the form of bringing her flowers occasionally, taking her out for dinner, or arrang-ing a special quiet event. Often my patients will go away for a brief vacation to "leave the scene"; this is sometimes helpful and allows them a respite. They often return feeling more positive and hopeful. Most importantly, however, the partner and other family members need to allow her to grieve in *her* way—as it feels right to her.

In the third stage of grief, *reorganization*, the person slowly turns her attention again to the outside world, to the life roles she plays, and to the future. Our society, which discourages emotional display and ad-mires the "stiff upper lip" of emotional control, often expresses great impatience with people who do not move on to this final stage quickly.

Dorothy's story is one that shows the extremes of the first stage and the kind of support that can help as the person works through grief.

DOROTHY'S STORY

Dorothy, a 38-year-old woman, lost a long-awaited baby at birth entirely without advance warning. At the time, she and her hus-band Paul had been married about eight years, and through most of their years together he had been firmly opposed to their having a family. He had been one of nine children and, in his words, wanted a marriage that was "child-free." Dorothy's feel-ings, as she got older, were quite different. After some marital therapy, they decided to go ahead and have a child.

When their daughter was born after a normal pregnancy, she was found to have a serious congenital heart defect, and she died immediately after birth. Because she was over 35, Dorothy had had a number of ultrasound examinations at different stages in her pregnancy, and this condition had been completely missed. Within 24 hours after the baby's birth, Dorothy became acutely suicidal.

Normally, suicidal patients are admitted to a psychiatric ward, but another psychiatrist on staff and I decided that it was better for Dorothy to go home, as there were relatives who could provide her with careful monitoring. Weighing all the pros and cons, my colleague and I felt that she was responding acutely to the birth/death of her little son and that support for her grieving process, rather than acute psychiatric care, was indicated. This judgment proved to be accurate; Dorothy's acute suicidal feelings passed once she was in her own home.

An elderly aunt came to stay with Dorothy and her husband. The aunt was a gentle, sympathetic person whose sole interest was Dorothy's well-being. She was constantly present and always willing to listen, no matter how many times Dorothy wanted to talk about her loss and the events surrounding the birth. Paul, too, was very supportive, and the shared experience brought the couple closer together. Having made the initial decision to begin a family, Paul had changed a great deal during the pregnancy and was deeply affected by the loss of their daughter.

Dorothy saw me weekly in therapy for a number of months. She felt a great sadness that she had not been more clear-headed in the hours after the baby's birth. She cherished the photos that Paul had taken of the little girl, but in her actual memory the first few days after the tragedy were "like a dream." She was very preoccupied with the role her age had played in the baby's condition, although her obstetrician had assured her that this was not an issue; initially, she felt "doomed" to having had only this one pregnancy in her life, at which she felt she had failed.

Dorothy and Paul saw me together for a number of sessions and, after several months, they began to consider the possibility of another pregnancy. I advised them to give themselves at least six months before they tried again, and I understand that some time after ending her therapy sessions with me, Dorothy did in fact have another pregnancy with a successful outcome. She was 40 years old at the time of her son's birth.

SOME QUESTIONS YOU MIGHT HAVE
ABOUT BIRTH DIFFICULTIES AND TRAGEDIES

I am a 40-year-old woman, a publisher in a big metropolitan firm. I have a three-year-old daughter, and I seem to be sitting on the fence about deciding to have a second child. I had a difficult birth the first time—an emergency admission to hospital followed by 20 hours of labor. Also I'm afraid of the possibility of having a child with birth abnormalities because of my age.

We are addressing two different problems here—the first is your age, the second is the birth experience, which seems to have been traumatic. The memories of your hospital experience and birth have understandably stayed with you a long time, and no doubt you will relive some of these fears if you become pregnant again. That is no reason for avoiding pregnancy, however. Every birth experience is unique and different, and the probability of the birth experience repeating itself in such a negative way the second time is quite small. You might want to talk to professional caregivers about your fears and feelings before making your decision.

You should also ask your doctor to refer you to a genetic counselor, who can give you expert information on the effects of maternal age on fetal abnormalities and the kind of monitoring that can be done should you become pregnant. As you already know, you haven't a great deal of time to do this. Becoming pregnant at age 40 is rarely as quickly accomplished as at age 20 though happy outcomes are certainly possible.

I am a 28-year-old woman who lost a baby a few hours after birth. The baby was born with congenital heart defects. It has been two years since her death, and I feel I have dealt with this loss through meeting with a grief counselor and participating in a support group for some time. I want to be-

come pregnant again, but I'm terribly worried about possible heart problems in another baby. Do you think my second baby could also have congenital heart defects?

Losing a baby at birth is terrible, and your fears are completely understandable. You need to find out exactly what kind of congenital heart defects your baby had. Some types happen completely by chance and may not happen again. A genetic specialist could talk with you about the specific problems your baby had and the chances of these recurring in a second child.

The memories of your first pregnancy and your first infant will always be with you, and it's possible that these may be very troubling for you in a second pregnancy. Supportive counseling throughout your pregnancy might be very reassuring, and you should not hesitate to seek support from a counselor should you feel anxious or fearful.

? *I lost my first child at birth and am pregnant again, this time with twins. From what the doctors tell me, there was no particular reason the baby died, yet I'm afraid that I might lose one or both of the babies again.*

Your feelings are completely understandable, and it's reasonable that you would want reassurance. If a genetic problem was not identified as the cause of your first baby's death, the chances that something similar will happen again are very small. I suggest that you concentrate on relaxing and approaching this pregnancy in a positive manner. I'm sure you will be very closely monitored, and you should make sure that you have your spouse with you whenever you go for tests. Various techniques could help lessen your anxiety and avoid a negative preoccupation with your previous loss—stress reduction, meditation, reading relaxing things, taking walks. It would be a good idea to talk with your doctor about your concerns and decide if you would benefit from a referral to a therapist or counselor who could instruct you in relaxation techniques.

? *At 38, after many years of infertility, I successfully became pregnant. However, I lost my baby two weeks before the expected date of delivery, and nobody was able to find exactly what was wrong. I was told it was a full-term healthy infant, and they could not find the cause of his death. I'm pregnant again* *and thoughts of my baby dying the first time continually haunt me.*

It is not uncommon for women like you, who have gone through a traumatic experience, to think about their previous loss during a subsequent pregnancy. This is especially so if they have not been able to deal with that loss by talking with a health care professional. It sounds as if you have many feelings of grief and anger related to your previous loss and you might want to express your feelings with the help of a counselor now.

However, you should make it clear that you do not want to get into any intense psychological issues that might affect your present pregnancy. It is not a good idea to explore in-depth interpersonal conflicts or issues from the past when one is pregnant. We know that there are strong links between the body and mind, and we do not want to get the mother feeling anxious and upset when she is pregnant. It may be important to explore such issues, but at a later time. Usually, my advice to the patient and to other therapists is that there is time to explore these underlying issues once the mother gives birth; there is no urgency to address such issues during the pregnancy. Nonetheless, you need to cross the hurdle of unresolved grief in order for you to feel happy about this pregnancy and allow you to bond with the new baby.

WHAT I TELL MY PATIENTS

When I counsel mothers who have lost a baby at birth, I almost invariably must spend time helping them examine their feelings about loss and blame. This same message bears repeating in so many instances involving perinatal loss, termination of pregnancy, or birth abnormalities: *This is not your fault. You did not will it, you certainly did not wish it, you and your body have not "failed."*

When a baby is stillborn or dies at birth, I encourage mothers to follow their instincts in wanting to hold and spend private time alone with their baby. I encourage them to take photos of the baby, just as they would have taken photos in the first happy hours of a healthy newborn's life. These things are very important, both at the time they happen and also for the mother's lifelong process of accepting and remembering this loss of a precious baby.

In some cultures, women do not take part in the funeral arrangements for such a death, and even in modern Western society, the family and community might offer mixed messages of support—trying to "spare" the mother by diminishing the need for a normal funeral. Attitudes like this tend to force the mother to suppress her grief and tend to ignore the reality that a living person has died. These are not healthy attitudes, and they do nothing to promote the expression of genuine emotion and the healing process. The suppressed grief may resurface later in different ways, including serious clinical depression.

The family should be encouraged to commemorate the baby's death with anniversary remembrances. Some religions have organized bereavement rituals, which the family can arrange. Whether or not this is the case, the family can develop its own rituals—lighting candles on the baby's birthday, for instance, or taking the day off from work. These are important steps in the long-term healing process and in confirming the identity and history of the family's experience—both the joys and sorrows in the unique life of this couple and their children.

Finally, I tell my patients that tragedies don't happen again and again. One loss is not a judgment that there is something wrong with their bodies. Grief and loss are terrible experiences, but they are part of what human beings encounter and they can be sources of great insight, strength, and self-development. Parents need to allow time to grieve, but ordinarily there is no reason not to try for a pregnancy again.

When a baby is born with a genetic defect, coping with it will be a lifelong commitment. There is no set method for raising such a child. Ongoing patience, devotion, and a willingness to make sacrifices help parents through this bumpy and sometimes painful journey in life.

CHAPTER 5

"I JUST DON'T
FEEL LIKE MYSELF
ANYMORE"

Postpartum Depression and Mood Disorders

My interest in postpartum emotions began after the birth of my own two children, when I realized that "postpartum blues" were very common. My knowledge of the subject and expertise in the field made me aware of the emotions of feeling blue, and I remember wishing that there was someone I could relate them to. In those days—the 1980s—although there was awareness of the types of emotional upheaval a woman might experience after birth, certainly there was no service such as the one I have worked to establish over the past 15 years—a service staffed by psychiatrists with particular knowledge in obstetrics. The efficacy and importance of this kind of specialized counseling should not be underestimated, since it can play as large a role in the family's well-being as medical counseling for a pregnant woman with diabetes or genetic counseling for the woman at risk.

The postpartum (literally, "after birth") period is a challenging time. The first-time mother may be understandably apprehensive about meeting the new 24-hours-a-day responsibilities of motherhood and developing routines for as yet unfamiliar tasks. The mother whose new infant joins a family with older siblings goes home to a busy household where the needs of her other children must be given equal importance with the newborn's. Commonly, the woman who has recently given birth is tired and may have few uninterrupted nights of sleep. Demands may seem unrelenting and emotional responses may be heightened, and thus a wide range of vivid emotions and new behaviors is quite normal at this time.

The special demands of the postpartum period are better recognized and attended to by the helping professionals in some places than in others. In localities as diverse as Hawaii and Great Britain, for example, the family physician normally spends time discussing the woman's home situation and personal adjustments in the course of postnatal visits. In these places, too, it is common for nurses to make visits after a baby goes home from the hospital, and to provide emotional support and practical advice to the mother as a matter of routine. In other places, however, it is more common to view the baby's arrival home as a signal that the woman and her family are "back to normal"—and there may be little recognition of and support through what can be a uniquely stressful time.

EARLY WARNING SIGNS OF POSTPARTUM MOOD DISORDERS

In discussing postpartum mood disorders, I will be describing some conditions or states that may be quite normal. I will also describe some symptoms or warnings that should not be ignored. When you are feeling profoundly disturbed and troubled, your first priority must be yourself. In order to get the right kind of help, you need to involve trained professionals, so you must be very specific with your caregiver about exactly what you're thinking and feeling. For example, your doctor will naturally focus first on your physical condition and well-being, so be sure to tell him or her precisely what kinds of feelings and thoughts are troubling you.

If you feel overwhelmed and suicidal, the time to seek help is NOW. Feeling overwhelmed by new responsibilities and competing demands is usually normal; feeling that life is no longer worth living is not. There is a useful time guideline for normal postpartum blues. If you feel unbearably distressed for longer than two weeks after giving birth, please talk candidly to your doctor about your feelings and anxiety. This is a point where intervention—professional care and attention—may make an immediate difference in your ability to cope and alter the course of your condition.

EARLY SYMPTOMS OF DEPRESSION YOU SHOULDN'T IGNORE

1. Feeling that you might harm yourself or take your own life
2. Feeling that you might harm your baby
3. Continued sleep difficulties over a period of two to three weeks or feeling continually exhausted
4. Feeling that you do not enjoy your baby
5. Feeling continually sad and hopeless

EARLY SIGNS OF ANXIETY YOU SHOULDN'T IGNORE

1. Unexplained episodes of feeling dizzy, with numbness or tingling in toes, feet, or hands
2. Feeling that your heart is beating unusually fast, with skipped beats at times
3. Sensation of fear or impending doom, or feeling that you might die or go crazy
4. Feeling nauseated, feeling like you're going to vomit; extreme diarrhea
5. Feeling as if you are "outside" your body; feeling depersonalized or "weird"

SYMPTOMS OF PSYCHOSIS

1. Hearing voices that are not present
2. Hearing voices that are asking you to perform certain tasks or do certain things
3. Unusual body sensations or unusual sensations of touch or smell, e.g., feeling that a certain person may have a specific smell or that "the uterus is dead"
4. Seeing images or things that are frightening and do not exist
5. Feeling that others are "out to get you," or are laughing or talking about you
6. Feelings of being unusually happy that you recognize as being strange
7. Feelings of extreme energy

8. Speeded-up speech or thought; having other people comment that your speech is speeded up
9. Feeling exhausted but having no time to sleep
10. Having ideas for the future that seem extravagant to other people

POSTPARTUM MOOD DISORDERS

Over the last half century—since the days of your mother's and grandmother's pregnancies—a great deal of progress has been made in recognizing and treating emotional disorders of all kinds, not just those experienced by new mothers. For one thing, it has become clear that certain disorders result from an imbalance in the body's chemistry, and it has become accepted that biology—the body's physical condition and functioning—is very likely an important factor in many emotional and mental disorders. The recognition that physical factors are at work in emotional disturbance, at least to some degree, is beginning to take some of the mystery out of the treatment and experience of "mental illness." This new understanding has prompted researchers to develop medications that relieve emotional symptoms by treating specific biochemical imbalances; I will discuss how these medications are used in Chapter Eleven.

Researchers and caregivers also recognize, however, that there is still much that remains unexplained in regard to emotional problems in general and the puzzling emotional disturbances of expectant and new mothers in particular. While body chemistry almost certainly plays a part in severe emotional disorders, it isn't yet possible to define exactly how it relates to various disorders or to understand clearly the roles played by stress, by heredity, by environment, and by the dynamics of interpersonal relationships. Emotional illnesses cannot be pinpointed with X rays or lab tests, and there is still no clear-cut explanation for the fact that some expectant and new mothers become emotionally disturbed with one childbirth but not with another, or that many women have virtually no emotional upsets at all. The latter is especially perplexing, as one of my patients said after the birth of her fourth child. "Why is this happening? What did I do wrong?" Eileen asked me. "All of my pregnancies have been wonderful, and with my first three children, I felt only a little bit blue before I left the hospital. Once I got home, everything was fine. But not this time!"

With these questions still unanswerable, it is not surprising that new mothers and their families find it difficult to understand and accept the situation when suddenly, emotional problems overwhelm the expected joy of new parenthood. If this happens in your family, one of the most important things for everyone to realize is that the mother's severe emotional problem is a *medical* condition—it is *not* the result of a weak personality, lack of willpower, a character flaw, or being a "poor mother." Almost invariably, there is some biological and psychosocial basis to the problem—and almost invariably, there is a known, effective treatment that will lead to recovery. After seeing me and receiving a six-week course of antidepressant medication, a patient of mine named Terri said, "If someone had told me six weeks ago that depression was an illness—like diabetes, maybe—and that medicine, like insulin, was needed to treat it, I wouldn't have believed them. I felt ashamed—that I was just 'weak' or 'lazy'—and I felt so guilty about what I was feeling. Now, I see it entirely differently. I had a medical condition, and I came to you—a doctor—and you've treated me. And now I'm beginning to heal."

I hope that similarly troubled new mothers and their family members will realize how outdated it is to view this emotional problem as a shameful "weakness" that should be hidden. Researchers haven't yet identified precisely what causes postpartum mood disorders, but a wide range of treatments and therapies is available. In many instances, a patient who receives professional care will quickly gain relief of troublesome symptoms, and there are very few cases in today's world that, with proper care and support, do not eventually have a positive outcome. Suzanne, a first-time mother who was referred to me, said, "At first I was ashamed about coming to see you. But now that I'm feeling better, I realize the most important thing has been being able to experience the joy of my new baby, to really care for her, and appreciate every moment of her new life—all the things I had expected to feel about her birth. Now that I'm feeling happy again for the first time in six months, I wish I'd realized sooner that someone could help me."

I will now discuss the various categories of postpartum mood disorders: postpartum blues, postpartum depression, and postpartum psychosis.

POSTPARTUM BLUES

"Postpartum blues" is a very common emotional state that affects some 45 to 80 percent of new mothers about three to five days after their baby's birth. The most common symptoms in a new mother are weeping, feelings of sadness, irritability towards her husband or partner, hostility towards the baby, emotional instability, fatigue, anxiety, and sleeplessness. Symptoms of postpartum blues tend to peak on the fifth day postpartum and then diminish.

What Causes Postpartum Blues?

There are several possible explanations for postpartum blues, and research has as yet given us no firm answers. Postpartum blues tend to occur in women from all socioeconomic levels. Marital status is not directly related to the occurrence of postpartum blues, but a poor marital relationship might be a factor in some cases. Many research studies have investigated the relationships between postpartum blues and psychological factors, hormone levels, the woman's reproductive history, and experience of pregnancy. Although individual studies have suggested some possible relationships, there are no overwhelming findings that help us pinpoint why blues affect some mothers and not others.

How Long Do Postpartum Blues Last?

Typically, women recover fully and naturally from the blues within two weeks, and only rarely, when a new mother becomes exhausted through lack of sleep, need her doctor prescribe a mild sedative. Usually, all that is required is support and reassurance from the woman's doctor, the hospital's nursing staff, and family members. A new mother may benefit simply from talking through some of her uncertainties about her new role and her worries about her inability to be a good mother. There are no long-term effects of postpartum blues on either the mother or on the child's development.

Janet's case was one in which supportive care for "maternity blues" helped her cope during the postpartum weeks.

JANET'S STORY

Janet, a 34-year-old married secretary, waited several years after marriage to have a baby, then had an uneventful pregnancy. Her husband was in the delivery room with her, and both of them were filled with relief and joy at the birth. Janet had anticipated this moment most of her adult life and was thrilled at the prospects of motherhood.

Around the third postpartum day, she looked at the baby sleeping in the crib next to her and suddenly felt very anxious—and quite negative toward the infant. She was surprised at these thoughts and felt uncomfortably that she "was not supposed to have thoughts like this." She became very sad and was unable to sleep that night.

Just before her discharge on the fourth day, she decided to confide her feelings to one of the nurses, and a referral was made to me. In talking with Janet, I found her feelings fit the typical pattern of postpartum "blues." However, I had her visit me once a week for a month afterwards to be sure that she did not develop acute depression. While she needed a lot of encouragement, she also had the support of her mother, who was staying with the family. Janet's symptoms did not require any medication, and after about a month's time she was back to her normal self, adjusting comfortably to the joys and demands of motherhood.

In therapy, Janet and I discussed practical ways and methods of handling the new baby and new responsibilities—establishing a new nursing routine, waking in the middle of the night to nurse the baby, her feelings of anxiety about being able to stop the baby from crying, and so on. Her husband helped and supported her by caring for the baby when he came home from work so that Janet could have a nap before dinner, helping with the nighttime feedings, and so on. Having her mother with her, she told me, was a godsend. Her mother was kind, helpful in a practical way, but did not interfere.

Not everyone suffering from postpartum blues needs the support of a psychiatrist—that is obvious. For instance, a new mothers' support group in the neighborhood can also help by offering the shared experience of other women. Talking with group members lets you know how other women experience postpartum emotions and may also provide practical suggestions about coping with your situation. Alternatively, your community may have home nursing services or a public health nurse who can visit you at home for the first few weeks.

Those mothers who experience intense feelings of blues beyond a period of two weeks, should actively seek advice on what they are experiencing. For some women, this is difficult, because the postpartum period may be the first time they have ever sought—ever required—the supportive care of a professional who is trained to recognize, support, and counsel patients who experience emotional disturbance. This person might be a family doctor, a psychologist, a specialized nurse, or a psychiatrist. In the discussion that follows, I use the general term "counselor" when any of these caregivers might be of help; in certain instances, however, I will emphasize that a psychiatrist's involvement is essential.

POSTPARTUM DEPRESSION

In the earlier discussion of depression during pregnancy, I introduced the concept of depression as a mood disorder in which extremes of emotion interfere with one's normal ability to function. The condition of *postpartum depression* goes beyond the normal "blues" described earlier and is experienced by 10 to 15 percent of new mothers.

Both men and women can experience depression as a disorder of mood, but women tend to experience it more commonly than men. Frequently, postpartum depression has the added complications of *anxiety disorder, obsessional thoughts,* or—very rarely—superimposed *psychosis.*

The signs and symptoms of postpartum depression can be both physical and emotional. Some new mothers in this state experience extremes of sleep disorders. They might consistently wake in the early morning hours, be unable to fall asleep easily, chronically lack energy, and feel totally exhausted day and night. Some women may sleep147 excessively and still feel tired. Often, depression is accompanied by lack of appetite or an aversion to the sight or smell of food. On the other hand, a new mother in this state may instead have an excessive appetite and start to eat in a way that is unusual for her. Her way of coping with anxiety may simply be to eat too much. Almost always, depressed patients feel a total loss of sexual interest.

Emotionally, some women feel uncontrolled and unpredictable tearfulness and have spontaneous crying spells that occur without any obvious cause; or they feel burdened with guilt. New mothers in a depressed state sometimes feel a pervasive sense of sadness—in some patients, this is especially noticeable in the morning. Other women may be aware that they feel angry inside but feel too tired to express that anger with anything other than a continual feeling of melancholia.

They may have a general feeling of apathy or despair, or an over-whelming feeling of worthlessness. Sometimes, forgetfulness or memory problems are part of the depressive syndrome. Many women also experience difficulty in making decisions; some complain of inability to concentrate. My patient Marji said, "I can't even watch or enjoy my favorite TV show!"

But during this time of new experiences, interrupted sleep due to the baby's nursing patterns, and marital readjustments to new roles, how does one distinguish "normal" emotions of a depressive nature from those of a clinical depression that require treatment? First of all, all of these symptoms must be present every day for a period of two weeks before a diagnosis of clinical depression is made. Secondly, the symptoms must interfere with the woman's life in a major way, making her almost dysfunctional. This is different from the normal "ups and downs" of pregnancy and postpartum—or indeed, from any periods of stress and change in one's life. Thirdly, the symptoms must be severe. The woman who feels pervasively guilt-ridden and hopeless, who sees not a single ray of hope ahead, is entirely different from the woman who feels occasionally sad or guilty because she was not able to quiet her crying baby easily! Thus the normal emotions of postpartum, with fluctuating range of feelings, are quite different from those of a major depression, a state in which the woman has signs or symptoms that are intense and prolonged and do not go away with reassurance. A woman's withdrawal from her infant, her partner, her friends and family is also a telling symptom—one that should alert the woman and those around her that "normal" behavior has become abnormal. In the most extreme cases, the new mother might think of harming herself and/or her baby. It is critical that a mother experiencing these feelings seek help immediately.

Postpartum depression can begin from a few days to weeks after delivery but, in some women, it may appear after several months. If untreated, it can continue up to a year after the birth. Of course, the earlier a condition of depression is recognized and the earlier the new mother receives treatment and care, the better.

What Causes Postpartum Depression?

Biological, psychological, and social factors are thought to contribute to postpartum depression. One possible biological explanation is shifting hormone levels which create a biochemical imbalance in the woman's body. As a result, the levels of the chemical substance that is responsible for keeping one's mood stable fluctuate. It is unclear whether chemical imbalance is directly or indirectly related to fluctuations of hormones that the woman experiences during pregnancy. This, in combination with intense emotional stress, can lead some women to a state of depression.

Genetic factors also seem to play some role in causing postpartum depression, and this is why women whose mothers have experienced postpartum depression are themselves at greater risk of developing depression after childbirth. Different studies report the risk of recurrence as varying from 64 to 100 percent. A history of depression in any blood relative, as well as a personal history of depressive illness, are also known risk factors for postpartum depression.

Among the psychosocial factors, the woman's relationship to her own mother is an important issue. If the woman's own mother was a poor role model, then becoming a mother herself for the first time may create conflict. As Olive, a 27-year-old patient, said to me, "How can I be a mother when I'm still a child myself?" Olive had been struggling with her relationship with her own mother for a number of years, and in general they had little to do with each other. Olive, still feeling herself to be a child longing for her mother, was now confronted with the imminent arrival of a baby who would need Olive to become herself the loving mother.

Every first-time mother must come to terms in some way with the loss of her previous lifestyle in exchange for a new and demanding role. For some new mothers, though, the conflicts between raising a baby and having a career or giving up the freedom of couplehood for the new responsibilities of being parents are especially intense. Margie was a patient of mine who had been deserted by her partner as soon as he learned of her pregnancy. She had been struggling with mixed feelings towards her pregnancy and had quite intense feelings of anger towards her partner. Then, following the birth of the baby, he had returned and had tried to rejoin the family and be supportive. Margie developed postpartum depression, and her feelings were centered on his abandonment during her pregnancy.

Some women are unable to deal with their anger and resentment because they feel these emotions at odds with the sterotype of motherhood as a uniformly happy and fulfilling role. Some new mothers simply feel hopeless and overwhelmed by the new and constant demands of caring for their infants. For instance, Leslie came to my office a few weeks ago with her colicky baby. "This is hell for me," she said. Her nights and days seemed to be all the same. She was unable to see any

future beyond the "nightmare" of constantly trying to soothe the crying infant and was unable to focus on practical solutions and alternatives. With her past history of depressive illness, it was not really
surprising that the extra stress of a "difficult" baby led to her postpartum depression.

The mixed emotions of anger, guilt, and insecurity can reach a critical stress point if the woman's partner is not supportive, if the infant
was not particularly welcome, or if the woman's own mother was a
poor role model. Although every case is different in its particulars, it is
clear that there are certain universal risk factors for postpartum depression. These are a poor marital relationship, low family income combined with a weak social network, and past personal or family history
of psychiatric illness.

What Can Be Done for Postpartum Depression?

Treatment for postpartum depression usually combines several approaches: medication and supportive counseling or psychotherapy for
the mother, along with involvement of her partner and family to help
them understand and deal with the situation and assist in the mother's
care. The types of medications prescribed vary with the individual's
case, and I will discuss some treatment approaches in Chapter Eleven.
Often, treatment takes place on an outpatient basis, and the mother is
able to remain in the family home. In treating women with postpartum depression as outpatients, I usually see the mother and her partner, as well as any other member of the family who is part of their lives,
such as the woman's mother, sister, or mother-in-law. I discuss the arrangements that can be made to allow the woman regular relief from
the demands of caring for the infant and any older children in the family. This allows the woman a restful break from daily stresses. We also
talk about the baby's feeding patterns and night routines, which inter-
rupt the mother's sleep. As a unit, the woman and her partner need to
consider nursing routines, and I help them by talking about breastfeeding versus bottle feeding and how the partner can help with night
feedings. These are some of the practical ways of helping the mother
while allowing her to be in close touch with her baby without feeling
overwhelmed.

In very severe cases, treatment in hospital may be necessary. When
this happens, the woman is usually very ill during the first few days,
and attempts are made to stabilize her with medications. She is often
not in a state to interact with her baby, and many doctors prefer to

wait until her symptoms improve before suggesting that the baby be brought in for visits. At first, these visits are likely be limited to perhaps a half an hour, with the partner or the baby's grandmother remaining with the mother during the visit. As the mother's condition improves, longer visits may be possible on weekends, or the mother might have a weekend pass to go home to the family. Before the mother is discharged from hospital, it is common to allow her to begin reestablishing confidence and familiarity by gradually extending the length of visits and allowing time for the mother and baby to be alone, without supervision. During these later visits, a caregiver is generally easily accessible should the mother feel that she needs reassurance or assistance.

Since postpartum depression takes a number of different forms and its symptoms range in severity, there is no simple answer to how long a particular bout will last. In general, the length of the illness depends greatly on how early the condition is recognized and how soon the mother receives treatment. As discussed, supportive involvement of her partner and family also seems to make a distinct difference to the course of the illness.

POSTPARTUM DEPRESSION WITH ANXIETY DISORDER

It is not uncommon for *anxiety disorder* (sometimes called *panic disorder*) to accompany postpartum depression. In Chapter One I described anxiety disorder as an emotional disorder that may surface any time during pregnancy. You might want to read the earlier chapter again, since this condition may show up in the same way in the postpartum period—either as a first-time event, or as another episode in a woman who experienced anxiety disorder earlier in her life. Anxiety disorder is not necessarily related specifically to either pregnancy or the postpartum period.

As I pointed out earlier, the symptoms of anxiety disorder—sweating, pounding heart, shortness of breath—may at first suggest physical conditions or illness. When women seek treatment for these troubling symptoms, they're likely to be tested first for physical illness, sometimes subjected to repeated examinations and a variety of investigations. They may find themselves returning again and again to their family doctor or even to emergency rooms, feeling frightened and frustrated that their alarming symptoms continue to go unexplained.

A description of a typical case of postpartum depression with anxiety disorder shows how disturbing this illness can be and how truly the term "panic" describes the range of sensations the woman feels: The new mother arrives home from hospital, and on the third or fourth postpartum day wakes suddenly in the middle of the night. She's bathed in sweat, her heart is pounding, her chest feels crushed, and she's terrified. Can this be a heart attack? Is she going to die? If she gets up and walks around, she might feel dizziness or numbness in her hands and feet, an overall tingling sensation. She might have diarrhea. Surely, something is drastically wrong. And then the symptoms pass— only to return the next day. Occasionally, the woman may feel an overwhelming dread that she may actually "go mad" if she does not receive immediate help.

Panic attacks like this might occur one or two times a day and gradually increase to a frequency of four to five times a day. After she has experienced a number of panic attacks, the woman becomes anxious between attacks, fearful that another one will occur—a condition called *anticipatory anxiety*. Panic attacks may start without any apparent reason, or they may occur under extreme conditions of stress. However, if they are associated in the woman's mind with a particular situation, she may come to fear and avoid similar situations. If the first attack occurred while she was driving or shopping, for instance, she might stop driving her car or going to shopping malls. She might become so afraid of experiencing a panic attack on leaving home that she finally refuses to leave home completely (a condition called *agoraphobia*). The reverse can also take place: A woman who has panic attacks in her home may leave the house and be afraid to return. A further complication is that it is very difficult for her to establish nursing patterns, because her thoughts are dominated by fear of dying or going insane.

For example, Louise, a 24-year-old legal assistant, began to have anxiety attacks every time she returned home from shopping, and was settling the baby in again. If the little boy began crying, Louise would break out in sweats and her heart would begin to pound. At such moments, she told me, "All I can think of is running away." Luckily, she felt close to her mother and when she realized that these feelings were not going away and that she was actually becoming afraid of interacting with the baby, she was able to talk about her feelings. Her mother helped her realize that these were not normal feelings and encouraged Louise to talk with her doctor, who subsequently referred her to me. "What a strange feeling this is to have your heart pounding when you see your baby crying," she said. "I should be comforting him, and instead, I'm feeling frightened and in need of comfort myself!"

The course of panic disorder is variable. Some women have a fluctuating course, which means that they will have a few weeks of acute anxiety and their symptoms may disappear without treatment. Other women may continue to have frequent attacks for a period of weeks or months, becoming increasingly dysfunctional without treatment, and in addition developing symptoms of depression. Under these circumstances, a woman can eventually come to experience an almost 24-hour vicious circle of acute anxiety, fear of the next attack, and memory of the previous attack—which only serves to bring on another attack. She can become almost paralyzed by fear, and the situation becomes truly dysfunctional for the entire family.

A new mother with fully developed symptoms of depression with anxiety disorder is a heartrending picture: She has difficulty concentrating and remembering, is unable to make decisions, and can't complete simple tasks like doing the laundry or making dinner. Her insomnia leads to exhaustion, she's unable to eat, and she may have suicidal thoughts. She may experience daily variations in her mood—some women feel worse in the morning and others feel worse in the evening—but she comes to feel completely without joy in life's events and becomes extremely withdrawn.

Fortunately, anxiety associated with depression is treatable. Both panic attacks and the related mood disorder can be alleviated relatively effectively with medication, behavioral therapy, and supportive therapy, as I will discuss in Chapter Ten. The key thing is making a correct diagnosis—and this depends on your being very frank with your doctor about just what you are going through. Remember, this is not an uncommon condition for new mothers, and you are not "going crazy." When you seek care for the kind of symptoms I've described, *it's important to give your doctor all the information you can about your feelings and moods during this difficult period as accurately as possible.* This will help your doctor come to the correct diagnosis and recommend the best treatment.

Anxiety disorder is not unique to the pregnant or postpartum woman. However, as with depression, women in general tend to suffer from it more than men do. The cause is still unknown and is a major focus of current psychological and biological research. What is known, however, is that stress can precipitate or perpetuate anxiety disorder. In the postpartum period, of course, any emotional disturbance is complicated by the mother's new responsibilities for her infant and the challenge of sorting out new relationships within the family. Any new mother with shaky confidence may be a candidate for this disorder.

Anxiety disorder may become more pronounced if the new mother is dealing with other stressful issues, such as discord with her partner or having to move the family home or cope with inadequate family income.

SALLY'S STORY

Sally was a 40-year-old lawyer whose first baby had been stillborn. When she became pregnant again, she tried hard to put her loss behind her—and in fact, she completely repressed it from her memory. She gave birth to a healthy baby boy, and, shortly after leaving hospital, began to experience typical panic disorder.

Each night when she went to bed, images of the stillborn infant—also a boy—flashed before her eyes. She would lie awake trembling, suffering nausea and diarrhea. Slowly, nights became such a dread to her that she stopped sleeping completely. She began to lose interest in her baby's care and in her own personal care, and she stopped eating. The panic attacks became more severe and occurred three to four times a week. Depression set in, which was moderate to severe by the time she came to see me some weeks later.

Sally's husband was a successful lawyer, working long hours in anticipation of becoming a partner in his firm. He had been rather removed from events due to these pressures at work. Typically, he would return from a long day at work, play with the baby for about an hour, bathe the baby, and then fall asleep, exhausted. As a result, Sally had little emotional contact with him during this difficult period. At night, she found herself sitting alone, watching her husband sleeping peacefully, watching the baby who was now also sleeping through the night—and suffering from her own intense depression and panic. When this had continued unabated for four or five weeks, Sally finally confided in an old classmate, who was a doctor. Her physician friend contacted Sally's family doctor, who asked me to see her right away.

When I saw Sally, she was severely depressed and panicky. Not surprisingly, she had found it difficult to establish a nursing pattern, and this had also added to her anxiety. It was not difficult to persuade her to begin immediate treatment with antidepressant medications; it did not seem necessary to admit her to hospital.

Within seven to eight weeks, Sally was completely free of her symptoms. I continued her treatment for a year, and she is now back at work practicing law. She and her husband are quite happy with their healthy three-year-old boy.

POSTPARTUM DEPRESSION WITH OBSESSIVE-COMPULSIVE DISORDER

In Chapter One I described *obsessive-compulsive disorder* in early pregnancy. This disorder can also occur in company with postpartum depression, usually in the form of disturbing obsessive thoughts rather than as compulsive behavior or rituals. These thoughts take on an especially frightening quality in the postpartum period because often they tend to focus on harming the vulnerable new member of the family. This is a truly terrifying condition for a new mother, and in describing its characteristics, I want to emphasize that women in this situation do not carry out the actions they continually imagine. However, they can become virtually paralyzed by the recognition of how horrible and unusual their thoughts are and by the fear that they may act on them.

I have chosen to discuss obsessional thoughts in some detail for several reasons. First, although obsessional thoughts are really quite rare in the general population, a significant number of women with postpartum depression suffer from them as a part of their depression. Second, women who experience these thoughts find them so frightening that they rarely are willing to talk about them, even with loved ones. Further, though these women are in touch with reality, they often have an overwhelming fear that they are "losing their minds." It is my hope that any woman with obsessional thoughts who reads this chapter will realize that she is by no means alone and will feel comforted to know that other mothers have suffered with this condition and that it can be treated.

There are several predominating themes to postpartum obsessional thoughts, and I will describe the most common ones. The mother may imagine that she will smother or stab her baby, and so start to hide things such as kitchen knives, which she begins to see as instruments of violence. Or she may imagine that she will somehow sexually abuse the baby, particularly if she herself has been a victim of sexual abuse. A woman may become so afraid she will act on her thoughts that she will neglect her infant. She may avoid bathing the baby, changing its diaper, or seeing it naked because of her terrible compelling fear of touching the baby in the wrong way. Another common obsessive disturbing thought concerns a woman's distressing conviction that she has murdered her baby in the past. This is specifically experienced by women who have previously terminated a pregnancy and are now experiencing motherhood for the first time. Yet another possible theme for her obsessive thoughts is suicide. She imagines that only a horrid, worthless person could think about harming her own child, and her intrusive thoughts begin to dwell on self-destruction.

For the woman so afflicted, the thoughts are terrible and obtrusive; and she has to fight very hard to keep them away. Her fear of what she might do may literally paralyze her to the point of immobility. And because she is very aware of just how abnormal and extreme her thoughts are, she is afraid to discuss them with anyone.

If the woman does not receive treatment and support, symptoms of anxiety may accompany the obsessional disorder—shortness of breath, heart palpitations, numbness. It is not uncommon to find anxiety and obsessional disorder occurring at the same time.

Though depression with obsessional thoughts is quite horrific, treatment is available, and specific medications can alleviate the symptoms quite effectively. If you are a new mother and are experiencing these kinds of disturbing thoughts, it is important to realize that you are neither "crazy" nor alone. You are experiencing a condition that other new mothers have experienced and for which a course of treatment exists. The destructive acts the obsessional person imagines are seldom acted upon, but obviously, the new mother will benefit from exploring these feelings with a professional caregiver.

LAURA'S STORY

Laura, a 32-year-old nurse, was referred to me about six months after the birth of her baby. Before her decision to seek help, she had endured some months of inner struggle. From about the third month postpartum, she knew something was not quite right about her feelings, but she felt embarrassed and ashamed at the thought of needing a psychiatrist—even though she was a nurse.

When Laura and her husband came to see me, they told me they were shocked that she had developed obsessional thoughts around harming their baby. They are a dual-career couple with a stable marriage and had planned and achieved this pregnancy just as the husband completed his university degree. Laura was happy in her job, and had planned to return to work about six months after the baby's birth. Their circumstances seemed ideal, and the question of something going wrong in the postpartum period had never occurred to them.

After the baby's birth, Laura developed all the classic signs and symptoms of depression—she couldn't eat and couldn't sleep and was exhausted and despondent. Any time she prepared meals, she became terrified that she would use the kitchen knives to harm her child. Eventually, as the baby started to sleep through the night, Laura moved to another bedroom in order to be as far away as she could get. She was terrified that she would awake in the night with an irresistible urge to go to the kitchen and get a knife.

Laura came to see me weekly for about two months. Together, we explored her emotional state as the combination of anxiolytic and antidepressant medication took effect. (Anxiolytic medicine, as I will discuss in Chapter Eleven, gives relief from the symptoms of anxiety). After two months, Laura was well, and I saw her periodically but less frequently for a total of one year, after which we felt comfortable in discontinuing the medication.

Recently, I saw Laura at work in the hospital, and she is pregnant again. She has asked that she be referred again to my care because she knows that her risks of becoming depressed after the birth are quite high.

POSTPARTUM PSYCHOSIS

Postpartum psychosis is the most extreme—and *rarest*—psychiatric illness experienced in the postpartum period. I want to emphasize how very infrequently psychosis occurs among new mothers, striking only 1–4 in every 800–1,000 pregnant women. It is recognizable as an obvious disorder, and when it occurs, it constitutes an emergency psychiatric situation. Some studies show that a woman having her first child is at higher risk for developing postpartum psychosis. I have chosen to discuss this unusual illness in some detail so that it will not be misunderstood. For one thing, readers should be aware—as will be clear from the descriptions—that obsessive-compulsive disorder, with thoughts of harming one's infant, is *not* the same as psychosis. Even within the small group of women who have had postpartum psychosis, the tragic cases of infanticide or lifelong withdrawal are very uncommon. It is important to realize too, that those cases you might recall from half-remembered family histories might well have had different outcomes with today's modern psychiatric care.

Psychosis is defined as a state of being out of touch with reality. People in psychotic states generally feel alienated from what is going on around them, and to others they appear obviously disturbed, sometimes truly frantic with excitement. The most common type of postpartum psychosis is *postpartum manic-depressive psychosis* or *bipolar illness*. A woman with this illness has extreme polarity of moods. At the start, she is quite *hypomanic*—that is, she exhibits a low degree of "manic" behavior and is in a state that we ordinarily describe as "high" or "hyper." She is physically hyperactive, has an increased rate of speech, speeded-up thought patterns with no connection between one thought and the next, and expansive or grandiose ideas; in addition, she develops fixed and unshakable false beliefs called *delusions*. These delusions usually center on the special powers she believes she has; for example, she might imagine herself to be a powerful figure such as the queen of England or the president of the United States. The woman also becomes sexually preoccupied, exhibiting an increased sexual drive and bizarre provocative behavior. When a mother is in this state, there is always the possibility that she will incorporate the baby into her delusional thinking, and the risk of infanticide cannot be overlooked. After the initial period of excitability and frantic behavior, the opposite mood may occur, and the woman will display all the classical signs and symptoms of deep depression, as described earlier.

When manic-depressive psychosis occurs, it is most likely to be apparent in the first few days or weeks after birth, and its dramatic symptoms are very obvious. It might, however, also occur later in the postpartum period when the woman stops nursing her baby. The sudden shift in hormones when the woman discontinues nursing may contribute to the onset of clinical depression in some women. In a few women in my practice who have had a prior history of bipolar illness, the cessation of nursing has triggered psychotic symptoms. Again, I want to emphasize that postpartum depression occurs in relatively few women and that postpartum psychosis is truly rare. However, among the different types of postpartum psychosis, manic-depressive psychosis is most frequently seen.

The second type of postpartum psychosis is depression with super-imposed psychotic features. In this mood disorder, which generally goes undiagnosed for weeks or months, the woman starts to become *paranoid* or suspicious. She might imagine people are laughing at her, talking about her, and even conspiring against her or her baby.

The third and least frequent type of postpartum psychosis is *schizo-phreniform psychosis*, a disorder in which there is a combination of schizophrenic symptoms and affective symptoms. A woman with this illness will display a great degree of emotionality, but she might have a complete blankness of thought or she may exhibit tangential (discon-nected) thinking, imagining that whatever she is thinking can be broadcast on radio or read aloud by a TV reporter. She might have both auditory and visual hallucinations. The visual hallucinations can be very frightening and can present her with distorted images of her baby and the people around her. She might imagine people are talking about her or hear voices. This kind of delusional state can be very dan-gerous, particularly when the imaginary voices begin to issue com-mands—a condition called command hallucination. This form of psychosis occurs usually in women who have a previous history of schizophrenia.

Another type of postpartum psychosis presents itself as confusion, when the woman does not recognize who she is, where she is, or what time of day it is. Her orientation is disturbed, she does not remember things, and she is almost "delirious." This is called an *acute organic brain syndrome*, where the woman is out of touch with reality. In the rare instances in which this type of psychosis occurs, it is often related to some other medical condition that occurs after delivery or to simple imbalances in the woman's body that occur after birth. Its course is usually short, and it clears without presenting any long-term problems.

Women with any of these forms of psychosis are severely ill and need immediate treatment and hospitalization. Although the woman herself may consider her behavior and delusions quite plausible, family members will recognize immediately that there is a problem. In these unusual cases, family members must act quickly to see that proper care is given and any possibility of family tragedy is averted.

What Causes Postpartum Psychosis?

Even today, postpartum psychosis is described by medical professionals as a "puzzle." As is the case with depression, it appears likely that there are both biological and psychological triggers to this illness. In fact, some medical professionals consider postpartum psychosis as a severe form of chemical imbalance that takes place in the woman's brain. The majority of researchers believe that "neuroendocrine" (biological) factors play a significant role in the causation of this disorder.

One focus of research is the impact of changing hormone levels on postpartum emotional states. Why this perfectly normal and necessary change in body chemistry provokes profound disturbance in a small number of new mothers is part of the puzzle. It has also become clear that certain factors place a woman at higher risk for postpartum psychosis: a history of previous psychosis, low socioeconomic status, and being a first-time mother.

What Can Be Done for Postpartum Psychosis?

As I discussed, postpartum psychosis occurs extremely infrequently. When it does occur, however, it is an emergency situation. The mother must be hospitalized under the care of a psychiatrist, and a range of treatment must be started immediately. Depending on the woman's particular symptoms, a combination of medications may be called for. With appropriate medication, the psychotic thoughts usually take eight to nine weeks to disappear, and treatment of depression somewhat longer. Meanwhile, the woman must be reassured that her delusions do not represent reality.

Although hospitalization rarely extends beyond two to three months, it is certainly necessary for a number of weeks. During this period, the family will also be offered supportive attention and will be involved, to the extent possible, in the mother's care. Today, psychiatrists consider it essential that arrangements be made as soon as possible to maintain regular contact between the mother and infant. When the mother is well enough to leave the hospital, she will receive medication and continuing therapy as an outpatient. It is important that this treatment be maintained for an adequate amount of time in order to avoid a relapse.

After an episode of postpartum psychosis or depression, many couples want to know what they can expect with the birth of the next child. While postpartum psychosis or depression is not a contraindication to pregnancy, the chances of a repeat illness are very high. If the woman chooses to become pregnant, her condition should be monitored throughout the pregnancy to ensure that appropriate treatment is not delayed.

HELEN'S STORY

Helen, a 29-year-old lab technician, had "felt unwell" when pregnant with her first child, but never sought treatment for her uncomfortable feelings during the postpartum period. When she became pregnant again, she was at first happy at the thought of the new baby but then became increasingly anxious, in some way reminiscent of her feelings in the first pregnancy. She remembered being unusually happy after the first birth but thought nothing more of it, assuming that most women felt the same way after the birth of their child. In any case, she settled down into a routine without any problems.

After her second child's birth, Helen started to experience unusual thoughts, imagining that she was the Virgin Mary. On her second postpartum day, she began to dress in a sexually provocative way and began flirting with any man who came onto the ward, including the husbands of other patients. That day, she also announced she had won the world over and was going to war with the pediatric hospital next door, and I was called for a consultation.

When I came to Helen's room, she was sitting on the edge of her bed, singing away, very happy one moment and irritable the next. She spoke very fast, her thoughts racing a mile a minute; it was obvious that this woman was psychotic and in a "hypomanic" state.

Helen was transferred from the maternity hospital to a psychiatric facility and started on antipsychotic medications. She stayed in the hospital a total of eight weeks. After about three weeks, when she had begun to respond to medication, the baby was allowed to room in with her on a periodic basis under medical supervision, and then regularly for the final four weeks when her thinking was much more controlled.

She had a repeat psychotic illness with the birth of her third child. She has been my patient since I first saw her and requires continual monitoring and medication. With this continued care, Helen actually functions very well.

Though postpartum psychosis occurs very infrequently, it is a frightening illness. For this reason, women who have personal or family histories of psychotic illness *must* take their partner and their doctor into their confidence early in their pregnancy—better still, even before their pregnancy begins. Some researchers believe that a woman with a history of manic-depressive illness has a one in two chance of developing a psychotic illness in the postpartum period. Women who have blood relatives with manic-depressive illness have approximately a one in five chance of developing bipolar illness or manic-depressive illness when they give birth. Similarly, women who have schizophrenic relatives have about a one in four chance of developing postpartum psychosis. If you have a family history of these conditions, it is important that you share this information with your partner and your doctor. With this knowledge, your doctor will be able to follow you carefully throughout your pregnancy and early motherhood, and your partner will be able to provide informed support.

As you read Sylvia's story, consider how different it might have been if those close to her had realized that a woman with Sylvia's family history requires special care throughout her pregnancy and postpartum period.

SYLVIA'S STORY

Sylvia, a 38-year-old mother of two, was planning to return to work after nine months' maternity leave. The only unusual event to mark her two pregnancies had been a two-month depression after the birth of her first child. She had kept this to herself, however, and the depression had gone undiagnosed and untreated. What she had also kept to herself, not realizing its importance, was the fact that her maternal uncle and a cousin both suffered from manic-depressive illness.

As the end of her maternity leave approached, Sylvia decided to wean her baby abruptly. Within five days, she started to experience extreme changes in her mood. Her job was a demanding one as administrator responsible for a key department in a large department store, and now she faced the prospect of ensuring that two children at home were properly cared for. She began staying up all night, making long lists of everything she had to do before going back to work. Quite unexpectedly, she visited her store manager before her return to work and regaled him with the grandiose plans she'd developed for the store's new season. She started using the fax machine at work in a bizarre way, and made several inappropriate long-distance calls to the store's main office.

It was shortly after this that her doctor called me for an urgent consultation, and I met Sylvia and her husband in the emergency room and admitted her immediately. Her shaken husband told me that his mother-in-law, who was staying with them, had run into the baby's room that morning having heard some disturbance. She had found Sylvia wild-eyed and singing inappropriately, just on the verge of smothering her baby with a pillow.

The husband was able to intervene and calm Sylvia sufficiently to get her to the hospital. When Sylvia talked with me, she described her baby as the devil and said she'd received messages that only by killing this devil in disguise could her own life be salvaged.

Sylvia was hospitalized under my care for a number of months and was treated with both medication and psychotherapy. Other counselors were enlisted to help her husband deal with his added family responsibilities and to lend support as he developed understanding of Sylvia's illness.

Sylvia continues under my care as an outpatient. She has had two more children and all together, she has had three psychotic episodes, two of them postpartum. Her illness is going to require psychiatric care for a long time to come. For a few more years, she will need to be on medication such as lithium to maintain her in stable condition, since the more episodes of psychosis a woman has, the longer she will need to be on maintenance doses of medication in the future.

When a woman has had an episode of postpartum psychosis, she and her partner often meet with me and ask if they should have more children. My advice to them is to weigh the pros and cons. Statistically speaking, a woman who has had one psychotic episode runs a one in two risk of having another during a subsequent postpartum period. Some couples will choose not to have another child; other couples may decide it is important to them to pursue another pregnancy. In the latter case, it is important that the woman be followed throughout the pregnancy and postpartum period. The psychiatrist's role is to lay out the facts as fully as possible, let the couple make their own decision, and then arrange for proper support.

WHY A PSYCHIATRIST IS SOMETIMES ESSENTIAL

Throughout this book, I talk about a wide range of emotional states in pregnancy and new motherhood. Some of these are upsetting but quite normal, and others are so extreme that they become incapacitating. I also describe a number of support systems, ranging from the tried-and-true comfort of understanding friends and the empathy of other new mothers to a variety of formal support groups and professionals that may be available in the community. In Chapter Ten I describe in depth about how various support groups and professionals can provide assistance.

In this chapter, I have talked about some of the most extreme emotional disorders that can occur, and I feel it is important to emphasize that in these cases, *a psychiatrist's involvement is essential*. Psychiatrists are medical doctors with additional years of specialized training in the diagnosis and treatment of emotional/mental disorders. The medical qualifications and experience of a psychiatrist are essential because some of the emotional disorders described may have an underlying physiological component. With specific experience in treating a large number of patients with emotional disorders, a psychiatrist is specially qualified to investigate the interface between physical conditions and emotional illnesses and to discern situations in which a physical illness or a prescribed medication might have contributed to an emotional state. For example, some blood pressure medicines, when given over a period of time, can cause depression. Similarly, depression is one of the symptoms of certain diseases, such as Parkinson's disease and multiple sclerosis.

As medical specialists, psychiatrists can admit patients to hospital and direct their hospital care. In addition, medical doctors can prescribe medication, and as new medications become available for the treatment of emotional disorders, the psychiatrist's role in prescribing and monitoring medication in the context of an overall treatment plan is essential.

The understanding and empathy of friends and partners are always important in resolving difficulties, and a variety of trained caregivers can be enlisted for support and continuing therapy, as I will discuss in Chapters Nine and Ten. When a patient is critically ill—that is, psychotic or suicidal—it is the psychiatrist who is best able to plan effectively an approach to therapy and ensure that the support network is coordinated to best effect.

SOME QUESTIONS YOU MIGHT HAVE ABOUT THE RISKS OF POSTPARTUM DEPRESSION

Recently I read an article that linked postpartum depression to a family history of psychiatric disorders. My aunt has been diagnosed as schizophrenic. Am I more likely to have depression?

Doctors continue to debate over the exact link between a family history of psychiatric illness and postpartum depression. In fact, the role of heredity in psychiatric illness continues to be a subject for medical research.

Just as there are known "risk factors" for certain physical illness or conditions in pregnancy, we can suggest some risk factors for mental illness. Since the association of psychiatric illness in one's family with postpartum depression has not been clearly established, it's worthwhile to consider family history as a *possible* risk factor for postpartum depression. You would be wise to alert your doctor to your family history and express your concerns. Just as you would pay particular attention to certain symptoms if you had known risk factors for a physical illness, so you should be particularly aware of and open about your emotional state during the course of your pregnancy and postpartum.

After the birth of my first child almost three years ago, I experienced a postpartum depression that affected my ability to function and look after my baby. I am now pregnant with my second child, and I am scared of repeating the experience.

The chance of experiencing a second postpartum depression is higher for you than for the average woman awaiting the birth of her second child. If your doctor is not the same one as before, let her or him know of your previous postpartum depression and your concerns about experiencing another. Be receptive to an early referral to a psychiatrist, even in the absence of any pronounced symptoms.

A previous depression, like family history of psychiatric illness, is another indicator that might be considered a risk factor for postpartum depression. It's a reminder to you to place as high a priority on your personal well-being as on your baby's. Keep in touch with your feelings and emotions, and keep in touch with your doctor about anything that troubles you.

? *I am afraid of becoming pregnant because I have a past history of manic-depressive illness. I have had two episodes of illness and was hospitalized both times. Currently, I am on medication—900 mg of lithium per day—and I feel wonderful. What are my chances of becoming ill during pregnancy or the postpartum period? I also have an aunt who suffers from manic-depressive illness.*

With your personal history and your aunt's history, you are at higher than average risk of becoming psychotic after the birth of your baby. The good news is that, having had two episodes and being in remission (free of symptoms), you can be tracked carefully throughout your pregnancy. There's only a small chance that your symptoms will flare up *during* pregnancy, but should that happen, your doctor can discuss treatment with you. I would suggest that while you are on lithium, you should not become pregnant. Most doctors try to avoid giving women lithium in their first trimester.

Unfortunately, your risk of illness in the postpartum period is quite high. We don't know the exact mechanisms involved, but it seems that in women who have had manic-depressive illness, the postpartum shifts in hormone levels can provoke another manic episode.

This said, there's no reason for you to choose against pregnancy. It's critically important that the doctor who cares for you during pregnancy be made aware of your history and that you are followed very closely throughout your pregnancy and for some time after giving birth. Ideally, you should become pregnant only after careful planning, and you should consult with your doctor regarding the effects of medicine during pregnancy. The important factor here is to weigh the risks versus benefits of continuing your medication when you become pregnant.

WHAT I TELL MY PATIENTS

Many women experience general concern and anxiety about how they will handle motherhood, and this is quite natural. But nowhere earlier in the pregnancy does anything prepare them for the idea that serious depression or anxiety can occur after the "happy event." Often, women who develop these problems are completely shocked because what they are experiencing is so contrary to the image of future happiness that pregnancy promises.

Even for women who are not depressed, motherhood is a difficult task. No one ever teaches us how to be mothers—it is something that most women learn by making mistakes and falling down along the way. This demanding—but normal—experience becomes overwhelming when a woman is depressed, constantly irritable, unable to concentrate. The process of bonding with the new infant can be disrupted, and this has long-term consequences for the future relationship between mother and child.

Even when the woman is healthy, the process of bonding is a prolonged one. With depressed women, health care professionals are concerned about the delay in developing attachment and also about the possibility of child abuse or neglect, which may appear in different forms. For instance, the mother may not be very nurturing to the infant, or she may have little or no interaction with the infant. Some women in a depressed state may outright refuse to have anything to do with their infant. Recently, a corporate executive who came to see me said, "I don't even know that my baby exists." This woman had returned to work, even in her state of depression, had kept herself busy—and had left the care of her baby entirely in the hands of her paid house-keeper. At the end of three years, she suddenly realized she had no relationship at all with her child—a frightening awakening. A depressed mother may also show anger or resentment of her child, feeling that it has caused too much emotional upheaval and physical change in her life. Women who experience obsessional thoughts may be so afraid they will harm their child that they avoid even touching their baby.

As you've read in the stories I've related, women too often suffer alone—through lack of knowledge or fear that admitting their emotional state will show to others that they are less than a "Super Mom." Too much silent suffering and too many tragedies have happened because women have been afraid to seek help. As I hope you've seen, the problems of postpartum depression, anxiety, and even psychosis can be treated. And when they are left untreated, they can be detrimental not only to the woman herself but to the entire family. This is why I cannot emphasize enough how important it is to seek help.

CHAPTER 6

"I'M GOING TO BE
THE BEST KIND
OF MOTHER"

Breastfeeding and Psychiatric Illness

W hen a woman has an emotional disorder in pregnancy or
postpartum, treatment of her illness involves more than the
well-being of the patient alone. In pregnancy, the health of
the developing infant must be considered. After birth, treatment of
the woman's condition must also take into account the health and
well-being of the entire family—the often overlooked partner, the
older children in the family, and most critically, the new infant. Family
needs and relationships are so complex that a mother's emotional illness often results in more difficult conflicts than might be the case if
she had a physically incapacitating problem, such as a broken leg. In
Chapter Eight, I will examine some of the difficulties faced by the father and the rest of the family when the mother has a psychiatric illness. But now, let me look at the very sensitive issues of the mother's
relationship with her infant and the potential conflict between breastfeeding and the appropriate treatment of psychiatric illness.

BREASTFEEDING: EXPECTATIONS AND REALITIES

The "Modern" Mother

In the industrialized West, the last fifty years have been marked by
repeated revolutions in the image of motherhood, including the distinctly maternal role of nursing. Different practices have been intro-

157

duced by "experts" of one sort or another, and mothers who have wanted to do the best for their children have quickly taken to each of the "modern" approaches. Some of these practices have been real milestones in better child care, and others have been short-lived fads that seemed valid at the time but proved not to be.

Earlier in the century, the development of infant formulas was quite a revolution, and there was a time when conscientious mothers rushed to move their infants to the formula stage, believing that this innovation was nutritionally superior to mother's milk. Today, we know that mother's milk in the first three months of an infant's life provides a remarkable boost to the baby's immune system. Studies have confirmed that breastfed babies are likely to develop fewer allergies and to have better resistance to illness. At one time—it might have been your grandmother's day—there were persuasive arguments advanced that infants' feeding should be highly regulated, with meals on exact timetables. Too bad for the crying infant who was hungry between scheduled feeding times! Now we recognize that babies are individuals, and that no one feeding schedule will work for all infants.

At the same time, great changes have taken place in the dynamics of the North American family. The "working mother" is more the norm than the exception, and new mothers often take only a brief maternity leave before they return to work. If the "typical" North American family with traditional roles ever really existed—and that is by no means certain—those families are now few and far between. Families have their individual personalities, too, and must make unique choices that fit their own needs and aspirations. Fortunately, the normal parental desire to do the best for one's children has been supported by advances in scientific research and broader public education. In making choices about child rearing and child care, families today have better awareness of nutrition, better information about the psychology of children's development, and better access to information.

As you read this chapter, you'll be reflecting on your own attitudes towards motherhood and breastfeeding. As you do so, I encourage you to remember that you, your baby, and your partner are individuals, and you need to make family decisions with an awareness that your situation is unique. Remember, too, that the benefits of modern communication and education will probably always be accompanied by fads related to childbearing and family behavior. It is true that every year we have more and more information to support the decisions we make about family life, but it is also true that lots of other people stand ready to interpret that information and influence the decisions we make.

Sometimes, the influence of these self-appointed decision makers and advice givers is very subtle. One example of the persuasive power of suggestion is the magazine with "how-to" articles that suggest that all mothers are alike and promote the idea that "all good mothers will want to" grind their own baby food or teach their babies to swim or run their own preschool program. Another example is the media message of TV shows and commercials with their often unrealistic and certainly unreal portrayals of family behavior. Other influential—and aggressive—voices abound. There are a number of organizations that provide education to new mothers on the techniques of breastfeeding—and also issue very powerful messages that breastfeeding is desirable and possible *in every instance*. The messages can persuade women that breastfeeding, and the prolonged breastfeeding of children to the ages of three or four, is the only option for a "good mother." This no-compromise approach to childbearing does not take individual personality into account and can be a tragic setup for the woman whose circumstances are not compatible with breastfeeding.

Expectations About Breastfeeding

Many expectant first-time mothers look forward with joy to the idea of breastfeeding their infants. Breastfeeding, like pregnancy, is a distinctly female experience, and there are deep psychological reasons why women want to take part in it. As well, we know that breastfeeding offers certain benefits to the baby. Research has confirmed the value of mother's milk to the infant's developing immune system, and many women want to be sure that their babies get this additional protection that only mother's milk can provide. Additional arguments come from the area of developmental psychology. Mothers and fathers who have taken an active interest in pregnancy are likely to be just as interested in how their children will grow emotionally and how the dynamics of their family relationships will evolve. This has led to an increased emphasis on breastfeeding as a psychological-emotional event, an area which continues to be a focus of research.

A first-time mother's feelings towards breastfeeding will also be colored by the experiences of her friends or sisters, as well as her own mother's recollections. If she's a career woman whose friends have breastfed for a few months before returning to work, she'll likely have the same expectations for herself. If her circle is one in which women place great emphasis on breastfeeding and are able to be at home with their children, she'll probably assume that this will be her pattern, too.

In either situation, there tends to be the societal expectation these days that a woman *will* breastfeed, at least for the early months. Just as prenatal classes help parents approach pregnancy with knowledge and enthusiasm, they also provide equally enthusiastic information on the benefits of nursing. Taking this positive view of the joys and benefits of nursing, most new mothers assume that they will readily and easily be able to undertake breastfeeding.

Expectant mothers who have enjoyed breastfeeding in previous pregnancies often look forward to the remembered pleasures of nursing. The intimacy of nursing can be deeply satisfying to a mother, and the variety of nonverbal and verbal exchanges between mother and child during nursing contribute to the infant's developing awareness of the surrounding physical and psychological world, in addition to promoting bonding.

When it "works," nursing is indeed special and, in quite a complex way, pleasurable and beneficial to both the mother and baby. There are several reasons, however, that nursing might be impossible or inadvisable. When this is the case, it's important for a woman to try to separate social expectations and her own emotions from facts and to make a guilt-free decision best suited to her own family's needs.

Realities of Breastfeeding

Breastfeeding is assumed to be a "natural" activity that women have practiced almost instinctively and certainly with little difficulty over the centuries. This is not quite the case—either in past times or now. The physical act of breastfeeding requires certain technique and a fair bit of practice and experimentation. The production of sufficient milk for the baby depends on the mother having good nutrition, adequate rest, and a supportive environment. Women adapt differently as individuals to the routines and requirements for good nursing, but adaptation is certainly needed—nursing is not something that all women can "instinctively" do with success.

In past times, the art of nursing was taught from generation to generation, with plenty of coaching available from the female members of large extended families. In addition, the woman's need for rest in the early months of motherhood was recognized and supported with practical assistance. The extended family could take on responsibility for older children and for housekeeping. However, even with these traditional supports, the production of adequate milk has been an uncertainty for nursing mothers throughout history. Thus, we see across some cultures the traditional use of wet nurses—nursing mothers who produced more than enough milk for their own babies and were able to nurse another's child as well.

Today, for many North American women, the traditional familial and societal supports are unavailable, and ironically, expectations of breastfeeding success are in some circles more rigid than ever before. Typically, a normal stay in a maternity hospital may be over in 24 hours. Hospital beds are too expensive for the once-common seven-day stay, and women typically make a quick entrance, give birth quickly, and make a quick exit. Nurses are highly trained medical-care specialists and their emphasis in a maternity ward is on caring for high-risk patients. There's no longer leisure time in the hospital; gone are the days when a new mother could count on abundant attention from matronly nurses eager to provide coaching in breastfeeding techniques. A quick "demo" in bathing and holding the baby, and some basic directions on how to start breastfeeding may be all a new mother gets before she's at home again and on her own. Then follow weeks, sometimes, of trying to perfect the routine of nursing through trial and error—often to the accompaniment of a crying baby who is just not getting enough to eat. Her own inexperience and expectations and the easy assumptions made by family and friends can lead a new mother to hide her concerns from both her doctor and from friends who could help. Her difficulties might be recognized only at her first postpartum appointment, when her doctor realizes the baby is not gaining enough weight. A usual suggestion at this point is that the mother supplement her feedings with infant formula.

This suggestion can present additional difficulties for the mother. She has had the joy of her tiny infant's complete dependency on her, and now she feels guilty that she has "failed" in satisfying this dependency—but doesn't want to give up the relationship of dependency that is to her mind symbolic of motherhood. If her doctor has talked in terms of *replacing* instead of merely supplementing her breast milk, she may indeed feel that she is being replaced in her maternal role. After all, anyone can now feed her baby—her husband, the nanny, her mother. It's normal that as a woman becomes a mother, her self-identity changes. Sometimes, even in an emotionally stable woman, the inability to nurse, to carry out what she perceives as a key role of motherhood, may be a real blow to her self-esteem. The experience of Melanie comes to my mind in this regard. She had had repeated infections of the milk glands and nevertheless had tried to continue giving her baby breast milk by using a breast pump. Finally, she realized that the only way the infection could be brought under control was for her to discontinue nursing completely and take massive doses of antibiotics. While she quickly became better physically, she also experienced a lot of emotional turmoil because she had so looked forward to nursing as an integral part of being a mother. She said to me, "I thought I could handle every part of motherhood. I was sure that for me breastfeeding would be a breeze—little did I realize!"

There are many perfectly normal and common reasons why a woman may be less than 100 percent successful in breastfeeding, such as the demands of caring for older children, anxieties about family finances, or problems in marital adjustment. Some women are unable to nurse for biological reasons such as inverted nipples, clogged milk ducts, or breast infections. There are women who would like to nurse but are separated from their infant because one or the other is hospitalized. Women who are faced with these concerns are often unfairly confronted with someone else's judgment that they are less than "good mothers" if they cannot breastfeed. Even more difficult, and potentially tragic, are the impacts of these societal expectations on women who are emotionally ill.

WHEN PSYCHIATRIC ILLNESS MAKES BREASTFEEDING IMPOSSIBLE

Breastfeeding can become an extremely sensitive issue for mothers who have emotional disorders. First of all, the disorder itself may make it difficult for the woman to establish a nursing routine. This is the case, of course, for a severely ill woman—for example, a woman hospitalized with psychosis, a mental state characterized by hallucinations and delusions. It's also the case, though, for women who are at home with their families and receiving treatment on an outpatient basis for a disorder like depression. A woman with depression is herself coping with symptoms such as insomnia and inability to concentrate, and she very likely lacks the energy to focus on a nursing routine.

Secondly, there are some severe disorders that *require* treatment with psychotropic medications, and there are also disorders for which medication is the best course of therapy to relieve symptoms quickly. When a nursing mother is taking medication, the drug enters the baby's system through breast milk, and therefore the possible effects of a particular drug on the nursing infant must be considered before the drug is prescribed. In this chapter, I will discuss medications and lactation; I discuss medications in pregnancy in Chapter Eleven.

Reviewing current medical information is an important part of the decision-making process between doctor and patient. Equally important is an awareness of how a woman's own expectations and view of her role as a mother can interfere with reaching an unbiased decision. Most women in North America today are aware that a doctor's advice is required before taking any kind of medication during pregnancy and breastfeeding. Many times, women who require medication (for whatever reason) need a great deal of persuasion from both their doctors and their partners, before they can even consider the possibility of taking medicine that they truly need. A woman's reluctance to take psychotropic medications during pregnancy or lactation is just somewhat farther down this continuum of normal concern for the well-being of the fetus or infant.

Some women in this situation are unable to look beyond their image of breastfeeding to a realistic picture of health for themselves and their infants. These women need support and encouragement to be open to alternate possibilities. How important is it for the infant to be breastfed by a mother who is depressed, inattentive, anxious, and hardly able to relate to the baby? How does this compare to a focused, comfortable mother who enjoys the closeness and contact of relating to her baby while she offers feeding from a bottle? What are the short- and long-term consequences of these two different scenarios?

If you are confronted with a decision like this, keep in mind that many women have faced the same choice. As you'll read in this chapter there is nothing unusual or unnatural about being unable to breastfeed or choosing not to breastfeed for your own individual reasons. When mothers can breastfeed comfortably and produce sufficient milk, there are benefits all around for both mother and baby. But neither breastfeeding nor motherhood is an "all-or-nothing" situation, and there are many individual variations in how healthy babies and healthy family relationships grow and thrive. A mother who chooses to give up breastfeeding in order to take medication she requires for her own health has made a positive choice for her family's health, as well.

GINA'S STORY

Gina was 24 when she became a first-time mother of twin boys. One of the twins was completely healthy, but the other developed lung problems immediately after birth. This second twin was placed immediately in the intensive care unit and remained in hospital for four months before he could go home. I've talked about the complex feelings that women often have when one of a pair of twins is not healthy; Gina was no exception. She felt guilty about the sick twin's medical condition, and she was also guilt-ridden because, right at the start, the healthy twin was getting "preferential treatment" in being able to go home!

She was determined that, although she could not nurse the twin in hospital, she would be sure that he received his mother's milk. Gina had no nearby family and no extra help in the home. Her husband, Ray, was a busy high school teacher who also coached one of the school's baseball teams. He was a friendly, extroverted man, delighted at the prospect of raising twin sons, but not at all aware of the complex demands their situation placed on Gina. He was very optimistic and never doubted that the hospitalized infant would be anything less than fine "as soon as he was big enough to come home." In fact, he thought there was almost a positive benefit in having to bring home only the one twin at first, since he was busy in his job and spent many evenings at school with his coaching duties.

Meanwhile, determined to do the best for both sons, Gina established a punishing routine centered on breastfeeding. She would nurse the twin at home, then use a breast pump to extract more milk, deliver the milk to the intensive care unit for the second twin, and then, almost immediately begin the whole routine again. Since Gina herself took this routine almost for granted, no one else seemed to be aware that it was almost a superhuman effort. Ray was confident that Gina was doing all the normal tasks of motherhood. Since he was away from home much of the time, he didn't see everything she was doing, and he thought her evident exhaustion was probably normal for a new mother. Most of Gina's friends had young babies, whom they had nursed. They, too, had taken it for granted that Gina would want both twins to have the benefits of mother's milk.

Gina was referred to me when she broke down during a visit to her doctor's office. Her doctor spent a long time talking with her and uncovered the whole routine of Gina's day. This tired young woman had essentially become a milk machine, with little energy and little joy. Yet she would not consider her doctor's commonsense advice to decrease the exhausting routine of breastfeeding and breast pumping. She did, however, agree to meet with me.

Gina and I had to spend several sessions exploring her feelings of guilt and the picture she had drawn for herself of what "a good mother" did for her children. She finally agreed that "getting a good rest" would be helpful to her, and she made the decision to adjust her nursing routine. Changing a baby from a demand-feed to a routine-feed is itself a very challenging task, and Gina had to work hard on getting the routine of the infant at home organized to the point where he would feed only every four or five hours, giving her some time to breathe and not feel so overburdened. It was not easy for Gina to give up the self-imposed pattern of trying to feed two infants on demand, by which she "proved" herself to be a good mother, and she continued to feel guilty, especially about the hospitalized infant. I involved her husband in several discussions and later referred this couple for some conjoint marital therapy to help them examine their relationship in regard to parenthood.

NURSING AND THE MOTHER–CHILD RELATIONSHIP

Bonding and Breastfeeding

Much attention has been given in recent years to the importance of breastfeeding in establishing a "bond" between mother and infant. This emphasis on the child's emotional development and long-term relationship with its mother makes many women fearful that giving up breastfeeding will do their child life-long damage. When a woman requires medications that are not compatible with breastfeeding, she's likely to have a difficult time making the choice not to breastfeed. And when women cannot breastfeed, for whatever reasons, they're likely to feel guilty that they are failing their children. However, the idea that bonding depends on breastfeeding is an oversimplification of a psychological process that depends on a multitude of exchanges between parent and child. The view of breastfeeding as essential for bonding also overlooks the fact that fathers bond with their child and that adoptive parents bond with their children. Without diminishing the importance of bonding or the value of breastfeeding, let's try to put these issues in perspective.

Bonding is the development between a parent and child of a deep, sometimes almost unconscious, relationship between two individuals. For an infant, this emotional and psychological relationship has profound consequences indeed. The infant's mother is its link to the world and its first link to developing as an individual personality. All the signs and signals that pass, even without benefit of speech, between mother and infant help the child learn and grow, from the first days and weeks of its life. Bonding between the two provides a pathway for communication, and through the rapport of their relationship, the infant is able to express its needs and wants long before it learns to talk. Without this intense, highly personal and individual bond to an adult dedicated to its well-being, a baby may "fail to thrive." This may be the very tragic case in hospitals that care for babies orphaned by war; the children may receive adequate nutrition and physical care, but when no one person is exclusively involved, minute by minute, in the life of each individual infant, they may not survive.

For the mother, bonding is also an experience of growth and development. After all, when a woman becomes a mother, she becomes in a sense a new person and her new self must learn and grow. This transition begins in pregnancy as a woman begins to realize that "mother" will soon be a major part of what she means when she begins a thought with the words, "I am . . ." From the mother's point of view, bonding also has very practical consequences. As the mother accepts the reality that this new baby is *her* child, she makes the child's well-being identical with her own. She comes to "know" what the baby needs and what it is feeling and to care intensely that those needs be met and those feelings responded to. Without this bond, how easily would any adult undertake the 24-hours-a-day responsibility for the care and growth of a child?

On one hand, bonding seems the most natural thing in the world, but on the other, we know that the mother-infant bond cannot be taken for granted. A number of things can interfere with bonding, and both families and health care professionals need to learn what they can about how this "natural" process unfolds. It is known that certain circumstances can discourage bonding—parental inexperience, insecurity, physical separation, severe marital or financial problems, lack of a role model for mothering behavior. But families and women respond differently, and the presence of one of these barriers does not mean that bonding can't take place.

The mothers of premature infants may have difficulty bonding if their infants must be in hospital for a number of months. Physically separated by respiratory equipment, the mother is not able to hold the baby or comfort the baby, and this physical separation is an important factor in delaying bonding. Severe emotional illness can also be an impediment to bonding. A woman who is hospitalized with severe psychosis is unable to care for her infant, and the baby's care is taken on by other family members or caregivers. Sometimes, it might take a number of months for the woman to heal enough to resume care of her baby. These mothers will often speak of their hospitalization as "time lost" even though they may have been able to see their babies for brief visits. Similarly women who must return to work for financial reasons very soon after the baby's birth and leave their babies with caregivers often speak of having "missed out" on their children's early development. As her children grow older such a mother might feel that by not staying home longer, they have missed out on a critical part of their relationship. She may look at her adolescent children, whose behavior she cannot understand, and feel that she would have known them better if only she had spent more time with them as babies. Women who were themselves raised in foster homes, or who were adopted, may perceive that as children they were raised "differently," and they may not feel they have the emotional guidelines for raising a child of their own.

There is no one "recipe" of requirements for bonding. While breastfeeding is a wonderful opportunity for the mother-child bond to develop, it is certainly not the only ingredient of bonding. Nursing a child for three to six months can be an important milestone for the mother and child, but their relationship is a continuous one over a period of time, and bonding takes place in various ways regardless of whether or not the mother nurses the child.

Prolonged Nursing

Professionals hold a number of views on the subject of prolonged nursing, the practice of breastfeeding a child into the late toddler stage. Prolonged nursing can be viewed as an attempt on the mother's part to keep the nursing child dependent on her. Others suggest that prolonged nursing replaces the intimacy the woman and her partner had previously enjoyed with an unusual attachment for the child. Certainly, many women have said that the experience of nursing establishes such an intimate closeness with the baby that the sexual touch of their partners is sometimes unwelcome.

Recently, a woman came to me who had been nursing her daughter for two and one-half years and was now eight weeks pregnant. In answer to my questions about her feeding her daughter, she said, "I haven't stopped nursing her and I'm not going to!" Her situation is rather unusual, but many women will continue secretly nursing a baby many months longer than they had expected to—a fact that may be unknown even to their partners.

There are many reasons why mothers may prolong nursing. A common reason is that there is a pattern of nursing at night to comfort a crying child and letting it fall asleep in the security of its mother's arms. While this is a very loving picture, the continuation of this intimate bodily contact between mother and baby into childhood results in a variety of social and psychological difficulties that mothers who extend nursing have discussed with me. For instance, a woman shopping in a mall can find it embarrassing to have her two and a half-year-old child tugging at her blouse when he becomes suddenly hungry. In spite of this, some women continue to prolong nursing far beyond society's norms. These are often women who have a need to find some sense of purpose, and they find this in prolonged breastfeeding. This one aspect of motherhood comes to stand for all the protective, nurturing roles of motherhood.

Prolonged nursing may also delay or prevent resumed sexual intimacy in the marriage, because there is always a "third party" in the bed. Some women may use this as an excuse to put off reestablishing sexual relations. Some women also tell me that it makes financial sense for them to continue nursing because they cannot afford the expense of baby foods. Of course, this is understandable for the first months, but a child's nutritional requirements change and it needs to have food in addition to milk. Thus as a long-term argument, this makes little sense.

I mention prolonged nursing to illustrate that breastfeeding can evoke deep and complex emotions that are much more complicated than the basic wish to build the child's immunities or the desire to promote bonding.

A QUESTION YOU MIGHT HAVE ABOUT BONDING

? *My sister had a severe postpartum depression and was hospitalized. She was put on a medication that her doctor told her would be harmful to my nephew if she continued to* *nurse. This little boy is three years old now, and my sister is quite impatient with his independent behavior. I have no experience as a mother, but I wonder if it's possible they didn't bond properly because she couldn't breastfeed?*

It would be a mistake to draw the sweeping conclusion that your sister and her son have not "bonded properly." A three-year-old's independence and a young mother's impatience are not at all uncommon, and the relationship between a mother and child goes through many stages. Their relationship as mother and son is in a constant stage of change, and in a sense their relationship is growing, too, just as your small nephew is growing. A great deal of mystique has developed around the concept of bonding, and this has led some mothers to believe that bonding depends on breastfeeding. In fact, bonding refers to a whole range of interrelationships between mother and baby, and breastfeeding is only one of a whole lifetime of shared activities that contribute to the bond between parent and child. Your sister should be applauded for seeing the importance of getting proper treatment for her depression and for being willing to forgo the pleasures of breastfeeding in favor of a quicker restoration to health.

MOTHERS' EMOTIONS WHEN BREASTFEEDING IS NOT ADVISED

When a woman's psychiatric illness requires treatment with a medication that is not compatible with breastfeeding, a number of emotional reactions can complicate the decision-making process. Although the decision may be medically clear-cut to the doctor, it is the family's decision to make. The doctor's role is to be open and honest with current findings from the medical literature and to clarify for the patient, along with her partner, the possible approaches to therapy and the consequences of various alternatives.

The partner is less likely to have deeply held expectations about breastfeeding and can help the woman look at the choices objectively. He also has a stake in how their decision will affect their child and their family life, and he needs to be involved in facing the issues and sharing the consequences. Whatever the final choice, the woman should not be expected to make the decision on her own—unless she happens to be a single parent and cannot call upon others for help.

In some families, a decision can be made quite easily. In others, the decision can provoke significant emotional upheaval, perhaps even delaying appropriate treatment. The stories that follow show how several individuals expressed, in their own ways, emotions common to women who face the loss of breastfeeding.

SHEELAH'S STORY

Sheelah, a 24-year-old Indo-Canadian woman came to Canada with her parents when she was three years old. The family had three children, all daughters, and when Sheelah gave birth to a son, her parents were ecstatic. In their culture, the birth of a son is a momentous occasion, and the grandparents sponsored a glorious "naming ceremony" ten days after their grandson's birth. Over 500 people, including many family members from India, attended this event. The little infant and the remarkable mother who had produced a son were shown off as family treasures.

Within the next few days, Sheelah felt a bit weepy and tired, but the female members of the large extended family assured her that this was not uncommon and that she'd soon feel fine. Before the baby was two months old, the family visitors had returned to India, and the young mother set about trying to establish a routine for nursing the baby. This did not go easily for her—she was irritable and her breasts were sore, and the baby was restless and cried frequently.

Sheelah began to have negative feelings towards everyone around her—the baby, her husband, and her widowed mother-in-law, who lived in a suite in their house. She had always gotten along well with her mother-in-law, but now couldn't stand her around and rudely told her so. Sheelah's husband, a carpenter, had made a point of adjusting his day so he could come home early to help with the baby, but she accused him of interfering too much in his little son's life.

At about ten weeks postpartum, Sheelah's family doctor referred her to me. Sheelah had arrived at her doctor's office without an appointment, and when this experienced practitioner saw Sheelah's unkempt appearance and the sad state of the infant, whose diapers hadn't been changed in hours, she examined Sheelah's story closely and diagnosed a severe case of postpartum depresion.

When I met with Sheelah, it was clear that she was in the midst of a major clinical depression that would require treatment with medication. When I presented her with the choices of treatment and addressed the issue of her stopping nursing, she almost had a fit of rage. This suggestion was truly unthinkable to her—it was too far outside her family's cultural norms. Besides, she could not imagine living with the stigma of being a woman who could not nurse her baby.

Feeling that Sheelah's condition was very serious and that the only chance of her agreeing to medication was to have her family "approve" of this choice I made an appointment for her to return the next day with her husband and mother-in-law. I talked with the three of them about the seriousness of Sheelah's illness, about the need for medication, and the necessity of Sheelah's discontinuing breastfeeding while on the medication. I also talked with them about the way bonding occurs, stressing that it is not dependent on nursing. They received this information without much comment.

I gave Sheelah a prescription for an antidepressant and scheduled an appointment for the next day. They must barely have reached home when I received a phone call from Sheelah saying she would not be in the next day and that she felt she could handle her own problems. When a patient decides not to return to a doctor, there's little the doctor can do unless there is a real concern about the patient's safety. Though I was concerned about Sheelah, I also felt she was safe in the care of her mother-in-law and husband and that she could make her own decisions.

Many weeks passed, and I happened to be on call in the emergency department when a frantic call came in from Sheelah's husband. He said she was suicidal and quite out of touch with reality. He brought her into the emergency room and we admitted her to hospital right away.

Sheelah had to be placed on major tranquilizers, and she remained in hospital for six weeks—completely separated from the baby whom she had refused to stop nursing. Had she followed a course of medication a few weeks earlier, her psychological state would most likely not have disintegrated into a suicidal condition that required hospitalization and intensive therapy.

During her hospital stay, Sheelah talked extensively about having to give up nursing. She was filled with rage and disbelief that she, of all people, had to be afflicted with an illness that prevented her from nursing. In the first weeks, fruitful dialogue was impossible, and basically, I listened to her vent her anger and guilt. She was overwhelmed, feeling that her inability to nurse set her apart from what was expected of women in her culture, and she actually went through stages of grief about the loss of breastfeeding.

As her recovery progressed in hospital, Sheelah had the opportunity to talk with other health care professionals—nurses, occupational therapists, social workers—many of whom were mothers themselves. Their approach, both as professionals and as women with the similar experience of motherhood, helped Sheelah find some balance in her feelings towards her baby. She left the hospital looking forward to interacting with him in different ways that would provide them with as much closeness as when she was nursing.

Sheelah was, after all, a very lucky mother from her family's point of view. She became pregnant again a year later and gave birth to another son. This time, the celebration ceremonies did not end in postpartum depression, and she was able to enjoy nursing the second time around.

Sheelah's story carries a bittersweet lesson. On one hand, the cultural expectations that formed her view of motherhood resulted in an unnecessary delay in treatment. Her illness became much worse, and the resultant hospitalization separated her from active involvement with her infant and family for six weeks. On the other hand, her experience also shows that an experience with postpartum depression following one pregnancy does not necessarily ensure that a postpartum depression will occur in later pregnancies.

Nita's story reveals a refusal to give up breastfeeding for quite different, deep-seated psychological reasons. Her illness and her life would surely have been much less complicated had she agreed to an early course of medication.

NITA'S STORY

Nita was a 28-year-old woman who had come to Canada from Switzerland to work as a nanny. She spent three happy years in a family with four children and was so attached to them that she felt she was more their mother than was the mother of the family. Nita passionately wanted to be a mother herself, and the question of a stable marriage or partnership was quite unimportant to her. As it happened, though, she met Bob, and after a few months' relationship they decided to marry.

Nita was thrilled to become pregnant, and she gave birth to a healthy baby boy. She began to develop panic symptoms in the postpartum period and when she was referred to me she was having four or five panic attacks a day. The attacks had begun in a perplexing and frightening way. Each time she began to nurse little Mark, she'd begin feeling panicky, her heart would begin to beat rapidly, and she would start perspiring profusely. The baby would respond to her nervousness and anxiety by starting to cry, and they could rarely settle down enough for him to nurse. Because of her anxiety, she was also unable to produce enough milk.

She was at first astonished that nursing made her anxious. As a nanny, she had gone through two pregnancies with the mother of the family and she had watched that woman nurse contentedly with little difficulty. Breastfeeding was one of the very things she had most eagerly anticipated about being a mother.

At Mark's eight-week checkup, the doctor diagnosed "failure to thrive" based on the baby's inadequate weight gain. He told Nita that she must begin to supplement her breast milk with formula, and this threw her into a complete frenzy. She felt he was unsympathetic and should have given her more encouragement to continue with breastfeeding, and she refused to go back to him. She insisted that Mark was doing fine, and that with a little more time, she would have the technique perfected. She began attending her church more often, receiving a great deal of comfort from some of the older women there.

Meanwhile, Nita's panic attacks became worse, and Mark himself became the focus of her fears. She wanted to nurse, but as soon as he began to suck, she would become shaky and fearful. The cycle descended into a round of the baby's cries of hunger, the attempt to begin nursing, and the feelings of panic— baby, nursing, panic, baby, nursing, panic, over and over. Eventually, when the baby even came close to her, she would have a panic attack.

This did not go unnoticed by her husband, who was becoming concerned and worried. Bob had heard an abbreviated version of her visit to the family doctor, and he felt that surely putting the baby on a bottle would end the ceaseless crying and Nita's anxiety about the nursing sessions. It was one of Bob's friends who suggested that Nita needed help. This man, a father of two whose wife had had a postpartum depression, was aware that women sometimes had emotional problems after childbirth, and he suggested that Bob contact me.

Bob said later than he almost had to "trick" Nita into coming to my office, by not being specific about the kind of professional care I could provide. When I spoke with her, it was clear that she was suffering from a severe anxiety disorder. I explained to them both that anti-anxiety medication would give her immediate help and told them that, if the situation didn't improve, she might have to discontinue breastfeeding. This she absolutely refused to consider, but she agreed to return the next day so we could continue our discussion.

The next day she confided in me that she had devised a solution. She, too, had played a "trick." She had convinced her husband to buy an airline ticket for her to Switzerland for a relaxing holiday. What she had not told him was that in Switzerland, she expected to "feel very safe" and to "be taken care of" by her mother; in fact, Nita had never even told Bob of the very complicated family situation she had left behind when she came to Canada.

The story Nita told me, with a great deal of emotion and resentment, suggested a very complex basis to her anxiety about nursing. As an infant Nita had been cared for by her mother's aunt, and then had been brought up by her mother's sister. She had been told that her mother was dead. Nita's aunt was kind to her, but their relationship was not close. She had never come to terms with the loss of her mother, and the idea that her mother had never known her, never been able to care for her, had been deeply troubling as she grew older.

When she decided to emigrate to Canada, her aunt expected that she would never see Nita again and decided to tell her the truth. Nita's mother had had a severe psychosis after Nita's birth and had been placed in an institution. When she was released from the institution, it was decided that Nita would never be told the truth about her mother's illness. What's more, her biological mother was in fact the "aunt" who had raised her as a niece! Although she had indeed been cared for by her biological mother, the two had never had a mother-daughter relationship.

For Nita to plan to return to Switzerland in her illness, believing that her mother—with whom she had never established a close relationship—would be supportive and take care of her was quite unrealistic. Nita was very interested in telling me this story, and since I hoped that we were making some headway in addressing her anxiety problems, we booked another appointment.

Just a few days later, I had a phone call from her husband saying that Nita had taken off with the baby and gone to Switzerland. I have never heard from this couple again.

Nita's panic disorder was essentially a symptom of her long-standing problems. She felt cheated, angry, and disappointed that she herself had never been "mothered" and she was convinced that, as a mother, she would do things entirely differently. To give up breastfeeding would be like abandoning her baby—just as she felt abandoned, first by her mother's "death" and then by the fact that her mother hadn't acknowledged her after she recovered from her illness. These very frightening feelings resurfaced as she faced, in the person of Mark, all the possibilities for good or ill in the relationship between mother and child. One cannot help but wonder what became of them.

Elizabeth was another mother whose expectations about breastfeeding were influenced by childhood experiences. When she developed an emotional disorder that required medication, she was spared making a choice between medication and breastfeeding because she was no longer able to produce milk—and to this occurrence, she had an extreme psychological reaction.

ELIZABETH'S STORY

Elizabeth was a 25-year-old woman whose dreams were coming to fruition. She had no great interest in a career and wanted most of all to be happily married, with a nice home in the suburbs complete with a friendly dog and white picket fence. She dropped out of university to marry Joe, and they were a "perfectly happy couple" who had their first baby within a year of their marriage.

Joe and Elizabeth pored over books on pregnancy and childbirth, went to prenatal classes, and attended a breastfeeding clinic before the baby was born. The pregnancy and the delivery of baby Maria went perfectly—a "natural" birth with no anesthesia, no forceps needed, almost a blissful experience. Elizabeth couldn't wait to launch immediately into a "breastfeeding program and routine," as the breastfeeding society had promoted. Even though she knew that in the first three days postpartum, the breasts produce colostrum, not breast milk, she was acutely disappointed that her breasts did not produce milk from Day One.

Even before Maria's birth, Elizabeth was obsessively preoccupied with the idea of breastfeeding, a preoccupation that resulted from her childhood experience. When Elizabeth was eight years old, her mother had given birth to a second daughter, and Elizabeth's feelings of jealousy focused on the closeness her mother and baby sister shared as the infant nursed. The little girl asked questions and learned that her mother had been unable to breastfeed Elizabeth because of a series of infections. As the two children grew up, Elizabeth continued to feel that her sister was the favored one. Surely, Elizabeth felt, she had been disadvantaged from the start because her mother had not nursed her. In her mind, nursing equaled attachment, and lack of nursing meant the child would never bond with its mother.

After the birth of Maria, Elizabeth intensely set about breast-feeding. She was greatly concerned with how to position the baby, how to position the towel, which breast to begin with, how long to nurse at the first breast, how to hold the baby at the second breast, and how long to nurse at the second breast. Much later, she admitted to me that the whole routine became so mechanical it almost "killed the joy" of sharing this intimate experience with her daughter.

In spite of all this, she did establish a successful nursing routine and planned to nurse Maria until she was three and ready for preschool. However, when Maria was about six months old, Elizabeth started to experience mood changes, which then developed into postpartum depression. As a result of her anxiety, she found it difficult to nurse the baby—and the fact that she was no longer producing enough milk for the baby was a great blow to her.

When she was referred to me, at seven months postpartum, Elizabeth was completely unable to produce milk and nearly unable to come to grips with this fact. She was quite willing to take antidepressant medication, which began to relieve her symptoms of depression. However, in our sessions, we had to work through a profound grief reaction—complete shock, numbness, and disbelief that she, the loving mother, was no longer able to nurse her daughter. She became quite withdrawn and looked for others to blame for this terrible "curse" that had befallen her. While she seemed to be mourning the loss of the ability to nurse and the perceived loss of intimacy with her daughter, in fact she was mourning the absence of nursing by her mother in her own infancy. I eventually had to involve her mother in her therapy so that Elizabeth could pass through all the stages of grief resolution.

In time Elizabeth faced the fact that her feelings about nursing were tied to her feelings as a child. She came to realize that she would continue to love her baby whether she nursed or not. It was about seven months after she stopped nursing that she began to be able to look rationally at her relationship with her own mother, and consequently at her relationship now with her daughter.

A QUESTION YOU MIGHT HAVE ABOUT
EMOTIONAL RESPONSE TO CESSATION OF NURSING

? *In my first pregnancy, I had to stop nursing abruptly after about a month because of breast infections. My healthy little son adjusted easily to formula, but for several weeks afterwards, I had periods of tearfulness and loneliness, which I managed to keep to myself. It's hard to explain, but I felt terribly sad that I could no longer nurse. I'm pregnant again and feeling a bit unsettled about having those feelings again.*

There's never much to be gained in keeping troubling feelings to yourself, and I'd encourage you to talk with your doctor now about these feelings you had in your first postpartum period. Many (though not all) women have felt the same way after having to give up nursing for one reason or another, and these feelings are a kind of grief reaction. As we have learned about the process of grief, we've realized that grieving occurs not only at the death of a loved person, but in reaction to many different kinds of losses. For many women giving up nursing is seen as a loss. In losing this special type of emotional and physical intimacy with her infant, a woman may feel the loss of dependence her infant has on her. She may feel that because she has stopped nursing, her baby might not want or need her any longer. One can understand the feelings of women who grieve when they stop nursing.

It's important to recognize that your feelings of loss were quite normal. It's also important to realize that there are ways to work through troubling emotions in a positive way, and that there's a risk that hiding your feelings may make you feel worse—lonely in addition to sad. You shouldn't hesitate to talk with your doctor or counselor about what you're feeling; sometimes, just understanding what's going on can help you feel better. Keep in mind too that the breast infection may not be repeated with this pregnancy, and you may be able to nurse your baby and enjoy the experience for a longer period of time.

LACTATION AND MEDICATION

What We Know from Current Research

Medical research into the early 1990s has given only a few guidelines for breastfeeding and psychotropic medication. A number of research studies have been published, but their conclusions are often contradictory and the designs of some of them make their findings questionable. In an environment like this, it's very difficult for a psychiatrist, pediatrician, or obstetrician to offer an opinion on the infant's safety when a breastfeeding mother is prescribed psychotropic medication.

The older medical textbooks traditionally recommended that the mother not breastfeed when taking prescribed medication. However, newer research has incorporated more recent scientific findings. I would like to emphasize here that *no* medication is totally "safe." With some drugs, adverse effects are seen, while this is not the case with others. As yet, the long-term effects of these medicines on breastfed infants remain unknown.

In short, the issues surrounding breastfeeding and psychotropic medication are complex, and medical research has not yet provided definitive information for a number of these medications. It's not at all uncommon for psychiatrists to have opposite opinions on whether or not breastfeeding should be discontinued. Any decision about whether to take medications and if so whether to discontinue breastfeeding must be made with the full involvement of the patient, her partner, and her physician. The physician's role is to bring forward the most reliable current information on the subject and to help the couple examine the impact of various options.

Reaching an Individual Decision

With some medications, there is thought to be a considerable degree of safety for the infant in the short term. It's important to remember, though, that the organizational tasks of a nursing routine may be difficult for a mother with illness, even if she is at home and is being treated on an outpatient basis. The physician and the partner can help the mother have a flexible attitude towards what is best in her individual circumstance. Certainly, the woman should not feel pushed to breastfeed just because the medication is thought to be safe.

In some cases, the potential risk to the infant can be clearly identified. If the family decides to proceed with medication and discontinue nursing, a number of other issues must be considered by the family, with support from medical professionals. The family doctor or pediatrician must become involved in offering advice on the infant's transition to a substitute for breast milk, and the infant's adjustment needs to be monitored. The mother's condition, too, must be carefully monitored in regard to her adjustment to giving up breastfeeding. As we've seen in this chapter, the mother's reaction to giving up breastfeeding can complicate the treatment and progress of the original emotional disorder. In addition, there are different opinions on whether abrupt weaning may in itself contribute to emotional disorders; in my practice I have occasionally seen the onset of postpartum depression when the woman stops nursing abruptly. One wonders about the role hormones may play in bringing about a depression at this time. There is also a possibility that, in some women, the natural increase in hormones required for nursing may have emotional impacts. When women nurse, the hormone prolactin is increased, and the prolactin level abruptly drops when they stop nursing. The role of hormones in the onset of emotional illness, then, remains an intriguing question. This question is a subject of medical research, and although still unanswered, it shows the importance of closely monitoring the woman's illness when she gives up breastfeeding.

The most difficult cases are those where there is virtually no choice but to hospitalize and medicate a mother with severe emotional illness. Here, too, there are a number of options, depending on the type of illness and type of medication. In some hospitals in England, psychiatric units are organized to admit the infant to hospital along with its mother. The nursing staff cares for the infant as much as is needed but at the same time, helps the mother continue to have a relationship with her baby as her illness permits. North American hospitals lag behind in this approach, but even so, it's common practice to encourage regular and frequent visits from babies to their hospitalized mothers. Sometimes, a hospitalized mother with an abundant milk supply might be able to pump her milk for the baby at home and thus maintain her lactation until she is released from hospital.

There are many possibilities for treatment programs that help the mother recover quickly and at the same time give the family flexible options for the care of their infant. No two families are alike, and neither medical professionals nor family and friends should make assumptions about what's best or force their judgments on the family. I encourage couples to take part together in decision making and to be open-minded as they consider alternatives with their physician. The decision they make should reflect their unique needs as individuals and as an individual family—rather than be "programmed" by someone else's agenda.

A QUESTION YOU MIGHT HAVE ABOUT
MEDICATIONS AND BREASTFEEDING

? *I had a severe episode of manic depression in my late teens and took lithium for two years. Now I'm 25 and in my third trimester of pregnancy. My doctor knows of my history and has talked with me about the possibility that my symptoms could come back after the baby's birth. I've been really well all through the pregnancy, and I'm looking forward to nursing my baby. What if I'm ill in the postpartum period? Are there medications I can take safely while breastfeeding?*

You have been very wise in keeping your doctor informed and following your own emotional state during pregnancy. Your doctor is right in counseling you that your previous personal history places you at risk for postpartum illness. Should your symptoms occur again, the question of whether or not you will be able to breastfeed depends a great deal on the type and severity of your symptoms. Lithium is not compatible with breastfeeding, but this is not necessarily the only option. Breastfeeding can be a great joy to a new mother, and you should keep your doctor informed about your wish to do this. However, if you become ill, remember that there are many ways to enjoy the pleasure of relating to your new baby as long as you are in a healthy state to do so. Your overall stability and composure is more important in relating to your infant than your ability to breastfeed.

MEDICATIONS YOUR DOCTOR MIGHT PRESCRIBE

General Precautions About Medication in Nursing Mothers

In this section, I will look specifically at the impact of *psychotropic* medications on the nursing infant. For some medications, there is reported to be considerable safety for the infant whose mother chooses to continue breastfeeding. These conclusions are based on several factors: research studies on the effects of the drug on nursing animals, knowledge of the drug's specific effects in the mother's body, and measurements of the amount of the drug that is passed to the infant in breast milk.

Studies like this give us an indication of immediate or short-term risks to the baby. However, the long-term effect on the neurological and behavioral development of these children as they grow older is a big unknown in assessing risks. Many of these psychotropic medications are just too new for long-term studies to have been completed. (My own research on long-term effects on children whose mothers take antidepressants is one of a number of worldwide studies in progress on this subject.)

As specific types of medication are discussed, it's important to remember that the prescription of medication always takes into account the mother's individual health picture and the characteristics of her illness. Medications are prescribed in different dosages depending on the individual and the progression of her disease. Some of these medications may be used in combination with others. In some illnesses, the doctor may start the woman on a very low dose of medication and gradually increase it until she begins to show improvement in her symptoms. In other conditions, a large dose will be given at first to address acute symptoms, and then tapered gradually. These factors, in addition to the health of the infant whose mother continues nursing, play a role when a medication is prescribed to the mother.

A table summarizing the following discussion of types of psychotropic medications and nursing can be found at the end of Chapter Eleven.

Major Tranquilizers and Breastfeeding

When tranquilizers are prescribed, the amount of drug excreted in breast milk is quite small. Most research studies have shown that less than 30 percent of the amount of the drug in the mother's blood will be contained in her breast milk. The drug haloperidol (Haldol) may be excreted in the breast milk in slightly larger amounts. In general, major tranquilizers are thought to be fairly safe in their impact on the nursing infant, with only minor side effects such as drowsiness. Some animal studies have suggested later behavioral abnormalities in the offspring, however.

In actual experience, the infant's safety is almost an academic question, as breastfeeding is rarely possible. Mothers who are prescribed major tranquilizers are those who have severe psychotic symptoms, such as hallucinations and delusions. When in this condition, these mothers are too out of touch with reality to nurse successfully, and as their recovery proceeds, they may continue to have difficulty concentrating and organizing the nursing routine.

DOREEN'S STORY

Doreen, a 22-year-old woman who had an episode of manic depression at age 19, married at age 20, and became pregnant two years later. She was under psychiatric care when she became pregnant, and she knew that she was at risk of a postpartum recurrence of her illness. During her pregnancy, I talked with both Doreen and her husband about the possibility of postpartum illness, and the distinct likelihood that she would require hospitalization and major tranquilizers. We also discussed the use of major tranquilizers while nursing since this was something that Doreen hoped she would be able to do.

During her first week postpartum, Doreen became acutely psychotic and was admitted to hospital, where she was started on chlorpromazine (Thorazine), a major tranquilizer. The hospital had no facilities to admit infants of psychiatric mothers, and it was not easy to organize nursing. However, since the baby was a full-term healthy infant and since the mother wanted to nurse him, we thought it might be possible. Her husband and the baby's grandmother took turns bringing the baby to hospital every four hours so that he could be breastfed.

The nursing sessions were not highly successful as Doreen was unable to focus for very long, and the infant did not get enough nourishment. Further, Doreen's delusions had begun to incorporate the baby; although a nurse was always with her and the baby, we became concerned that the baby was at risk since the mother was experiencing delusions.

In a family conference, it was decided that the infant would be brought in to see his mother on a regular bais but that she would discontinue nursing. Doreen and her husband agreed that her treatment, aimed at getting her back to reality as soon as possible, was what was urgent, and her wish to continue breastfeeding was quite secondary to this goal.

Doreen remained in hospital for about nine weeks and then was well enough to go home. She eventually was prescribed lithium medication, which is incompatible with nursing.

Antidepressants and Breastfeeding

There are a number of different kinds of antidepressants (see Chapter Eleven for more details), and their effects differ. There are mixed views about the effects of tricyclic antidepressants (Elavil or Tofranil, to name just two) on infants who receive the medication through breast milk. Early studies suggested that the amount of medicine passed into the breast milk was quite small. However, there are also studies that indicate that the amount of tricyclic antidepressants in the mother's milk is quite high. More recent studies suggest that tricyclics are quite safe in the short term, but their long-term effects are unclear.

In short, some antidepressants are probably safe, while on others, we do not have enough information to make a judgment either way. Studies on this subject have suggested that tricyclic antidepressants are safe during nursing but that the possibility of later side effects needs more investigation. I am currently one of several psychiatric researchers conducting long-term studies, including one looking at possible long-term effects on children who were breastfed while their mothers took antidepressants. The children's progress in reaching developmental milestones is being followed for a five-year period and is being compared to that of similar children, matched for age and sex, whose mothers did not take antidepressants. The new antidepressants like Prozac or Zoloft have not been around long enough for conclusions to be reached about their safety in lactating mothers.

When a recommendation is made that the mother should go on medication, her nursing infant should be assessed by the family doctor or pediatrician before medication begins to establish a baseline for evaluating the infant's developmental progress. As long as the mother continues to nurse, the baby should be assessed at regular intervals to assure that its progress is following normal patterns. The doctor might also have routine laboratory tests performed to measure the amount of drug in the baby's blood, and sometimes even in the mother's breast milk when such testing is possible. The child is then assessed at age three before entering a preschool and again at age five before entering kindergarten. This behavioral assessment should be conducted by trained psychologists.

MONICA'S STORY

Monica was a 35-year-old lawyer who delivered a healthy baby and planned to resume her busy law practice after being at home with her new baby for three months. She began to experience depression at about six to seven weeks postpartum.

Together, we examined several possibilities. The first was for her to take one of the serotonin uptake inhibitors—Prozac or Zoloft—which are currently contraindicated during nursing. Another was to take a tricyclic antidepressant such as Elavil and to continue to nurse, and as it happened, Monica had a friend who was doing just that. However, she was very concerned that she be mentally well as quickly as possible in order to go back to work. Monica opted for the serotonin reuptake inhibitor medication and stopped breastfeeding. Certainly in her profession she was used to dealing with evidence, and she wasn't entirely comfortable with the incomplete evidence on long-term effects of tricyclic medications on the child.

HANNAH'S STORY

Hannah was a 32-year-old woman who owned her own business as a landscape architect. She and her husband had what might be called an alternative lifestyle and were committed to a "natural" approach to everything in their lives. When Hannah gave birth to their little daughter, she of course planned to nurse the child, perhaps for a period of some years.

She was diagnosed with depression about three months after the baby's birth. While Hannah recognized that she needed help, she was adamant that she would not consider any medication that would require her to give up nursing. In this, her husband agreed fully. I reviewed with them both what is known about the safety of tricyclic antidepressants, and they felt this was the route to follow.

Hannah continued on medication for some months, and meanwhile she maintained the normal routine of nursing. While she continued in therapy, she resumed her business projects, taking great pleasure in being outdoors and carrying her baby daughter in a pouch while she worked.

Hannah and her husband Jes are very absorbed in their daughter's well-being and in giving her as healthy a lifestyle as possible. They were very interested to learn of my research project and their little girl is now enrolled in my study.

Both Hannah and Monica and their partners made decisions that could be supported by their psychiatrist. Giving equal attention to the health of the mother and the infant, and weighing the information available from medical research on the medications the mothers were prescribed, they chose different—and successful—paths.

Mood Stabilizers and Breastfeeding

In general, the mood stabilizer class of psychotropics—the most common of which is lithium—are not compatible with nursing. In the case of lithium, studies have shown that 50 percent of the amount of the drug in the mother's blood will be found in her breast milk, and the levels of drug in the infant's blood are almost at the same concentration as in the breast milk. Lethargy, hypotonia (weak muscle tone), and cyanosis (inability of the heart to process oxygen completely) have been observed in nursing infants whose mothers are taking lithium. For these reasons and because I do not know the long-term effects, mothers taking lithium are strongly advised to discontinue breastfeeding.

STACY'S STORY

Stacy, now a 38 year-old woman and the mother of two growing sons, was taking lithium when she accidentally became pregnant with the first boy. I tried to discontinue her lithium therapy, but she suffered a second trimester relapse so severe that it was necessary to begin the medication again. Stacy was monitored carefully throughout her pregnancy, and several attempts to discontinue the medication ended unsuccessfully.

Her baby boy, Trevor, was monitored throughout the delivery and had to be placed in the intensive care unit for some days after birth because of respiratory difficulties. Stacy was not about to expose him any further to lithium and, since her illness required that she continue with lithium, she did not breastfeed Trevor.

Stacy continued to see me as a patient, and by the time of her second pregnancy eight years later, she was no longer taking lithium. She gave birth to a healthy son, but had a relapse of her illness after the baby's birth. This time, Stacy responded well to chlorpromazine, a major tranquilizer, and was able to nurse little Brian for six weeks while on this medication. However, it was necessary for her to resume lithium medication, and she discontinued nursing—having had the joy of a successful, albeit brief, experience with breastfeeding.

The long-term development of these two boys is promising, indeed. Brian is a bright and happy first-grader. At age 14, his older brother Trevor has won a scholarship to a private school and is in a class for gifted children.

Anti-anxiety Drugs and Breastfeeding

The anxiolytic (anti-anxiety) medications, sometimes called the minor tranquilizers (Valium or Ativan, for example), should be used with caution in nursing mothers. Since anxiolytics are commonly used to relieve the acute symptoms of panic disorder, a nursing mother with this disorder may continue to nurse while she receives a *short course* of medication that immediately improves her symptoms. Over the longer term, however, the safety to the infant is less certain. Infants whose mothers continue on one of the benzodiazepines such as Valium (diazepam), may develop jaundice because their immature livers cannot clear their drug from their system quickly. In addition, some of these infants have been observed to be lethargic. For these reasons, nursing mothers on this medication must keep in close touch with their doctors, and their infants' condition must also be closely monitored. In choosing a benzodiazepine, short-acting ones (Ativan or Lorazepam) are recommended because they are cleared from the body in a few hours.

TRISHA'S STORY

Trisha, a 30-year-old woman, had a completely normal pregnancy and gave birth to a healthy baby girl. A week after the baby's birth, she began to have severe panic attacks and was referred to me. I talked with her about the apparent safety of a short course of benzodiazepine while she continued nursing.

Luckily, Trisha had an immediate and positive response to a low dose of this medication. Her severe panic symptoms subsided within about five days, and we decided to see how she would do off the medication. At the same time, I referred her to a psychologist who began coaching her in behavioral techniques to control her panic symptoms.

Trisha will continue to see me until her illness stabilizes. So far, she feels able to "live with" her infrequent panic episodes, and she is enjoying the experience of continuing to nurse her baby girl.

Such a quick alleviation of symptoms is not always the case with panic disorder and, when the patient is not a nursing mother, the medication can be safely continued for a longer period. Trisha's story has truly been a "best case scenario" and unfortunately, that cannot always be counted on.

WHAT I TELL MY PATIENTS

It's often a very emotional issue for women to face the decision to give up breastfeeding when their illness requires that they take a medication that could potentially harm their nursing infants. It is not a decision that a woman should make alone; her partner should be fully involved in discussions with the woman and her doctor so that the couple can together come to understand the specific risks of different courses of treatment.

When I talk with a mother and father about medications that are not compatible with nursing, I openly discuss with them the issue of bonding and nursing and try to alleviate any anxieties they may have. We know that bonding is crucially important to a child's well-being and development, but we also know that bonding does *not* depend on breastfeeding. Although the couple may have strong emotions about the woman nursing, both partners must be made to understand that the infant is not going to suffer in a major way because its mother cannot breastfeed. The couple together needs support in looking at the broad picture of the woman's health and its effects on their family relationships. A mother who is emotionally stable and relaxed is in a far better state to bond with her baby as she feeds the child with a bottle than is a distracted, preoccupied mother who resolves that she will breastfeed this baby no matter what!

The best guidelines are always: Discuss the current medical information with your doctor, be involved in decisions about your health care, recognize that your family has its individual needs, and put aside others' expectations and the fashions of the day. You and your partner are in this together, and you are going to need each other's support as well as your doctor's.

GUIDELINES FOR ANTIDEPRESSANT USE WHILE BREASTFEEDING
(American Academy of Pediatrics Recommendations)

Amitriptyline	Usually compatible with breastfeeding. Drug has not been detected in infant serum, but effects on infant are unknown and may be of concern.
Amoxapine	Usually compatible with breastfeeding, but effects on infant are unknown and may be of concern.
Buproprion	Effects on infant are unknown but may be of concern.
Desipramine	Usually compatible with breastfeeding. Drug has not been detected in infant serum, but effects on infant are unknown and may be of concern.
Doxepin	No recommendation, but serious and potentially lethal effects in one infant were noted in one study.
Fluoxetine	Effects on infant are unknown, but may be of concern.
Imipramine	Usually compatible with breastfeeding, but effects on infant are unknown and may be of concern.
Isocarboxazide	No data available.
Maprotiline	No recommendation. Effects on infant are unknown but may be of concern.
Nortriptyline	No recommendation. Drug has not been detected in infant serum, but effects on infant are unknown and may be of concern.
Phenelzine	No recommendation. Drug has not been detected in infant serum, but effects on infant are unknown and may be of concern.
Proptriptyline	No data available.
Tranylcypromine	No reports of excretion of drug into breast milk.
Trazodone	No recommendation. Effects on infant are unknown but may be of concern.
Trimipramine	Effects on infant are unknown but may be of concern.

Source: Adapted from D. M. Jermain (1992), Psychopharmacologic approach to postpartum depression, *Journal of Women's Health, 1,* 51.

CHAPTER 7

"I JUST DON'T NEED THIS RIGHT NOW!"

Marital Upset After Pregnancy and Childbirth

Many couples choose to begin families partially to celebrate their stability as a couple and as a way to make their relationship even stronger. The expectation is that the couple's life after childbirth will unfold as a natural extension of this choice—that the postpartum months will be a time of special tenderness, intimacy, and growing maturity. However, in recent years, it seems that more and more postpartum women are referred, with their partners, to marital therapists or counselors. This is not at all an unhealthy sign, but rather a recognition that the months after childbirth can be a stressful period that tests even the best of marriages. Such marital upsets are by no means limited to first-time parents. While new parents are the most likely to be stressed by role changes and lifestyle adjustments, more experienced couples can be equally stressed, perhaps by financial difficulties or the complicated demands of having several young children in the household.

In this chapter, I will examine some of the more common marital problems in the months after childbirth and explain how consulting specialists in marital therapy can help.

190

ADJUSTING TO BECOMING A FAMILY

The New Mother's Adjustment

Women at home with a new baby often say that their roles have changed so dramatically that they could never have predicted their response to this experience. "I get up at seven in the morning, watch my husband shave and dress for work, then leave the house as if his life is completely unchanged," one woman said. "And then I sit looking at the laundry and dishes, trying to decide which of five boring tasks to begin first. It's as if nothing is different for him, and he doesn't even realize that I feel like I've been given a life sentence to unending housekeeping and child care." These changes are especially acute for a woman who has previously enjoyed a challenging career outside the home—a court reporter whose most interesting assignment is now getting the bathroom cleaned; a lawyer whose only outlet for negotiating skills is persuading a three-year-old to finish lunch; a flight attendant whose big excursion is a trip to the park with baby in stroller!

The change to the role of mother is more than simply a change in "job description." Whether or not a woman worked outside the home before childbirth, whether or not she greatly enjoyed her job, she existed before motherhood as an individual in her own right. The friends she had and the work she did all provided a context for her individuality. The way she performed in that greater world was part of her unique identity as a person. Motherhood changes all of that. A woman finds that the familiar goalposts for "Who I am" have changed, and she is often unprepared for the magnitude of that change.

Who will she talk with about this change? Who is really interested in the concerns in her life, which range now from finding diapers on sale to developing a nursing schedule? If she's lucky, she has the support of friends or sisters who are going through early motherhood at the same time. But as often as not, in our mobile and diverse society, she may live some distance away from friends from her prenatal class and her friends may be busy applying to graduate school or investigating new job prospects. Her mother may sympathize and claim to know exactly how she feels, but in fact is delighted her daughter has "finally settled down to give her a grandchild at last." Her husband will perhaps find her feelings completely incomprehensible—after all, he may think, she wanted this baby so much, and she wasn't all that crazy about her job, anyway.

In addition, new mothers are typically dealing with reactions to their changing body image, reactions that they feel unable to discuss with anyone. Their breasts and nipples are changing; their hips have widened; their vaginal muscles have become slack. Their reactions to these changes are nothing like the mild dismay of the woman who suddenly realizes she's gained ten pounds over the summer. For a first-time mother, the realization that her whole body has changed may be a source of deep insecurity, fear that she will no longer be attractive to her husband, and a basic lack of confidence as she tries to adjust to a new version of "Who I am."

WHEN IS MARITAL THERAPY NEEDED?

When I counsel individuals for emotional illness related to pregnancy or postpartum, it is not uncommon for women to bring up problems in their marriages. When these problems are serious or of a kind that could be helped by marital therapy, my practice is to follow up the interview with a separate meeting with the woman's partner. After I have a better understanding of the situation, I talk with them together about the possibility of marital therapy. Then, although I might continue seeing the woman individually or the couple jointly for a few visits, I usually refer the couple to colleagues in the health care professions who specialize in marital counseling.

Dr. Michael Myers, a psychiatrist and expert in the field of marital therapy, sees couples in the Marital Discord Clinic located in the same hospital where I work, an arrangement that allows me to refer my pregnant or postpartum patients in marital crisis to the clinic with relative ease. Conversely, patients referred to Dr. Myers for conjoint therapy often end up in my office if the woman has emotional problems related to pregnancy and postpartum. In this chapter, I will describe several of the patients I have seen in therapy, some of whom were referred to the Marital Discord Clinic for further treatment.

The normal adjustment experiences of new mothers can, in themselves, create an environment ripe for marital misunderstandings and conflicts. New fathers have their own adjustment problems (see Chapter Eight), and the couple together are facing new and possibly troubling realities in their changed lifestyle and family relationships. These factors can all come into alarming collision when a new mother is experiencing postpartum adjustment. Marital therapy is indicated when a couple find that they are unable to resolve issues on their own. Not surprisingly, this situation becomes even more complicated when the woman is in the midst of postpartum depression.

CYNTHIA'S STORY

Cynthia was not the first new mother to tell me that she had the feeling her old friends from her workplace "felt sorry" for her. She had chosen to stop working after the birth of her baby and left her career as a bank teller. At the bank, she had been part of a group of women co-workers who had usually enjoyed dinner together about once a month. Not long after her baby's birth, her friends extended the usual invitation to her and were quite unsympathetic when she declined. Cynthia told them that her husband wasn't able to take care of the baby that night, but the real problem was that she hadn't yet developed a comfortable nursing schedule—something she didn't really feel like talking about with her friends from work. Two months later, she felt the baby's routine was sufficiently organized for her to join her friends for a night out. Midway through the evening, she found to her horror that her breasts were overflowing with milk. She not only made an embarrassed retreat home, leaving her friends without a clue as to why she had left, but resolved that she was not going to risk another such experience until she was completely finished with nursing—nine months later!

Cynthia was one of those mothers in whom the diagnosis of postpartum depression was missed. She became completely preoccupied with her nursing schedule, almost to the point of being obsessed. When she started to lose weight and started experiencing mood swings, she put it down to her failure to establish a comfortable nursing routine. Her husband, who was away on business often, did not realize that his wife was depressed and that her withdrawal from him was because of her illness. He in turn started to make more demands on her. He would ask, "Are my shirts ironed?" and then become irritated as he looked at the untouched pile of laundry. The more demanding he became, the more Cynthia retreated to her room with the infant. Her husband felt outraged, like a total outsider in his family! After about two months of "living in hell" as he described it to me, and on the verge of leaving the marriage, he decided to confide in Cynthia's family doctor about their marital difficulties. Her doctor referred Cynthia to me and I prescribed antidepressants.

Cynthia's story illustrates how a postpartum depression can affect the stability of a marriage. Adjusting to parenthood when everything is going smoothly is itself a monumental task. When the marriage is complicated by an emotional illness in one partner, the journey through the postpartum period can be a nightmare, as appropriately expressed by Cynthia's husband.

I saw Cynthia for about a year and was eventually able to take her off antidepressants. When she recovered, she was back to her old self again, an outgoing, extroverted, social person who enjoyed her baby and her marriage—a marriage that she and her husband had for a time dreaded would fall apart.

The New Father's Adjustment

In Chapter Eight, I discuss in great detail some of the common issues faced by expectant and new fathers; for now, I will confine myself to the most common situations. Beginning with the pregnancy, the expectant father may easily feel excluded from events and unable to deal comfortably with the focused attention on the mother-baby pair. Depending on his personality and the extent to which his partner "welcomes" him into—or "exiles" him from—the experience of her pregnancy, he may feel abandoned and unloved. These feelings can continue and even worsen when the infant is born and comes safely home to be the center of the household. Young fathers in particular may respond to this "competition" by themselves becoming like children again. They may tend to deny any responsibility and involvement and look for escape routes. Sometimes, new fathers will immerse themselves in a new interest, such as joining or coaching a sports team; or a career-oriented father might become the classic workaholic, spending endlessly long hours at his job. In other fathers, escape may take the form of substance abuse.

A father, too, has to adjust to the expectations of his new role, and to a large extent, his adjustment depends on his own experience of being nurtured as a child. If as a child he received little paternal love from his father and saw little evidence of his father's supportive attention to his mother, he will be somewhat at a loss as to how fathers are supposed to behave. If it happens that his parents were divorced or he saw very little of his own father for other reasons, then the new father may really have no clue as to how a father interacts on a daily basis with his family. Quite often these days, young couples find that the traditional behaviors and attitudes demonstrated by their own fathers are not sufficient models for today's ideal of co-parenting. Richard's father, while visiting with his new grandson, casually remarked, "Where's Marilyn? This little boy needs his diaper changed." He could not imagine his son, the baby's father, performing this unfamiliar "motherly" task—and it certainly never occurred to the grandfather that changing diapers was something he himself might think of doing!

Even a man who has been very involved in the pregnancy and childbirth, who is very interested in becoming "a good father," may be completely unprepared—as is his partner—for the realities of a family. Now he finds himself rarely getting a good night's sleep, being called on to do more than his previous share of fixing meals and grocery shopping, and feeling that even a Saturday night at the movies is a long-lost luxury. He may want to participate as a partner in the care of his child but feels embarrassed or inadequate because he perceives his wife as naturally having infant care skills that he lacks. He, too, can feel socially isolated. A casual inquiry like "How's the family?" may be the only apparent interest his contacts at work have in his new world—and how all the recent changes are affecting *him*. A man who has grown up in a traditional household may chafe at these new demands and, in fact, deny that any real adjustments are necessary.

In Western culture, extraordinary importance is placed on "the family meal." Some families have indeed made this a ritual, and the meal is viewed as one of the essential components of a harmonious and healthy family. You're familiar with the picture; it appears in movies, in commercials, in TV shows—but rarely on a daily basis in the real life of a family with young children! The idea is that parents and children of all ages will sit down together at the dinner table, eat a completely balanced, full-course meal, and enjoy a pleasurable time together as a family. How often I have heard young mothers criticize themselves for "not even getting a proper meal on the table"!

Rituals, of course, have importance because they symbolize attitudes and feelings, and the North American ritual of the family dinner symbolizes commitment to the family, shared experience, and physical well-being, among other things. It's fair to say, though, that many of the "ordinary" rituals of family life are carried out at great expense to the woman of the family—as Marjorie's story shows.

MARJORIE'S STORY

Marjorie was referred to me for treatment of her postpartum depression. She and her husband Craig are both lawyers. Craig's first marriage had ended in divorce, and he had custody of his two children, who were three and five. He was quite willing to have another child, but he had made it clear to Marjorie before their marriage that he expected things to be very different this time around. His first wife apparently had been very disorganized and, as it turned out, did not deeply care for the children. His complaints, though, tended to focus on her cooking. She had not enjoyed cooking, and he said he'd felt "starved" for years.

In speaking with them, I learned that Craig had drawn up, and Marjorie had signed, an explicit premarital document that detailed very specifically the duties she would undertake in marriage. She agreed first of all to care for the two children from Craig's previous marriage, and *no matter what,* she would prepare a "proper family meal" every evening, specifically to include meat and potatoes!

Now coping with a postpartum depression, Marjorie was struggling to meet this contractual obligation. While the meat and potatoes got on the table, these were scarcely the idyllic family meals of women's magazines. The three-year-old was not always interested, and the boy of kindergarten age had more interesting things to do than sit still in his chair. In addition, the newborn infant never failed to cry when the family sat down at the dinner table. Not surprisingly, Marjorie was exhausted. We discussed how she could explain to her husband about the dreaded dinner routine and plan more informal meals.

Her approach to this situation was quite philosophical. She

had decided to "tough it out" until her maternity leave was over, but admitted she could not wait to hire household help and get back to her law practice.

I began this discussion of potential marital troublespots with the new mother's viewpoint and her possible perception that her situation was not understood. It's important to remember, however, that misunderstanding easily works both ways. For her part, the new mother may be completely unaware of concerns that deeply trouble her partner. It's often the case that, just as the woman's attention is centered on the baby, the man is left on his own to contemplate the family's finances.

There's no doubt that having another mouth to feed is more expensive than ever. First-time parents are rarely able to predict just how quickly expenses associated with the baby will multiply. If the family has depended on two incomes, the mother is certainly bringing in less when she is on maternity leave. For some couples, the maternity leave is the time in which they face the hard fact that they can't get by on one income alone. The mother's return to an outside job is no easy solution since child care expenses then go up, family schedules become more complex, and the couple may feel that they see each other only when they're both completely exhausted. And although family finances are certainly a joint responsibility, the father may be left in the position of being the "bad guy" who has to force tough decisions about family financial priorities. That is why it is advisable for the couple to sit down and discuss their finances ahead of time to avoid future misunderstandings. My patient Jean told me, "I felt relieved and reassured when Roy agreed I could take time off from contributing for a while."

The father's role adjustment, social isolation, and financial pressures combined can contribute to symptoms of depression that often go unrecognized by the partner or friends. Sleep problems, difficulty concentrating, anxiety, overwork, hopelessness—all these symptoms of depression can be easily glossed over as routine reactions to the baby's schedule or to an altered lifestyle. At the least, they are likely to contribute to marital conflicts and a generalized feeling of inability to cope. At their worst, they can signal a clinical depression in the father.

The Couple's Adjustment

With the birth of a child—later children as well as the firstborn—couples to some extent have to begin anew. Just as they invested time and effort in developing mutual understanding and mutually acceptable routines at the start of their relationship, they have to renegotiate these routines and understandings in a new setting when a new baby enters their lives. Often this need for readjustment goes unrecognized, and it's very easy to take for granted old routines and assumptions that no longer apply. For example, a husband's typical greeting at the end of the day might have been, "Hi, what's for dinner tonight?" A more congenial greeting for the lifestyle of new parents might be, "How's your day been? What can I help you with?" It's not always easy for couples to be aware that their relationship is undergoing change and that extra attention and consideration from both partners is the only way to successful adjustment. It's likely, too, that the new baby's arrival means a fair bit of sleep deprivation for both partners and, despite best intentions, they may find themselves sometimes too tired to make an effort—or just plain cranky from lack of sleep.

For first-time parents, there is the new reality that their old priorities as a couple and as individuals must now be readjusted around the needs of an infant. Perhaps surprisingly, the readjustment period does not necessarily become easier with second or third children. The household schedule becomes even more complex, children of different ages have their distinct needs and express their distinct demands, family finances are spread even more thinly, and parents may be left with the feeling that their entire adult lives have been spent under an aura of diapers. Both parents can feel exhausted from both lack of sleep and the pressure of events—a state of mind in which it's often easier to strike out than to extend a helping hand. For some couples, what helps most is taking a breather to talk things over and finding a little time to be a "couple" again, even if it has to be scheduled on the family's calendar. "Steve and I felt like marathon runners in the months after our third child was born," Liz told me. "One evening we realized we couldn't remember the last time we'd just talked one-to-one. After that, we decided no matter what, Thursdays were 'our' night at home. I'd feed the children early so they'd be settled down when Steve came home, and usually we could enjoy fixing our own meal together and really talking with each other the way we used to."

These are normal transitional problems which every family experiences to some degree. The situation can be more difficult if it's complicated by other factors. Young couples who perhaps had not planned the pregnancy now find themselves with demands and restrictions that neither of them chose, but for which blame can easily be placed when tempers are short. The coincidental timing of other life events—loss of a job, the death of a parent, the need to relocate to another community—can add to the pressure on marital readjustment. Health problems in the new baby or in the parents themselves can be sources of great anxiety and conflict.

REGAINING SEXUAL INTIMACY

One of the most common readjustment problems for new parents is diminished sexual interest and/or loss of sexual intimacy. Sexual problems, in fact, can begin early in pregnancy, and hopes that things will "be back to normal" after the baby's birth are not always well-founded. Nausea and illness in early pregnancy naturally affect a woman's sexual desire. In addition, an expectant mother may have heard the old myth that sexual intercourse in the first trimester can cause miscarriage. This is not true, but both men and women usually find it difficult to talk about sexuality with their doctors, and too often keep their uncertainties to themselves.

As the pregnancy develops and the baby begins to kick, some women start to feel that it is somehow "wrong" to have sex while carrying the baby. Late in the pregnancy, the woman's large abdomen and the increased frequency of urination can make it more difficult to have sex comfortably, and often her changing body and her general fatigue can make her feel uninterested—and in fact, be less sexually attractive to her partner.

For some couples, pregnancy can develop into a long abstinence from sex, and their remoteness can continue after childbirth. Even if this has not been the case, the woman's slackened vaginal muscles may diminish the pleasure of intercourse for both partners. In addition, a woman who has had an episiotomy (a surgical cut to facilitate the baby's delivery) needs time to heal and at first will find intercourse painful. Breastfeeding, too, can inhibit sexual pleasure, either because of breast tenderness or because of attitudes that the woman's breasts are now "reserved" for the baby.

Differences in levels of sexual interest and response can be very painful sources of marital conflict. Not uncommonly, a new mother may feel "all touched out" by her intense physical and sensory interactions with her baby and may avoid any physical attention from her partner. For some couples, sexual intercourse is the only way they experience intimacy, and when this is absent, they have no other means of exchanging tenderness or expressing physical love. Men whose partners have turned away from them both physically and emotionally can feel extraordinarily betrayed and outraged. Some women, for their part, go along with having sex only because they fear their husbands will leave them or seek sexual intimacy elsewhere. Meanwhile, some women in this situation report feeling repelled by their husbands' touch and even "raped" within the context of marriage when they felt pressured to have sex against their will.

HEIDI'S AND DON'S STORY

Sexual problems in marriage are among the most common reasons why couples finally seek therapy, yet they are terribly difficult problems for couples to talk about—with each other and with a therapist. The perspectives of the man and woman may be so much at odds at the outset that sometimes it seems they can never be brought into alignment.

Recently, Heidi and Don came to my office for the first time. Heidi, at seven months postpartum, had been diagnosed as having postpartum depression and had been under the care of her family doctor. One of the main concerns of her depression, the couple told me, was that Heidi felt "sexually dead." As she began to describe her experience, she started instead to use the terms "feeling sexually assaulted." During the early months after childbirth, when she was experiencing a full-blown depression, Don had made overtures of wanting intercourse and she had repeatedly rejected him. When this continued for several weeks, he told her he'd had enough. If this was all there was to their marriage, he said, he was ready to leave.

Heidi had decided she had no choice but to give in to Don, and she bitterly described their lovemaking: "I would lie there and let him be satisfied, and then he would turn over and go to sleep. I would stay awake crying, my teeth clenched, and then I would have these terrible panic attacks. I would cry myself to sleep, knowing there was no chance of a good rest, having to get up in the night to feed the baby. It has been a nightmare."

Heidi's viewpoint was not really difficult to understand—nor was Don's. He was appalled that she described his behavior as "sexual assault," when what he wanted was the pleasure and closeness they'd shared before. This young father was one of those forgotten figures in postpartum depression, a man who was terribly isolated as he tried to cope within a world that had shifted around him. Although their doctor had talked to him about his wife's illness, he had not really understood how long it might last and what he could expect until she recovered.

This is not an easy stage for this couple to move beyond because they have wounded each other a great deal. Heidi continues to see me for individual psychotherapy, and they have agreed to go for conjoint marital counseling.

WHEN A MARRIAGE BREAKS UP IN THE POSTPARTUM

One of the first adjustments that couples make within a relationship is learning to interpret and adjust to each other's communication styles. Since men and women tend in general to communicate differently, particularly when it comes to dealing with emotional issues, this is an adjustment that is not always perfectly achieved. It's not surprising, then, that a basic theme in marital upsets is poor communication.

Marital problems, especially in the complicated setting of a new family, can operate in vicious circles. A misunderstanding occurs, the couple is tired, there isn't time to talk, abrupt words are exchanged, the woman is turned off, the man takes off, the misunderstanding worsens, and on and on. Common problems, any of which can start the vicious circle, can be lack of sexual interest, financial problems, arguments and fights, in-laws, the "workaholic" father and the lonely resentful mother, role adjustments, and different expectations about each other's roles. When a vicious cycle gets going, a new baby's entry into the family will make the lives of the couple even worse.

SASHA'S STORY

Sasha was a 32-year-old business executive with a major computer company who valued her university education dearly. Her husband, Ralf, was two years older than she and part owner of a business he had started with his father before he left for business school in another province. When he went away to school in Quebec, Sasha decided to remain in Vancouver and continue her career obligations. Although they met occasionally over holidays, their marriage began to show signs of strain because Sasha was pursuing one career path while Ralf was pursuing another.

Ralf wanted a baby very much although he realized that perhaps the timing of the baby might interfere with their career
goals. He knew that if they had a baby at this time, it would be
Sasha who would need to compromise, and she did not seem
willing to do that. However, with much persuasion on Ralf's
part, they decided that Sasha would become pregnant.

After the birth of baby Stefan, Sasha and the baby remained
in Vancouver while Ralf moved to Toronto after finishing his degree and getting his first job. The very thing that Sasha had most
wanted to avoid now became reality: with a small baby in tow,
Sasha had to follow Ralf to where his job was located and live
there in a tiny apartment. All of her worst dreams were now realized. Cut off from the life she had known, she felt stripped of
her identity. She longed to go back to Vancouver, to her friends,
her family, and to the job she had really loved. A daily life made
up of changing diapers and fixing Ralf's meals was not what she
had bargained for!

They decided to come back to Vancouver when the baby was
about five months old. Sasha immediately went back to work
and started working long hours. Although Sasha and Ralf had
employed a full-time nanny to look after Stefen's needs, it became a competitive issue as to who would stay longer at work
and who would look after the baby and supervise the household.

Sasha's job took her overseas occasionally, which meant the
baby was left at home completely in the care of the nanny or a
babysitter. Ralf was now quite occupied in looking for new career opportunities to make the most of his training. Somewhere
during this time, Ralf and Sasha became emotionally distant
from each other. When they were together at night, they were
both exhausted and could scarcely talk. All they wanted was to
get a good night's sleep before the start of the new day, with its
heavy schedule of work. A vicious cycle had set in, in which
there was no intimacy between the two, no means of communication at all. The occasional dinners-for-two had stopped along
the way, as had socializing with their friends.

Sasha confided the marital problems to her family doctor and
felt that she would like to explore the issues, provided that Ralf
wanted to do the same. I saw Sasha a few times in my office and

then eventually decided to meet with Ralf to hear both their stories.

In a way, they were both right. Having a baby at this time, when they didn't feel very anchored in their careers was probably not a good decision. Most important, each was trying to develop a personal sense of identity. Sasha came from a family in which career was considered very important, and her family had invested a great deal in her education. At no point was she willing to consider giving up the fruits of this expensive education. Ralf, on the other hand, came from a fairly wealthy family and was not as driven as Sasha. He was more laid-back and flexible about issues in life, including the baby and the marriage. It was obvious, though, that they both needed better communicating skills, and they both needed to work on their marriage. I therefore referred them for marital therapy.

The sad story of Sasha and Ralf demonstrates how a troubled couple who attempts to improve their marriage by having a baby will often find it even more difficult to keep the marriage together after the birth. The atmosphere surrounding a couple who are having trouble communicating, and have become emotionally distant is not one of love and nurturing, and the couple can then provide little love and nurturing to the child who has been brought into this environment. When a couple is troubled, their baby can suffer through neglect. This is not to say that children in the care of nannies or babysitters are necessarily neglected. Rather, the couple themselves will have expended their energy in fighting and disagreeing and have little energy left to spend on the child's well-being.

A child is a symbol of a couple's love and represents an extension of their commitment to each other. When this commitment is in question and the relationship is on shaky grounds, it is better to seek therapy, resolve the issues and conflicts that exist, and then carefully plan for the birth of a baby when the relationship is firm. A traumatic family breakup can then be avoided.

THE TRAP OF SUBSTANCE ABUSE

Substance abuse in our society is more common than we are led to believe. In the sixties, the drug scene hit the world for a short while, but alcohol has for centuries been a "recreational drug." When a person is lonely, alcohol can be a soothing companion. Sometimes, there is a very fine line between acceptable social use and abuse. To have a glass of wine or two with "business lunches" is almost the norm, and this consumption can gradually increase unnoticed as time goes on. Many people with alcohol problems are unable to recognize the addiction themselves until something disastrous happens.

Alcohol can be wielded as a very powerful weapon by one partner to explain a problematic marriage. A husband might say, "I drink because all my wife does every night is ignore me and pay attention to the baby; I feel left out and alone." Drinking is one way of "blocking out" problems. When a couple has a fight and cannot resolve issues, it is easy to retreat to a bottle of beer because it takes away pain temporarily. A woman whose partner usually works late might say, "I have to have that glass of wine to settle my nerves before I face the evening with my two daughters. Otherwise, my nerves are raw and I feel cranky."

Particularly in the postpartum period, a woman looks and hopes for support from her husband. Because some mothers elect to stay at home after the birth of the baby, their husbands feel that it is the wife's job to take responsibility for all domestic chores plus child care. At the same time, if he is the sole wage earner in the family, then the external demands on him are greater.

Long hours away from home are sometimes an integral part of one's profession. How many lawyers, doctors, or executives are home for dinner at five or even six o'clock? As these professionals become parents, it is more often the women than the men who cut back on their working hours to accommodate a new child. Not too many male doctors or lawyers take a leave of absence to raise a child! Many women married to workaholics ultimately resign themselves to not getting any help from their partners and "try to do it all." In those cases, marital problems can take many forms. Some women have extramarital affairs, others resort to drinking, while still others spend money excessively to seek comfort. But these "acting out" behaviors are signs of marital tension. Unless these problems are addressed, the birth of the new baby will likely turn the home into a battlefield.

SIMONE'S STORY

Simone, a 32-year-old doctor's wife, was under my care for approximately ten months after the birth of each of her three children. She had postpartum depression after the birth of all her children, and on one occasion, she had to be hospitalized. One day, I had a call from her husband, John, who was very concerned that his wife was abusing alcohol and taking more pills than prescribed. When I saw the two of them together in my office, Simone's distress was obvious.

John and Simone were both immigrants from Bulgaria. Their first few years after relocating in Canada had been fraught with tremendous difficulties. They had to learn to speak English, and John had to drive a cab for a few years while he was preparing for examinations that would eventually qualify him as a doctor in Canada. During that time, Simone had her first baby and she rarely saw her husband. But he promised that with time, once their lives were more "normal," he would participate in child care.

Three years later, John opened his practice and as he was one of only three doctors in the area very soon became extremely busy. Night calls, weekend deliveries, and twelve-hour days left him totally exhausted. All he did was eat, sleep, and work. By this time, Simone had had her third child and was hospitalized for her postpartum depression. Her mother flew in from Europe to look after the children, now aged six years, four years, and four months, while Simone recovered. John was too busy to visit his own wife in the hospital where he worked.

Evenings were very lonely for Simone who, in spite of having friends, felt isolated within the marriage. Her resentment and anger against John were gradually rising and Simone started to drink excessively as a means of coping with the stress of raising three children alone. I saw them together for a few sessions for assessment of their marital issues.

John told me he was quite aware of Simone's drinking habits and had found it easy to work late and avoid going home to a wife who became angry and argumentative when she drank. He felt little support from her for the demands of his busy practice, and he felt divided loyalties when he weighed his patients' needs against his family's. For her part, Simone felt if only she were not so lonely, if only he could be at home more, she would be able to stop drinking.

They were referred to the Marital Discord Clinic, where they began to make progress as a couple. John felt that he wanted to work on salvaging their family life. He put some limits on his professional schedule and expressed more interest in Simone and the children. In turn, she had less occasion to retreat into alcohol. They began to talk of taking a family vacation, the first they had ever had.

The stories of Ralf and Sasha, John and Simone, illustrate the kind of pressures that today's couples may experience. Traditional roles are changing, and these changes offer both men and women many possibilities for growth and fulfillment. At the same time, conflicts and pressures that were less evident in earlier generations can affect the stability of a marriage, particularly when children join the family. Women today have more options for individual fulfillment in a career, and many choose to pursue both individual fulfillment and fulfillment as the mother of a family. The father of the family can become involved in parenting to a degree that was unheard of in his grandfather's day. In these economic times, though, his ability to fulfill the traditional role of "breadwinner" is more difficult than it used to be, and for many couples, the ordinary requirements of establishing a home and starting a family require both of them to earn an income.

It is not surprising that some couples overlook the need to establish mutual understanding about their focus and priorities until misunderstandings result in conflicts. With so many complex issues in the life of today's family, neither is it surprising that the objective view of a trained professional may be needed to help a troubled couple assess their situation and find a resolution to their problems.

WHAT HAPPENS IN MARITAL THERAPY?

Various types of professionals specialize in marital therapy—family physicians, psychiatrists, psychologists, social workers, nurse-clinicians, as well as religious counselors. Referrals to these practitioners can be made formally by your family doctor. However, a non-physician marital therapist can be found through various resources including suggestions of friends, and you yourself can phone for an appointment.

The Therapist's Role

For some people, talking about one's marriage problems to a stranger is almost unthinkable. For one thing, the marriage itself has a deep meaning for both the identities and self-esteem of the two partners. The kind of relationship we have with our partner says a great deal about the kind of people we are, and most people are deeply hurt, to their very core, by the prospect of a "failed marriage."

Secondly, the marriage unit is by nature intimate and is accorded a distinct status in society. Unless a marriage becomes dysfunctional, most couples observe a great deal of privacy and loyalty in what they share with others outside the marriage. It is this very circumspect approach to the marital relationship that can make it so difficult for couples with problems to step back and objectively work on sorting them out.

A trained marital therapist can bring several resources to the process of working through marital upsets. First of all, she or he is an objective observer—someone who can interpret clearly what each partner is saying, and someone who has seen similar patterns before. Although it is true that every couple is unique, it is a fact that most marital problems center on common themes, such as finances, sexual intimacy, child care, and so on, and therefore most partners in the conflict will respond in ways similar to those of other couples in similar conflicts. Just as individuals who seek counseling can gain some reassurance by learning their situation is not unique, couples in therapy can also be supported by learning that their problem has been faced successfully by others. Sometimes, it's simply helpful to know that some of what the couple is experiencing is quite "normal."

The primary role of the marital therapist is to facilitate communication between the couple so that they can understand what their problems are and work to solve them. The therapist talks with the couple and helps them learn specific techniques to talk to each other. Couples who are enmeshed in conflict and misunderstanding usually need help in talking about their problems in an open and fair manner. For example, many couples don't know how to talk about their feelings without criticizing or blaming the other: "You're so insensitive, you never know how much you hurt me." They may have habits of talking in generalizations that are both meaningless and hurtful: "You're just like your mother!" Marital therapists are trained to deal with such miscommunications, and after working with a marital therapist, couples usually come away with improved skills in resolving their own conflicts.

How Long Does Marital Therapy Take?

Every marital therapist has a different framework in terms of tech-niques used and amount of time spent. At our Marital Discord Clinic, usually after their first joint consultation with a therapist, the partners will have separate interviews. After gaining an understanding of their two perspectives, the therapist will then arrange to see them together. Solo sessions are scheduled for conjoint visits. An upper limit for mar-ital therapy would probably be six months to a year. However, what's important to note is that often couples need only a few sessions to de-velop an understanding of their problems and gain insight into ways to begin to turn things around.

WHAT I TELL MY PATIENTS

The normal adjustment from being a couple to becoming a fam-ily can be difficult, and in these times, it's perhaps more difficult than ever. We have left behind the days when women's and men's roles were clear-cut, when a woman's destiny was always expected to be wife and mother, and a man was always ex-pected to be the provider and protector. Today, there are rich possibilities for varied and blended roles within the family, and it appears that today's young mothers and fathers have the po-tential to realize much more rewarding roles as parents than their own parents had.

Nevertheless, a societal transformation is in progress, and it's not always easy to match the dream of a different kind of par-enting with the reality of one's own individual family. In addi-tion, quite an extraordinary level of stress is placed on both men and women in Western society. In many instances, women are supposed to expect more than "just being a mother" and end up feeling pressured to be the Superwoman who will manage home, children, and career brilliantly. At the same time, men are expected to be more than just breadwinners; to be sensitive partners and caring and knowledgable fathers as well.

Coming to grips with these changing roles in the modern family can be trying for even the most stable couple. When one partner experiences an emotional illness, the strain can tip the balance into marital instability. I frequently see couples together in my practice, even if the woman has been referred to me for an emotional disorder. Sometimes, these couples have had marital problems that have never been addressed and have now become unbearable. In other cases, marital problems are the result of their joint attempts to cope with the woman's illness. In either case, these problems can often benefit from marital therapy, in addition to the individual therapy of the woman under my care.

Since our families and social institutions focus on marriage and childbirth, it's natural that they tend to project and anticipate only the positive side of these events. Regrettably, we miss preparing couples for the possibility that something can go wrong and they can feel terribly isolated and overwhelmed when unanticipated problems arise. Although it's true that some high schools offer courses in "family life," and some churches provide premarital counseling sessions, they offer only general guidance in advance of "real life," and usually do not focus on the specific problems of pregnancy and postpartum.

Many marital problems can be solved with the help of a trained therapist, the objectivity that the therapist brings, and with some changes in strategies that the therapist can suggest. I want my patients to realize that there are many types of therapies available to help them. There is no reason not to take full advantage of these therapies, and in today's world, there should be no stigma attached in seeking the specialized help of a trained therapist to address marital problems.

CHAPTER 8

"BUT I'M INVOLVED IN THIS, TOO"

The Father's Role During Pregnancy and Postpartum

In discussing the events and emotions of pregnancy and childbirth, I have naturally concentrated on the mother's experience, since my main purpose is to give information and guidance on women's emotional health. However, the new father's experience is equally complex and important, and his feelings and needs are often overlooked in relation to both the normal and abnormal events of pregnancy and childbirth. It's important to remember that he, too, is an individual involved in profound changes in his life and his relationships, and the extent to which he can face these changes with awareness and understanding has a great bearing on both his individual emotional health and his family's well-being. He, too, is deeply affected by these events—whether he is facing normal adjustments to his new role, emotional illness in his partner, decisions about termination of a pregnancy, or the tragic loss of an infant.

When a woman experiences emotional illness, one of the significant elements in her recovery is the involvement and support of her partner. But what about the partner himself? In this chapter, I will examine events and issues from the father's point of view and take note of his need for support in coping with these life-changing events, especially if they turn out to be traumatic.

SOME ISSUES FOR EXPECTANT AND NEW FATHERS

Living in Changing Times

This is a time of transition for the North American family, and more so than ever before, each family is experimenting with changing roles and relationships. As recently as thirty years ago, there were fewer variations in what the family looked like, and thus less confusion within individuals in regard to their lifestyles. The entry of more women into the work force and the widespread social philosophy of the feminist movement have started to change the stereotypes of men's and women's roles and begun to make alterations in the overall dynamics of interpersonal relationships within the family. But this transition is not complete, if it ever will be, and in many families of today, there's a great deal of uncertainty about the complex choices that confront them.

Let's begin by looking at some general issues in fatherhood and some of the stresses faced by the male partner with regard to pregnancy and parenthood. Men respond very differently to these issues than do women, because for centuries, men have been socialized differently than women. Consequently, their emotional responses to situations have been "gender specific." For example, even though supportive societal expectations are beginning to arise around the man's role in childbirth and child rearing, in the minds of many, there remains an underlying assumption that home life and care of the family is more closely related to the woman. While few people would state it in quite this way, there is often an unspoken assumption that men "feel" or "care" less than women do about things like the children's health or the quality of their schools—that these are essentially "women's issues." By and large, women are more likely than men to find tolerance for vivid expression of emotions such as crying or pronounced grief, while men are supposed to contain their emotions and "get on with it." These basic underlying expectations about male and female behavior are conveyed at a very early age to children, and we have all heard parents at the playground or hockey rink admonishing their sons with statements like, "Big boys don't cry," and "Act like a man!"

Therefore, finding one's own direction in the midst of these changes and choices is sometimes even more difficult for men than for women. The traditional guideposts on the road to fatherhood no longer necessarily point in the direction a couple has chosen to go. On one hand, the newly expectant father may feel excited about the possibilities of participating in the birth experience and being an equal partner in raising his children. On the other, he may feel that his own upbringing has offered him no guidance in this new role—or, he may feel uncertain about whether he really wants any role other than the traditional one he has seen males practice around him. Ron was one such expectant father. He came to see me with his wife several times before their child was born. "Doctor, I'm looking forward to having this kid," he told me, "but I don't know about stuff like changing diapers. My dad never did that!"

Today, fathers are allowed a very important role in pregnancy and childbirth. For many couples, this is a welcome development that gives both partners an equal opportunity to learn about and share in the emotional and physical developments that lead to their baby's birth. It's worth noting that a couple will not necessarily have the same views about the father's participation in pregnancy. For instance, some men have mixed feelings about their choices. If the couple's friends have had positive experiences with both partners having been active participants during pregnancy and childbirth, they may make an automatic assumption that every father naturally wants to be present at his baby's birth—an assumption that is not necessarily shared by the father in question. Alternatively, the expectant father may be quite eager to be fully involved and find that his partner subtly discourages his interest. After all, the woman can control the extent of her partner's participation by choosing not to invite any involvement or share information. Since so much attention is placed on the mother and baby, it's easy for fathers to be relegated to the sidelines. Expectant couples may need to discuss their assumptions at an early stage of the pregnancy so that they both feel comfortable with the other's attitudes and roles and have some sense of what to expect from one another in the future.

Men who choose to participate actively in pregnancy and childbirth will of course experience the whole process more profoundly and intensely than the traditional father whose role is confined to pacing in the waiting room. However, the father clearly experiences pregnancy much differently than his partner. He does not receive the physical cues from a changing body that for the mother begin very soon after conception. Even for a father who is fully absorbed in the progress of the pregnancy, the reality of the infant may not hit home until he, too, can feel its kicks and see the beating heart on the ultrasound screen. While the expectant mother is constantly aware from early in the pregnancy that her entire being is absorbed in nurturing her baby, the father's nurturing behavior must take place externally.

"Nesting behavior" by men tends to develop only late in the pregnancy through specific tasks like painting the baby's room, building an extension to the house, and so on.

Men can share certain of their partners' physical aspects of pregnancy more intimately these days and can be true partners during childbirth. However, their experience of pregnancy and approaching fatherhood is nevertheless still theoretical rather than practical. Prenatal classes and books on pregnancy and child care can help men develop a more realistic picture, which can provide a basis for the couple to share feelings and views about their transition from being a couple to being a family.

There is another sense, too, in which fathers experience pregnancy. Just as the woman's body carries out the major physical and emotional tasks of pregnancy, the expectant father must at least carry out some emotional tasks of pregnancy to prepare the two of them for parenthood. These emotional tasks include becoming aware that he must and can take on the responsibilities of parenting, that he will be functioning as a member of a family unit in which the father and mother must be concerned with the well-being of dependent children. Emotionally, he must come to terms with the change in the marital unit as he and his partner change from being a couple, absorbed in their own and each other's needs, to being parents who must begin to focus on the needs of the baby and the well-being of the family as a whole. These role changes for the father are signaled in our culture by joking remarks like, "It's time to trade in the sports car for a station wagon." While the father can have only indirect experience of the physical event of pregnancy, he is directly experiencing his own parallel incubation period as he prepares to become a father and to be seen as a father in the eyes of the world. This aspect of "male pregnancy" has been largely overlooked in Western culture, though in other cultures some expectant fathers are said to feel "labor pains" (Couvade's syndrome).

Sadly, many men who are eager to explore their emotions and feelings about themselves and their fatherhood find that they receive little social support for their interest. Many men feel fearful about their ability to handle the increased responsibilities of fatherhood; they may feel guilty about their occasional resentment of the baby and fear that it will be a burden on both family finances and lifestyle. They are unlikely to express these anxieties either to their partner or to male friends. Alternately, a man may be thrilled and eager to take part in childbirth and child rearing and find little understanding of this interest from the more traditional males among his father, brothers, and friends. While there is growing social support for men to be involved in prenatal education, many people still see pregnancy and childbirth as centered almost exclusively on the mother and infant. If the father's co-workers express interest in the pregnancy, they're likely to ask about the woman's health rather than the father's new feelings. Despite changing laws and attitudes, "paternity leave" is still a novel concept in our society. Under normal circumstances, most men can handle this philosophically, and many may not feel the need to share their feelings with other males. But when problems arise in pregnancy and childbirth, they can feel extremely isolated and resentful that their emotional needs are overlooked, sometimes by those to whom they're closest.

Experiencing Fatherhood in Today's World

In these transitional times, the family's immediate social environment can greatly help or hinder the father's adjustment to his new role. The most obvious way in which both men and women have traditionally learned to be parents is observation of their own parents, who can provide both practical knowledge and a model for behavior. Such observation is a learning experience even when young parents resolve that they'll do a better job as parents than their own mothers or fathers did. In today's world, because of a generational gap and our swiftly changing society, the guidance and suggestions offered by the expectant grandparents are not always as satisfying or acceptable as they used to be; the support of friends whose attitudes are similar to one's own may be more meaningful. A young father, in particular, may find himself disappointed when searching for answers from his own father; he may find himself turning instead to his mother or mother-in-law, who can be surer guides in some of the child care skills he wants to master. This is quite understandable, since his own father likely experienced childbirth and pregnancy quite remotely, as was the norm. In recent times, as more couples choose to embark on a joint participation in childbirth and child care, a new father may find it enlightening to talk to other men about his emotional response in the delivery room and his feelings toward his new infant.

There are many mixed messages these days about what is expected of a man and a father, and even within a cohesive social circle, attitudes may not be black and white. The two-income family is becoming a norm across North America, but there are still hidden messages and not-so-hidden expectations that the male in the family should be the main provider and bring in the bigger income. A great deal of attention has been given to changing roles within marriage, but studies continue to show that even when mothers work outside the home, most of them also carry the main load of housekeeping and child care responsibilities. Although fathers are expected to share equally in child care duties, the working world has an even lower tolerance for a father's "family problems" than it does for a mother's. Thus, fathers are expected to be jointly involved in parenthood, yet find themselves striving harder than ever to meet the current social "norms"—without a network of people in place in case they need support and guidance. For instance, I recall what happened when Derek, a chief executive officer of a large Canadian company, tried without success to persuade his company to allow him paternity leave. The president of his company was appalled that Derek had even considered making this request. For months, Derek was angry; the message he had been given was "Get your priorities straight!" when in fact he was working as hard at work as at home. He was helping his wife through a difficult post-partum period by taking on nighttime feedings and changing diapers so his wife could get some sleep. Then he was expected to show up at work, alert and bright-eyed, to make decisions on intricate financial dealings. These were practical problems, by no means uncommon for new parents, which a formalized paternity leave would have helped solve. In the United States, the new Family Leave Act allows families to solve such problems in their own way; it will be interesting to see whether fathers will be able to take advantage of its provisions or whether subtle and not-so-subtle pressure from above constrains them from taking time to be with their new families.

Living the Role in Times of Stress

These aspects of social transition have to be lived through in the context of each individual family unit. Addressing conflicts in roles and expectations can be a source of growth and fulfillment, allowing the family to become closer and to establish its own identity in society. But there's no mistaking that these are difficult challenges that can be a source of personal and marital problems, particularly when the family is faced with crisis. When things are going smoothly, most fathers can handle the supporting role status they're assigned fairly enthusiastically. However, when the family unit of father-mother-infant is disrupted, the father may find himself completely outside the focus of attention. When a couple experiences the loss of a baby, for example, the mother is generally the focus of family members' and friends' concern and support. If the family is faced with a new or expectant mother's emotional illness, the emotional needs of the father and the practical demands he's expected to meet may be completely overlooked by health care professionals, friends, co-workers, and even relatives. Thus, at a time that traditional expectation is that the father will be the family's "pillar of strength," he may actually be in a state of devastating isolation and vulnerability.

WHEN THE MOTHER IS EMOTIONALLY ILL

Social and Personal Stress for the Father

Our transitional society places some extreme demands on the father of the family when the mother becomes ill. Few North American families these days have the benefit of an extended family network that can easily rally to support the couple, so the odds are that the father will have to go at it alone somehow. The dynamics of the family unit change as the father, no matter how involved he has been in family and housekeeping duties, also takes on the duties of his dysfunctional partner. When the mother has a postpartum illness, the father will have to play even more than his usual role in caring for the new infant. If there are older children in the home, the demands on the father are almost unbearable. He will have to arrange for their practical needs—from regular meals and clean clothes to after-school hockey practice—while being their emotional lifeline, at a time when they are quite naturally worried and fearful about what has happened to their mother.

The father, distressed about his partner's condition, is sometimes not given enough basic information about her illness and its probable outcome to feel at all confident in the family's future. At the same time, health care professionals recognize that the attitudes, understanding, and support of the partner are key indicators for a woman's recovery from emotional illness. So even as his energy fades, the father continues to press himself to offer support and encouragement.

Financial worries often contribute to an already stressful situation. Depending on the family's insurance coverage, the costs of the woman's medical care might or might not be fully covered. Unplanned expenses related to the mother's illness, ranging from the cost of additional take-out meals to extra fees for babysitting and child care, are sure to pile up. For the father, the immediate financial worries are complicated by fears about how his new family demands will affect his performance on the job. Too often, careers and jobs offer no flexibility for family crises. The father may be simply too exhausted to concentrate on his work or he may have to place family demands ahead of a nine-to-five work schedule. Neither of these types of behavioral changes is likely to be tolerated long in any employment situation.

Sometimes he'll feel that he *could* handle it all without strain—"If only I could take a break for a bit...," "If only I could get my thoughts together...," "If I could just go out for a night with my friends...." But there's no time for a Saturday afternoon game of tennis, no time to linger over a beer with a few friends, no time to see the latest movie. There are no breaks in the cycle of getting the kids off to day-care, going to work, picking up the kids, doing the shopping, visiting the hospital, and so on. While this situation is at its most acute when the mother is hospitalized, it may be only slightly improved when a woman with psychiatric illness is being treated as an outpatient. In fact, this second situation—when the woman is at home but unable to resume her full role in the partnership and her previous meaningful relationships with both her children and her partner—can be almost more stressful.

Whether or not the woman is being treated in hospital, the kind of stress-linked marital problems that often develop in the context of an emotional illness can last well beyond the illness itself.

Some Common Emotional Reactions

Most individuals in a marriage or committed relationship like to imagine that, should their partner become seriously ill, they would have endless reserves of love and patience to support the sick partner. And luckily, we often find that we do have remarkable strengths we've never been called on to use before. But emotional illness in a family can test these strengths to the limit, sometimes even more so than a life-threatening disease or recovery from a debilitating accident. Part of the reason is that emotional illnesses can't be "seen" as concretely as, for instance, heart disease. Another part of the problem is that emotional illness alters for a time the sick individual's usual manner of self-expression and ability to relate to others. Finally, emotional illness offers a great test in that it challenges personal and societal attitudes and fears about a condition that has only recently begun to be understood.

When one's partner becomes ill, the usual responses are to show concern, to be empathetic, to be supportive in taking on the partner's responsibilities so he or she is relieved of worries and can rest and heal, to express strength and confidence in an encouraging way. When a partner's illness continues, it is not uncommon for these positive feelings to wear thin from time to time. It is completely normal to have a broad range of emotions, including resentment at the person who is ill, impatience for his or her feelings, anger that he or she is unable to fulfill usual family roles. These are all normal human emotions that any partner, whether man or woman, may experience. When a man is faced with his partner's postpartum illness, he has the additional responsibility of providing primary care and nurturing for a new infant.

As we have seen, along with one's concern and care for the sick partner, it is also common to experience a variety of "negative" emotions. When a woman becomes emotionally ill in pregnancy or postpartum, it is quite likely that the father will feel some guilt and blame. It is normal for him to feel that, somehow—perhaps simply by his role in starting her pregnancy—he is responsible for what has happened. It's easy to become involved in "what if" questions: "What if I'd been more considerate? What if I'd realized sooner that she was stressed out? What if I hadn't pressured her so much about going back to her job?"

The man can experience the same pattern of emotional responses as in a grief reaction—shock, anger, blame. After all, his world is inside out now. He can feel acutely that he's lost the loving relationship he shared with his partner and the happy pregnancy or early days after childbirth that they'd both looked forward to; he may even feel the woman he loved is a complete stranger. His anger and blame may well center on her—and what a setup for his own personal guilt this is! As her illness continues, he may come to feel she's malingering—that, really, she's not ill at all, just a little down, and if she'd only snap out of it, she could pull herself together. And when the mother's illness affects the healthy partner's ability to work and bring in an income, the family is indeed threatened by long-term conflict and disruption. Unfortunately, these personal demands on the father's energies may ultimately cost him his job—either because he's unable to perform to the expected standard or has to take time off. The old joke about new fathers falling asleep at desk or workstation is no joke for these sorely pressed men.

Feelings of anger and resentment can be fueled by the insensitivity and lack of understanding of family and friends. It is not uncommon for a woman suffering depression to place quite unrealistic expectations on her partner. He may be trying his best to take on duties that she has customarily performed—only to find himself criticized by her for not performing these to her usual standards! Perhaps he has neglected stocking up on the children's preferred cereal. Perhaps he has missed the usual day to change the sheets. Perhaps he is not ironing his own shirts as carefully as she has. Even less fairly, his wife might complain to family and friends that "Steve is no help at all" and he may find himself being berated by his mother-in-law or other outsiders to the family unit. On the other hand, the man may be fully accepting of the reality of his partner's illness, fully involved in the plan for her care—and find that either her parents or his own cannot grasp why a "healthy young mother" could "neglect" her new baby. Thus, he may find himself the center of the entire family's negative attitudes and reproaches.

Postpartum emotional disorders can also have the effect of distancing the couple from a particular circle of new friends—the other expectant parents they've become close to in prenatal classes. Sadly, there is nothing like any kind of complication of pregnancy or childbirth to cool off these kinds of new friendships. A husband with all the positive attitudes in the world towards this temporary derailment in his family's stability may find himself as his wife's only ally, stigmatized not only by friends but by his parents and in-laws, and left without the supports on which he had previously been able to rely.

The Need to Reconnect

Oftentimes in a marriage or a relationship of many years the partners come to take each other for granted, and in therapy, I talk with the couple about starting the courtship all over again. We talk about setting time aside, hiring a babysitter, going out again to the movies. We talk about finding time and opportunities to be together as a couple and becoming close again through talking things over—going out to dinner or just taking walks together. We talk, too, about a woman's need to feel "romanced again" before sexual intimacy resumes. When couples can respond with sensitivity to each other's needs, a joyful reconnection as a twosome is possible even as the family has grown to include a child.

A QUESTION YOU MIGHT HAVE ABOUT EMOTIONAL REACTION TO THE PARTNER'S ILLNESS

 I am a 35-year-old engineer, married for nine years with three children. After the birth of each of our children, my

wife had a postpartum depression, and my life was turned up-side down each time. She was hospitalized after the birth of our middle child, and I had to take a leave of absence from my company—and, as a matter of fact, lost a promotion because of that. I feel angry and resentful, and upset that there seemed to be no one to talk to as I went through a very tough time.

It's understandable that you feel angry and resentful. After all, you've sacrificed a lot in order to meet your family obligations. You probably feel that the efforts you made were scarcely appreciated, perhaps scarcely even recognized. Although no one seems to have lent a sympathetic ear while you were going through these crises, you would still derive a great deal of benefit in talking about your feelings now. I would strongly recommend that you seek a referral to a therapist who can provide individual counseling and help you examine and work through these feelings.

THE FATHER'S NEED FOR SUPPORT

Involving the Father in Treatment and Recovery

In my practice, a woman with emotional illness related to pregnancy or postpartum is always treated with her partner's involvement. The usual procedure is to spend time with both partners, together and individually, to explain emotional illness, to discuss the woman's particular condition, to explore options for treatment, to outline the course the illness might take, and to clarify how long treatment might be required.

It's important that the education of the patient and her partner continue throughout the course of treatment. It would be unreasonable to expect that either of them will absorb all the information they need at once, and they might not even realize the questions they want to ask until after the first interview. The woman's doctor needs to help with this by creating avenues for the couple to participate together in both information gathering and decision making.

If the woman is receiving treatment as an outpatient, her partner needs to understand some basics about how her medication might affect her. He, as much as she, needs to know the medication's possible side effects—for instance, drowsiness or having a dry mouth. If the illness occurs in the postpartum period, he needs to be equally involved in understanding the many issues I discussed in Chapter Six about breastfeeding and emotional illness. If there are decisions to be made about nursing and medication, he needs to participate with his partner in making these decisions. As her condition improves, the woman's doctor needs to help the couple together explore the long-term risks for recurrence of her illness and the implications for later pregnancies.

When the woman's partner is fully involved in the treatment, he is better able to be a partner in the true sense of the word—to support the treatment plan and participate in making decisions that shouldn't be left to the woman alone. He is also more likely to feel somewhat more in control of events because he knows what's happening and how long the recovery might take.

Removing the Mysteries About "The Psychiatrist"

The woman with psychiatric illness needs all the help she can get, from the treatment provided by her doctor, from understanding family and friends, and perhaps most important, from her partner. Some men have acknowledged after the fact that one of the biggest barriers to their being supportive of their partners was the fear and mystery that surrounded their own images of "The Psychiatrist." Some men have said that until they actually saw and met with their wife's doctor, they couldn't imagine "The Psychiatrist" as another human being, a person they could actually relate to. A partner may even discourage a woman from following her family doctor's suggestion that she see a psychiatrist because of his own fears about a remote, unknown specialist. Why is it necessary, he may think, for his wife to waste half a day making arrangements for an office visit with this mysterious entity, this "man in a white coat," whose role is quite unclear?

These fantasies usually vanish quite quickly when the man is involved from the start in his partner's care and treatment. When that is the case, he sees that the psychiatrist is nothing more exotic than a person who has experience helping other people with problems similar to his partner's, and he can relax a bit and feel reassured as he begins to understand her psychiatric illness. Just as important, psychiatrists must recognize that generally speaking, the patient should be treated in the context of her family, and that the support he or she provides should also be available to the husband in sorting out his emotions and reactions to his wife's illness.

A QUESTION YOU MIGHT HAVE
ABOUT SEEING A PSYCHIATRIST

? *My wife has been seeing a psychiatrist for the past two years. Each time she comes home from a session with her psychiatrist, we tend to have a fight, sometimes over very trivial issues. I get the feeling that there are things that are talked about in the sessions that bring about these fights. Is it because I'm being talked about?*

One can imagine that if a woman has been seeing a psychiatrist for a period of time, and the husband has not met the psychiatrist, then the husband might imagine that the two are "plotting against him." If there are ongoing problems in your marriage, you may easily begin to feel like an outsider standing by as your marriage and other intimate issues are discussed without your presence. This can be especially troubling if you feel that sexual issues are being discussed. Why not talk with your wife and with her psychiatrist about your feelings? It is in no one's interest for you to feel excluded and resentful, and your wife's psychiatrist will very likely be receptive to your attending a session with your wife or arranging to meet with the psychiatrist individually. If there are issues in your marriage that need to be explored, the psychiatrist would be in a good position to judge whether you and your wife might benefit from conjoint marital therapy. If there are issues that might be explored through individual counseling for you, the psychiatrist would also be able to refer you to an appropriate therapist.

Offering Practical Support

There are no easy answers to how to offer practical day-to-day support to the father whose partner is ill and whose duties have quadrupled. Often these issues will be brought to the psychiatrist, and some avenues of help may open up. With luck, the family may have some type of assistance from their extended family—a grandmother might be able to move in for awhile to look after older children or a new baby, or possibly the extended family might offer some financial support to help with the hiring of babysitters or nannies. Remarkably, one's social support system is sometimes more generous than one would have expected. A patient in my practice told me of unexpected help from a childless neighborhood couple who actually moved next door to help with the care of her three older children when she was hospitalized. Where immediate solutions are not evident, the woman's psychiatrist can sometimes suggest community resources or the help of other professionals, such as hospital social workers, who can contribute to finding solutions.

Families in crisis sometimes discover they lack certain useful skills in time management and financial management that really hadn't mattered to them before. One of the invaluable ways to develop these skills and to receive emotional support for the family's situation is through taking part in peer support groups. The woman's doctor will know whether there are ongoing support groups operating through the local hospital or other community health organizations. In working with my patients, I have organized both a casual support group for fathers whose partners are hospitalized and an informal telephone support group. Both groups developed quite naturally as I talked with fathers about their interest in meeting with others who faced similar problems. The telephone group developed spontaneously as "experienced" fathers said they'd gladly talk with others who were just beginning to face a family crisis. In both cases, the men involved come from many different backgrounds and various socioeconomic groups but have found a common ground in their situations—and developed friendships that lasted beyond the duration of their partners' illness.

Emotional Vulnerability

When attention is acutely focused on the woman's emotional state, it's very easy for everyone involved to overlook how emotionally vulnerable the father may also be. This emotional vulnerability is both understandable and normal, but it shouldn't be underestimated. Sometimes, support groups or individual counseling sessions with the woman's psychiatrist can provide enough of an outlet for expression of feelings to help the father cope. I feel it's important for family members and caregivers to acknowledge this vulnerability and "give permission" for him to express fears and emotions. In many cases, fathers "survive" by living out the male role of strong protector, doing what needs to be done and keeping their emotions tightly under wraps—but at considerable cost to themselves. If the father is truly isolated from any source of meaningful support, he may himself be at risk for developing an emotional disorder.

When I am treating a woman for postpartum illness, I always see her with her partner at the very beginning of therapy. Many times, after three or four meteings with the couple, I am contacted by the husband who wants to see me individually to talk about his feelings, which he feels he cannot express in his wife's presence. It is interesting to me that sometimes these are the men who have initially been reluctant to see me or who have been fearful about just what a psychiatrist is and does. Once they come to understand the process, however, they usually feel more comfortable in talking with me.

MICHAEL'S STORY

Michael is the husband of Lydia, a woman who was referred to me by her family doctor for postpartum depression. This very compatible couple had been married for ten years before they chose to have a child, and Lydia had had a happy and uneventful pregnancy. Michael had accompanied his wife on her first visit to me, and we had jointly been involved in deciding that her condition did not require hospitalization. Instead, I prescribed antidepressant medication, and they came to see me together for several sessions over the first few weeks of treatment. Michael is a writer, an intelligent and extraordinarily sensitive man, who was extremely supportive of and very "loyal" to his wife, never once breaking his role of attentive, patient, loving husband.

I will never forget the message this soft-spoken man delivered when he came for an individual appointment. To all appearances, he was "coping" completely, but inside he felt his whole identity, his whole world, was changing around him. "Where is the woman I've loved for ten years?" he asked. "She's gone crazy. Where is the baby we planned for and longed for? He's a sad little guy, born with asthma and crying for his mother. Where is my home, my nest, where I was safe? It's a mess, it's chaos. It seems to me, Dr. Misri," he said, "that the whole world is in a state of disarray—and I think I'm actually losing it too."

Michael was not emotionally ill, but he certainly needed and deserved immediate support through this excruciating time. He saw me for one or two more individual visits, during which he found he could express some of the frustration and disappointment that he felt would be heartless to express to his wife. He continued to be supportive of her, and as she recovered from her depression, they worked together on regaining their former compatibility and intimacy.

Michael's story, while very poignant, is neither extreme nor uncommon. The pressures of a spouse's emotional illness, the demands of carrying the load of two partners, the worries and uncertainties about the children involved, can be extraordinarily stressful. As much as possible, health care givers and family members need to offer understanding and support to the father carrying this load.

A QUESTION YOU MIGHT HAVE
ABOUT THE FATHER'S EMOTIONS

? *I'm a 29-year-old man married to a woman who is being treated for a depressive illness. I came from a home where my mother was depressed off and on through her life, and I never thought I would end up marrying a woman who would need the same kind of treatment my mother did. Now, watching my wife going through these depressions, I am reminded of the times I had to struggle with my mother's illness, and I wonder how much my two young sons are troubled by all this. Sometimes these dreams haunt me, and I find myself spending many sleepless nights thinking about it.*

Being married to a woman who is struggling with depression just as your mother did must be difficult for you to deal with. Your fears are quite legitimate, and it is understandable that you would be troubled by your memories and the sense of history repeating itself. It seems to me you were affected by your mother's illness, and you are quite naturally concerned about the responses of your children. Obviously, you need to talk about these fears and concerns, and you also need to know more about how the course of your wife's illness is likely to affect you and your children. At some point, you may have to talk openly to your sons about their mother's illness so that they feel less fearful. You may also ask their pediatrician to help you in picking up early signs of stress in your children. Many psychiatrists prefer not to provide individual therapy to both members of a couple, but your wife's psychiatrist should be able to recommend a therapist who could help you.

WHEN BOTH PARTNERS ARE EMOTIONALLY ILL

So far, I have talked about family crises that have been handled by men in normal emotional health. Sometimes, however, emotional illness in one spouse can be the stress factor that contributes to emotional illness in the other, particularly if that partner has a personal history of depression. These are not common events, but they do occur, and it's important to know that other couples have been through events like these—and survived. Both partners may be obviously ill, but sometimes the illness of one is only diagnosed when the other comes forward for care and consultation. As I have discussed, the postpartum period can be a time of great vulnerability for both partners in a relationship, and especially so if one or the other has a history of emotional illness.

DAVID'S AND ROSE'S STORY

David was a 30-year-old man who had had episodes of manic depression in his early twenties. He was under a doctor's care and had been on appropriate medications off and on for five years. His depressive symptoms are affected by the seasons and tend to worsen in winter. His wife, Rose, had given birth to their first child in the month of December. At the same time that David's symptoms were becoming worse, she developed postpartum depression.

Fortunately, the baby's grandparents were frequently able to take the tiny infant to their own home so that Rose and David could have short breaks from their new responsibility. I treated both of them with antidepressant medications and supportive psychotherapy, after which they also sought conjoint marital therapy to sort out the issues that had arisen because both of them were ill at the same time.

The concurrent illness of these two young parents was an uncommon situation indeed. I have chosen to include their story as an example of practical approaches to dealing with the illness of two partners.

David's case was indeed unusual in the severity of his illness and the coincidence of a winter-related depression with his wife's postpartum depression. Two other men who responded severely to their wives' illnesses were perhaps more typical in that their reactions were extremes of the conventional emotional reactions of anger, hurt, and abandonment. The stories of these two fathers also demonstrate in their own individual ways the heartening human capacity to grow emotionally through the course of an illness and so achieve deeper maturity and fulfillment.

RON'S STORY

Ron is a trained family therapist whose wife, Barbara, is a social worker. They are an upwardly mobile couple, proud owners of a house they love. Barbara worked up until the birth of their first child, and they planned that they would hire a nanny so both parents could work full-time and pursue their careers. They are intelligent people in their 30s; both were knowledgeable about postpartum depression and in their own practices had counseled many people with this problem.

Barbara had no personal or family history of emotional illness and certainly had not expected to experience postpartum depression. However, when this developed, she was well acquainted with the symptoms and sought me out immediately. She responded very well to supportive psychotherapy and antidepressants, but her illness created a major shift in Ron's and Barbara's relationship. Ron then made an appointment to see me.

Ron felt angry and disappointed, frustrated, and guilty—and on top of this, very vulnerable and embarrassed. "I know very well how it feels to be sitting in your chair, Dr. Misri, because that's how I've conducted my whole professional life. Little did I imagine that I would someday change places in the therapist's office!"

Ron was actually ashamed that the healthy and "powerful" person he saw himself as had to admit he needed help. It took

three or four sessions for him to come to grips with the fact of
being a patient himself, and then he finally realized he must
practice what he had always preached. And there were other aspects of his professional-personal self he had to face. In looking
after Barbara, he had found that he could not offer her the help
that was needed, couldn't empathize with her, and felt distanced and remote from the whole situation. He understood
where his feelings came from but he had few resources within
himself to help him change things around.

Ron's own mother had had severe depressions during most of
the time he was growing up, and he clearly remembered that
she had been hospitalized twice. When he was 14, he came
home from visiting her in the hospital and found his father had
packed his bags, having decided he would move out for a "temporary separation." Ron's parents never got back together and
later divorced. He chose to live with his father, who he considered "the well one," but a year later he returned to live with his
mother.

So his teenage years were traumatized by several things—his
mother's constant bouts of depression, the divorce of his parents, and his sense of having been abandoned by both parents.
Ron moved out of his mother's house at an early age, took part
time jobs, put himself through university, and eventually got a
master's degree in counseling psychology.

This hardworking, determined man thought he could con-
quer his feelings of anger at the world and anger at his family by
getting himself an education and helping other people with
problems. Through treating their problems, he thought, he could
forget his own. When his wife became ill, he was completely
surprised to find flooding back to him his whole childhood experience of loss and abandonment. He had an extraordinary
fear that he would now abandon his own child, and he could
not empathize with his wife's illness because he had never
worked through his anger about his mother's depression. One of
the things Ron talked about was how poor a role model his father had been. He was also somewhat resentful that his wife—
who had come from a nurturing and loving family—had
become ill, when he himself was "the weaker one."

Despite his fearful fantasies, Ron did not intend to leave his wife and child, and he recognized that he needed to work through these old problems, incorporating the events of his childhood, if he was to move on to become a good father and a good partner. He came to see me weekly for about 20 visits, and during this process he applied himself to coming to terms with his childhood conflicts and his emotional response to his wife's condition.

BRUCE'S STORY

Bruce was a 32-year-old man who, with his wife Maureen, owned a successful recording company. By the time this couple married and later decided to have a baby, Bruce had come a long way in progressing beyond what had been a difficult up-bringing and, together, the couple had had considerable success in conquering substance abuse. When Maureen developed a postpartum depression, they saw it as the result of their past years of heavy alcohol and cocaine abuse. Throughout Maureen's depression, Bruce was very supportive. I saw them together in the course of her therapy, and I was surprised when about a year after her recovery, I had a phone call from Bruce asking if I would see him.

I had learned during his previous visits that he had been raised in a very strict religious family, where everyone was tightly controlled by his father's criticisms and harsh standards. Bruce could never do anything right. His parents constantly told him, whenever he'd done something wrong, that he would be "punished by God," and as a result, he grew up with a sense of right and wrong so concrete that for him there were no gray areas.

One positive aspect of Bruce's home life as a child was that he was able to use his musical talent as a singer in the church choir. Bruce left home right after high school and began to get jobs with various bands, eventually joining a high-profile band that toured throughout Canada and the United States. It was in this group that he met Maureen, and they formed a close rela-tionship. Maureen was already addicted to drugs, and Bruce

easily fell in with the group's culture of heavy drinking and cocaine use. For a couple of years, though they both had careers
as singers, they were otherwise quite out of touch with reality.
When one of their close friends, a fellow musician, accidentally
killed himself with a drug overdose, they began to see the dan-
gers of this lifestyle. Together, they went to a rehabilitation center and were successful in breaking their habits. They decided to
marry and return to British Columbia, where their connections
in the music world enabled them to set up a highly successful
business.

When Maureen became ill, Bruce inwardly became very
angry at the fact that she was no longer able to provide him with
the extraordinary degree of nurturing that she had provided
when she was well. In fact, he felt that given the harshness of his
upbringing, it was only through Maureen's devotion that he had
survived. At first, he had felt good about being the one in the position of caregiver, but inside, he was still an insecure little
boy—a "bad child," as his parents constantly told him.

With the birth of their baby and Maureen's illness, he became
deeply angry. All of her attention tended to focus on the baby
rather than him. As is not uncommon in a woman with depression, she was sexually remote, and he sought love and affection
in two extramarital affairs during the course of her illness. While
superficially supportive, making sure she took her medications
on time, he was actively considering "running away from
home."

He came to see me partly because of his guilt about these affairs, but largely because he was feeling a loss of control of his
life and was again overwhelmed with a sense of feeling completely loveless. His parents had died since his teenage years,
and although he'd never been close to them and resented the
way he'd been treated, he also felt grateful to them for grooming
him to become the success he was now. Fortunately for Bruce,
he was able to renew contact with a brother fifteen years his se-
nior and found in him a kind of welcoming father figure.

Bruce came to see me regularly for about four months. In
therapy, he really had to work out his sense of guilt for having let

his wife down, his extraordinary dependency on her, and his inability to be an individual who could function on his own without having to be constantly told how terrific he was—in other words, that he really could survive without a woman being "completely devoted" to him.

Bruce and Maureen have continued their singing careers, and they are now considering having a second child. I feel confident that even if she suffers another depression, the experience will be met with a better understanding from Bruce and that their passage through the second pregnancy and postpartum will be much smoother.

WHAT I TELL MY PATIENTS

Whenever I treat a woman with postpartum illness, I always involve her partner in discussions and decision making. Sometimes at the beginning, the partner may not be fully supportive of the woman's need for treatment, for some of the reasons I've outlined. I usually find, though, that once we have had an opportunity to meet and talk, the partner becomes my ally—his wife's ally, really—in her treatment plan. At the same time, these men are often in need of understanding and support themselves. Certainly, their needs cannot be met solely by their wife's psychiatrist, but I have found it a very valuable practice to say, and to reemphasize with each visit, that my door is open— that this is a place the father can also come, as an individual, if he finds himself in crisis.

Often, the father will cope extremely well with the overall crisis, only to find that some small concern is deeply troubling. For example, if the mother is hospitalized, should he bring the older children to visit her? He has nowhere else to turn for answers, and he needs someone available to discuss and clarify these issues. For the family's well-being, as well as the patient's, the psychiatrist needs to be very receptive and to make it possible for the father to feel that he can get help easily.

As a rule, men have difficulty sharing their emotions, and despite all the changes in society, little boys are still told they mustn't cry, mustn't be too emotional, must "be a man." These messages from childhood can make it more difficult for a man to get help at a time of crisis, when the boundaries of roles are thrown into question. It is understandable that men will experience a great deal of frustration, anguish, and isolation during such times.

The role of the woman's partner in her recovery cannot be underestimated, but we must also bear in mind and pay attention to the subtle and not-so-subtle signs of despair in the partner—and offer prompt and empathetic help when necessary.

PART II

GETTING PROFESSIONAL HELP

CHAPTER 9

"MAYBE I SHOULD SEE SOMEONE ABOUT THIS"

When to Get Help

For most women, the events of pregnancy, childbirth, and the postpartum period go quite smoothly. Expectant parents don't expect either physical or emotional problems to occur, and in most cases, they do not. Although the physical course of pregnancy is not always easy or comfortable, the majority of pregnancies are healthy, and while the emotional and psychological transition to parenthood is not effortless, most mothers and fathers do come to terms with their new roles. The arrival of a new baby can be temporarily exhausting and even disruptive, but most families manage to cope.

Certain combinations of events, however, can contribute to extreme emotional reactions that may progress to serious emotional disorders if untreated. My purpose in this book has been to look specifically at emotional health and illness in association with the trimesters of pregnancy and the postpartum period. I have described the contributing factors in emotional illness, and the types of emotional disorders, and I will shortly move on to the kind of treatment that can help address emotional problems. Before doing so, however, I will offer some general guidelines to help individuals decide when and if to seek professional advice. In many cases, these guidelines can be useful to all individuals who are concerned with their emotional health, whether they're male or female, pregnant or not.

SOME GUIDELINES FOR SEEKING HELP

When You Experience Specific Symptoms

There are certain kinds of physical symptoms that may indicate a physical illness—and can also signal the presence of emotional disorders. If any of the following symptoms persist you should talk with your doctor so that your condition can be properly evaluated:

- Sleeping problems: insomnia, early morning wakefulness and inability to resume sleep, restlessness throughout the night
- Feelings of exhaustion or constant fatigue
- Pounding heartbeat or irregular heartbeats
- Change in normal eating patterns, whether loss of appetite or overeating
- Shortness of breath or the feeling that you can't breathe deeply
- Sudden sweatiness
- Tingling sensation or numbness
- Dizziness
- Crushing sensation in your chest

In addition, certain emotional symptoms are commonly described by people with emotional disorders. If you experience these symptoms, you should bring them to your doctor's attention:

- Constant crying for no apparent reason
- Feelings of dread or sense of doom
- Anxiousness about things in general, or exaggerated anxiousness about minor events
- A deep feeling of helplessness or sadness
- Fear of being alone
- Preoccupation with disturbing or frightening thoughts, such as suicide or harming your baby
- Constant need to check on things or to do the same thing over and over again
- Emotional numbness; feeling remote from people you care about
- Intense negative feelings towards people you care about
- Mood swings or major change in your usual personality
- Inability to concentrate; confusion
- Feeling unable to make decisions
- Lack of sexual desire

Many people experience some of these physical or emotional symptoms to a slight degree or infrequently—and they may signal nothing other than a passing emotional state. On the other hand, even one symptom that concerns or troubles you, recurs frequently, or continues over a period of time, is an indicator that your physical or emotional condition needs attention and treatment. However, one symptom that should never be viewed lightly is having thoughts of suicide. This is an indication that you need help immediately, and you should talk with your doctor about this right away.

In pregnant or postpartum mothers, many of the physical and emotional symptoms listed can be part of the normal, expected experience. However, it's always best to discuss these as soon as possible with your doctor so that she or he can help you determine whether your symptoms are normal or whether they indicate a need for treatment.

If You Feel You Can't Cope

The inability to cope with life events isn't necessarily expressed as one recognizable symptom. Instead, you might find yourself in a general state of ambivalence towards loved ones and your life itself; more intensely, you might feel that events are out of your control, that you "just can't handle it any more." Sometimes, when people feel this way, their state of mind is evident to others—as, for example, when a new mother begins to neglect her baby. By the same token, it's important to recognize too that an inability to cope with life can indicate the presence of an emotional disorder; it can also indicate a situation in which the individual could benefit from brief counseling to address specific lifestyle problems—for example, advice on how to manage family finances. In any event, the feelings associated with inability to cope or difficulty adjusting to your situation should be discussed with your doctor.

If Past Events Still Trouble You

Some people cope very well with life's events, but continue to be bothered by old feelings of hurt or anger from their childhood or from past disappointments or crises. Sometimes, these unresolved feelings resurface later in life in the form of emotional disturbances, such as depression.

Women who are deeply troubled by past feelings in relation to their parents or their childhood might consider seeking a referral to a therapist who can help them address these issues before they undertake a pregnancy. Similarly, women who have tragically lost a baby in pregnancy or childbirth need to work through their grief before they undertake another pregnancy, and professional counselors can be of great help with this process.

If You Have a Personal History of Psychiatric Illness

Pregnancy and postpartum are times of high risk for recurrence of psychiatric problems. If a woman is currently under the care of a psychiatrist and is on medication, some careful thought needs to be given to the effects of her medication during pregnancy, a subject which I'll discuss in more detail in Chapter Eleven. In some cases, medication must be discontinued, at least for the first trimester, while alternate therapies are tried and the woman's symptoms carefully monitored.

A woman who has had a past psychiatric illness and is pregnant or considering becoming pregnant should also consult with her doctor, even if she is not on medication, since certain emotional disorders may resurface in pregnancy or postpartum. The woman, her partner, and her doctor should all be aware of her past history and be involved in monitoring her emotional state during the pregnancy. With some conditions, it might be advisable for the woman to receive prophylactic medication to prevent such a recurrence. This, too, requires careful administration of the dosage for the infant's safety.

Beyond these precautions, it should be noted that in general, emotional disorders can follow three courses during pregnancy: they can continue the same, they can become worse, and not uncommonly, they can improve. A woman with a history of psychiatric illness should not automatically assume that her illness is incompatible with pregnancy, and she should seek consultation to make her pregnancy as healthy and comfortable as possible.

If You Have a Family History of Psychiatric Illness

When serious emotional disorders occur as a first-time event in pregnancy or postpartum, they tend to do so in women with either a personal or family history of psychiatric illness. If you have a blood relative who has experienced an emotional disorder, it's best to discuss this with your doctor and partner early in your pregnancy. Your doctor will want the three of you to be involved in monitoring your emotional state and addressing any problems that may arise.

I do want to reassure all my readers that my advice should not frighten them. When I ask my patients with a personal or family history of psychiatric illness to consult their doctors, I am being cautious. The goal is that the pregnancy should proceed smoothly. In most cases it does. Nobody becomes permanently ill after childbirth. Most women lead fulfilling lives despite these short-lived episodes of illness.

If You and Your Partner Are in Conflict

As I discussed in Chapter Seven, marital problems can easily accompany emotional problems related to childbirth and postpartum. Sometimes, the resolution of these problems can begin quickly, once a couple is able to put all the issues on the table in a neutral setting. Therapists with special training in marital discord can help this process along.

WHY PEOPLE AVOID SEEKING HELP

There are common reasons why people put off getting help for something that troubles them, or seek treatment but decide to discontinue a course of therapy or not to take prescribed medications.

Wishful Thinking

When we notice a new symptom or unfamiliar discomfort, whether it's a sore throat or an episode of fatigue, it's very common to ignore it and take the approach that "maybe it will go away." Given the pressure of our lives, it's also easy to put off making a doctor's appointment for a problem that's less than dramatic. And many times this turns out to be a fairly workable approach to our personal health care.

However, with emotional problems, it's important to set some personal time limits for seeking help. It's not easy to define these time limits, just as it's not easy to define how long you should put up with recurrent headaches before you see your doctor. You may have the sense that you're anxious or sad or tearful or have difficulty concentrating for very reasonable and specific reasons—a tax bill, for instance, or a problem at work. What you should realize, though, is that when an emotional disorder is present, it rarely "goes away by itself." The longer treatment is delayed, the more serious an emotional disorder is likely to become and the more difficult it can be to treat. With that in mind, it's better to be cautious at an early stage and talk with your doctor about what's troubling you.

Fear of the "Stigma" of Emotional Illness

Popular attitudes are still quite uninformed on the subject of emotional illness. Individuals themselves may not want to admit that they have an emotional disorder, and their families, too, may have quite old-fashioned ideas about the "shame" of emotional illness. Throughout this book, I have tried to provide readers with a great deal of information about what emotional illness is and how it can be treated, with the hope of dispelling old myths.

Misunderstanding About the Nature of Emotional Illness

Some of the old attitudes towards emotional illness stem from misguided beliefs that a person with emotional problems has a weak personality, lacks will power, or has some kind of "moral defect" in her or his character. As I've discussed in the course of this book, though emotional illness has its basis in a combination of biological and psychosocial factors, *a serious emotional illness is a medical condition.* While exact causes and processes in emotional illnesses are still being researched, what is known is that biochemical imbalances in the brain can cause emotional disorders, and these imbalances can be successfully treated with medication or other therapies. Obviously, it makes little sense to attribute such a complex illness to "poor will power."

Misunderstanding and Fear of Psychiatric Treatment

Throughout the history of medicine, there have been both medical treatments and surgical methods that we now consider primitive. Certainly, until early in this century the treatment of people with emotional disorders fell into that category, being generally inhumane and misguided. Psychiatry was only formalized as a medical specialty in the 1920s. Its development as a medical discipline for treating identifiable categories of illness with established methods, based soundly in both science and psychology, has come a long way since. Recent medical discoveries have given us an expanding base of knowledge about the body's process and about appropriate means of treatment, which are today administered under consistent and highly ethical guidelines.

Nevertheless, psychiatrists have received something of a "bad press" ranging from the popular jokes about "the men in the white coats" to very inaccurate portrayals of unethical psychiatrists in popular movies. Methods of psychiatric therapy, such as the administration of psychotropic medications and modern electroconvulsive therapy, have also been misunderstood and misrepresented. I hope that in reading this book, you have come to a better understanding of what psychiatrists do and how emotional disorders are treated today.

Should you feel hesitant about accepting your doctor's referral to a psychiatrist, you should ask your family doctor to spend time with you, giving you her or his insights into how psychiatrists care for their patients. Your family doctor should also provide you with background on the particular psychiatrist to whom you are being referred.

The Experience of Other Family Members

It's not surprising to find that individuals who have watched family members suffer from a chronic emotional disorder often have mixed feelings about seeking help for their own problems. For example, a person who has seen the experience of a mother or brother with schizophrenia, receiving prolonged neuroleptic therapy, may hate the thought of having an illness which needs to be continually monitored. This can result in a kind of denial—a feeling that they don't want anything to do with emotional illness and a distancing of themselves from the possibility that they could need help.

However, psychiatric illness in a family member is an undeniable risk factor for developing emotional disorders, particularly in pregnancy and the postpartum period. It's worth pointing out that early treatment of these emotional disorders is always the best course of action. Additionally, the methods of treating even chronic emotional illness and the medications available are constantly improving. Your mother's or brother's case might have been different if, twenty years ago, they had had access to the treatments we use today.

WHY SEEK HELP FOR EMOTIONAL PROBLEMS?

The most obvious reason to seek help for painful or disruptive emotional problems during pregnancy and postpartum is that treatment is available for them; in most cases, acute symptoms can be alleviated quite quickly. A second reason is that symptoms that appear to indicate emotional disorders might instead be signs of a medical problem or quite normal consequences of the discomforts of advancing pregnancy. When your doctor evaluates your condition, she or he can also decide whether some preexisting medical condition or a medication you are taking may be contributing to symptoms of emotional distress.

In deciding whether to seek help, you should also consider the possible effects of an untreated emotional disorder on your partner, your children, a new baby, and yourself. Emotional disorders can result in behaviors that are not easy to live with—emotional distance, sleeplessness, irritability, hopelessness—and that can fuel a vicious circle of marital problems. Your children are not going to benefit from their mother's care and involvement if she is abstracted and easily upset. If you experience emotional problems in the postpartum period, you're going to find it difficult to develop a healthy bond with your new infant, let alone enjoy the pleasures of new motherhood. And finally, untreated emotional problems rarely go away. They can sometimes go underground only to resurface with later stress, particularly during a later pregnancy or postpartum. One of the doctors who studied postpartum emotional illness in the early nineteenth century observed that probably many undiagnosed women "suffered in silence." Today, when treatment is available and accessible, there is no reason for this.

HOW CAN THE PARTNER HELP?

A typical scenario in the household with a new baby has the partner or husband up at the crack of dawn, off to work promptly, and returning home late in the evening. When he arrives home, he may be greeted by a wife who has had a trying day with a young baby and—in the kind of cases described in this book—a wife who is also experiencing a psychiatric illness. This is far from an easy situation for the new father. He needs something to eat, he wants to relax at the end of a working day, and he'd like to spend some quiet time with the new baby. Under these conditions, it would be the unusual partner or spouse who could "clue in" to his wife's symptoms and concerns. How is he to know if she's spent the day crying? How is he to know if she's struggled with terrible thoughts of harming the baby? How will he figure out that she is suffering from chronic feelings of sadness and hopelessness, especially if she puts on a smile in the evening when he arrives home? As the disease progresses, however, she will no longer be able to "pretend" and her symptoms of depression slowly start to become apparent. Having been unaware of her mood, the partner is bewildered as to why she is having outbursts of rage or episodes of extraordinary irritability and anger. Shouting matches over seemingly trivial things may eventually drive him to seek help—perhaps from the family doctor, or from a neighbor, his mother-in-law, or his own mother—though these nonprofessionals may be totally at a loss to understand what is going on. I want to emphasize that the partner should not feel guilty for not having recognized symptoms sooner. Not only is this type of illness not commonly understood, but he has been busy with the demands of his working life and consequently has not been constantly in his wife's presence.

Once the illness is recognized, however, a professional person should be involved as soon as possible. It is difficult for the partner himself to sit down with his wife and try to sort out the situation. She may be totally irrational, her judgment may be quite impaired, and she may feel very angry and slighted when he suggests that she needs help. A joint visit to the family doctor would be helpful. The doctor can then determine the extent of the illness and whether the woman needs a referral to a psychiatrist or any other health care professional.

In my opinion, it is very important for the partner or spouse to be routinely involved in the woman's treatment. It is my routine—one that I feel is invaluable—to meet with both partners early in my relationship with the patient and to give them together basic educational information about the nature of the illness and the course of treatment.

After the initial hurdle of seeking help is conquered, there are various ways in which the partner can be supportive in a practical way. It is not uncommon for a woman to refuse to accept the fact that she is ill. She may throw away the medications or refuse to take them, which only prolongs the illness and delays relief of symptoms. A gentle daily inquiry as to whether she has taken her medications shows that he is concerned and involved in her treatment; a caring and loving spouse who doesn't confront but accepts and encourages can be an enormous factor in recovery.

The partner can also take an active role in either arranging for some sort of paid help in the home or organizing various kinds of practical support from family or friends. Some small relief from the endless tasks of caring for a baby can give the woman a needed break and time to recuperate. In my practice, I have had many examples of the spouse who phones to confirm his wife's appointment—showing in this way his recognition that she needs professional care and his encouragement to her in the process. Depressed patients often have memory problems, and this practical assistance can fill a real need.

Although there are many different types of therapies available, the two main types of treatments I practice are pharmacotherapy and psychotherapy. Pharmacotherapy—treatment with medications—is recommended for those in whom there is a psychiatric disorder that will respond to medication. Supportive psychotherapy, or insight-oriented psychotherapy, is explained in Chapter Ten in detail. This is generally offered to the patient in addition to pharmacotherapy when the psychiatric symptoms are cleared and she is feeling relatively stable. Most often, these two types of therapies are prescribed together.

CHAPTER 10

"WHAT SHOULD
I EXPECT?"

Approaches to Therapy

Throughout this book, I have talked about many situations in which a woman will benefit from therapy. The term "therapy" means treatment, and treatment for individual or family problems can be provided in different ways by different types of caregivers. It used to be that patients requiring treatment were expected to be passive and receptive in receiving care, to accept advice that was given, and to "follow orders." Today, we all have very different expectations about patients' participation in their own health care. Medical professionals recognize that the better informed people are about their illness, the better they can contribute to their own recovery and continued good health. Patients, for their part, have benefited from the lessons of the consumer movement. After all, they're paying for professional services, and they expect to know what they're paying for and to have a variety of choices. With better general education about health issues, people have realized that their own lifestyle choices contribute significantly to their health and well-being. They expect complete and expert information from medical professionals, and they want to be involved in decisions about their treatment.

I hope that the discussion in this chapter will help women and their families realize the range of supportive services that may be called on and feel comfortable in seeking more information about them. Usually, a woman's family doctor or a community health service can advise on what is available in her community and put her in touch with those who can help. I should also mention that formal or informal "new mothers' support groups" can provide a very meaningful setting of ad-

245

vice and shared experience for the normal challenges and stresses of new parenthood. These groups often develop from prenatal classes and bring together couples in the same community whose babies have similar due dates.

In this chapter, I will describe the roles of various health care professionals and outline general approaches to treatment. Some of the discussion will focus on the role of the psychiatrist and the various kinds of therapies that might be suggested if you were to consult a psychiatrist. You will find that the general information on selecting a psychiatrist, professional ethics, and some types of therapy can also be applied to your relationship with caregivers other than psychiatrists.

WHO CAN HELP?

Various health care professionals with specific qualifications and areas of expertise might be involved in treating a woman for emotional disorders or family problems. Sometimes, an integrated team of professionals may be involved in a woman's treatment, and different professionals might become involved at different stages of treatment or for specialized needs in the course of a treatment program. Those who engage in counseling might offer *individual therapy, therapy for couples and families, and group therapy*. Sometimes, a patient might be involved in both individual and group therapy at the same time, as I will discuss later in this chapter. Your access to these professionals depends in part on where you live, since highly specialized professionals are less likely to be available in rural communities.

Family doctors (or "general practitioners") are medical doctors who have earned a medical degree through a four- or five-year program at medical school and have been licensed by their state or province to practice medicine. Family doctors may also have additional years of concentrated training in the practice of family medicine, as well as additional training in specialized areas on which they may choose to focus. Some family doctors devote some of their time to personal, family, or marital counseling; others may prefer to send a patient for counseling to another health care professional. In either case, your family doctor is a major resource and will be considered by other health care professionals as the key person to ensure that you are receiving a coordinated treatment plan. Your family doctor is aware that your emotions are an integral part of your overall being, and family doctors are often the first to diagnose emotional illness in their patients.

Ob/gyn specialists or obstetrician/gynecologists: An obstetrician/gynecologist is a medical doctor who has received further training of usually five to six years in the field of obstetrics (the area of medicine related to pregnancy and childbirth) and gynecology (the area of medicine related to the female reproductive organs). An obstetrician may become involved in your care during either a routine or a high-risk pregnancy. Depending on the country you live in and your health care coverage, your visits to an obstetrician may or may not be limited in number. These highly trained physicians are usually attached to a maternity hospital where they perform surgeries and/or deliver babies; many of them have outpatient offices or private offices. After the delivery of the baby, it is again the family physician who plays an important role in following the welfare of the mother and the baby.

Psychiatrists are medical doctors with four or five years of additional training in the specialty of psychiatry (mental health). In many cases, they may train for several more years in a subspecialty such as child psychiatry or addiction medicine. In Canada, a doctor who practices psychiatry must be specifically licensed to do so. In the United States, specialty licensure is not always mandatory in addition to a general medical license, as long as the doctor has had some training in psychiatry. Most well-known U.S. research centers and university-affiliated departments of psychiatry employ psychiatrists who are "board certified"—who have met the special requirements of a medical specialty board. Since a psychiatrist is a medical doctor, she or he is able to prescribe medication.

Psychologists have a university degree in the subject of psychology. A bachelor's degree is granted after a four-year program, a master's degree after an additional one or two years' program, and a Ph.D. after a further specialized program of two to three years. This overall degree program varies from one university to another in terms of training offered and the time required to complete the program. Regulations vary regarding private practice for psychologists in Canada and the United States. In most places, psychologists need a Ph.D. to conduct private practice. In general the Ph.D. (or doctor of philosophy) degree can be earned in almost any field of study. Anyone with a Ph.D. is entitled to be addressed as "Doctor," yet is not a medical doctor.

Some psychologists develop highly specialized practices in areas such as counseling people with eating disorders, agoraphobia, and so on. In addition to establishing private practices, psychologists may work as consultants in hospitals, insurance companies, workers' compensation boards, large industries, and so on. A psychologist is not a medical doctor and cannot prescribe medication.

Nurses have earned either a diploma at a school of nursing or a degree in nursing from a university. They, too, can earn degrees at the bachelor's, master's, or Ph.D. levels. Some nurses with master's degrees work in an area of specialized interest, such as counseling women with premenstrual syndrome or patients who have been sexually abused. Many work as "nurse-clinicians" in a hospital setting; other nurses with bachelor's or master's degrees work as administrators or in affiliation with government agencies, pharmaceutical companies, or large corporations. Nurses play an extremely important role in community health programs, where they may be the most accessible point of contact for a new mother seeking advice on infant care and emotional well-being.

In the treatment of emotional disorders, trained psychiatric nurse-clinicians might be involved in providing ongoing counseling and psychotherapy to patients who have first been assessed by a psychiatrist.

Social workers have earned university degrees at the bachelor's, master's, or Ph.D. level. The field of social work is concerned primarily with the integration of the individual into a healthy social unit, and social workers have an important role to play in a wide variety of areas which intersect with family health. Social workers are affiliated with government agencies, welfare departments, public health units, residential treatment programs, school systems, and hospitals; they may also have private counseling practices.

Occupational therapists have a university degree and three to four years of training in a recognized occupational therapy program. Occupational therapy is concerned with helping patients achieve personal balance and self-understanding through participation in such structured activities as handicrafts and building simple things. Occupational therapists are usually attached to hospitals and work mostly in inpatient psychiatric and medical wards. Some may have a private practice, depending on their area of expertise.

All of these health care professionals might also occupy teaching or research positions. They may combine teaching, research, and private practice during their professional lives.

Attitudes Towards Health Care Professionals

Depending on their personal experience and educational background, different patients might have distinct preferences for certain types of health care professionals. Sometimes, their preferences are based on attitudes resulting from lack of accurate knowledge. For example, some patients might be willing to consult a psychologist rather than a psychiatrist. It might be that to them, "seeing a psychiatrist" equates with "severe illness" while "seeing a psychologist" equates with "mild illness." Similarly, they may feel negatively toward seeing a psychiatrist, because they associate psychiatrists, but not psychologists, with "hospitalization." When unclear assumptions interfere with a suggested course of treatment, it's probably a good time to discuss attitudes openly with one's family doctor.

PSYCHOTHERAPY

What Is Psychotherapy?

Psychotherapy is a treatment in which a therapist attempts to provide a new interpersonal experience to a patient. The aim of any psychotherapy is to achieve certain goals through verbal and nonverbal exchanges. The key goals of psychotherapy, whether individual or group therapy, are:

- to alleviate psychological distress
- to bring about changes in maladaptive behavior
- to encourage personal growth

Before I go into further detail, let me first explain how psychotherapy works. There are several methods of psychotherapy used in the practice of psychiatry. This chapter can hardly describe all the modalities, but I will focus mainly on *psychodynamic psychotherapy*. The other major types of psychotherapy include behavior psychotherapy and supportive psychotherapy, which are also used as psychological treatment. Behavior therapy aims toward changing behaviors while supportive therapy offers emotional support. Psychodynamic psychotherapy basically emphasizes understanding of oneself while behavior psychotherapy is more task-oriented. Behavior psychotherapy does not aim to develop any insights into the patient's behavior or personality but uses instead techniques that provide relief of symptoms to the patient.

In reality, no form of therapy is rigid in following one theoretical model. Rather, a mixture of different types of techniques are used depending on the personality of the therapist, her or his individual style, and the needs of the individual patient.

Psychodynamic Psychotherapy

In my office, I practice two types of psychotherapy: *supportive psychotherapy* and *insight-oriented (or explorative) psychotherapy*. Supportive psychotherapy aims to alleviate symptoms and distress that have become apparent as a specific emotional disorder and sometimes can be identified as having been triggered by a specific event. For example, let's say that Susan is depressed and suffering from a grief reaction. She would then receive specific therapy aimed at examining issues connected to her grief. Many of the patients you have met in my stories have received supportive psychotherapy to address specific disorders or to help them grow positively beyond a certain life crisis. Supportive psychotherapy tends to be needed for a relatively short duration—several months up to two years—although counseling may be resumed at a later time, if the patient again faces similar problems. For many types of emotional disorders, supportive psychotherapy is used in conjunction with medication.

Insight-oriented psychotherapy (or *psychodynamic psychotherapy*) tends to be a longer-term process that is used to address deep-seated and ongoing emotional disturbances. Patients who are involved in insight-oriented psychotherapy may or may not have an obvious emotional disorder but are deeply troubled by unresolved feelings that affect their self-esteem and relationships. For example, a father who is extraordinarily strict and punishing to his teenaged son may not be able to understand when his wife points out to him that his anger is quite out of proportion to the son's behavior. The father's anger might originate with his feelings towards his own father, who treated him in this same strict, punishing way when he was a teenager.

In describing these two broad approaches to psychotherapy, I don't mean to suggest that there is a black-and-white distinction between the two. A patient may require supportive therapy to move beyond a specific crisis and then may find that she would like to continue, through insight-oriented psychotherapy, to pursue some of the emotional and psychological issues that arose in discussions. However, it's worth noting that some people's stereotype of psychotherapy is the process that I have defined as insight-oriented psychotherapy.

How Does Psychotherapy Help?

Psychotherapy helps in many different ways through a process in which the patient and the therapist work together in specific ways that ultimately result in restoring the health of the patient. The therapist offers an attentive, sincere, reliable presence, and patients who come for treatment come with the hope that the therapist has the capability in a benevolent way to alleviate their symptoms. This hope and trust underlies the majority of doctor-patient relationships in most areas of medicine.

As children, we are dependent on parents and other older adults to give us care, love, and nurturing; they also alleviate our fears and pain. This learned expectation of help is reactivated in different situations as we become adults ourselves and particularly when we consult with health care professionals. Those who have not learned as children to trust an adult or an older person in this manner and have been deprived of love and nurturing in their early infancy will obviously have problems relating to other adults. Much of their life will be spent being angry and suspicious of other human beings. In this situation, the role of a psychotherapist is to offer a different perspective in this person's life and, through therapy, help the individual overcome these conflicts.

Sometimes this self-improvement happens when the patient identifies with the therapist in a positive way and has a positive attitude towards the therapist as she or he did towards parents or teachers. A patient who has been self-critical all of his or her life can now identify with the tolerance of the therapist and gain the ability to be more flexible and less perfectionistic. Also, the patient learns in the therapist's office that she or he can discuss feelings or attitudes that have been forbidden, experiences that have been traumatic, and also situations in which he or she has felt punished, judged, or reprimanded. Developing a confiding, trusting, emotional relationship with a therapist is a considerable achievement for many inhibited people, and can then serve as a model for developing other satisfying relationships with other adults. As I will discuss, the therapy is safe when sessions have clear boundaries in time and space, and when the therapist is trained, professional, and reassuring.

Though psychotherapy cannot alter the existing problems of a patient, it can enhance self-respect and self-acceptance so that the patient can cope more effectively with the present environment. Sigmund Freud, who was born in 1856 and died in 1939, is generally acknowledged to be a major figure in the development of psychotherapeutic concepts. His assumption that our present is shaped by and is based on our experiences from the past still continues to be the key concept in many psychotherapeutic approaches.

Most psychodynamic theories focus on childhood, especially early childhood experiences, in an attempt to understand the psychological health of a person. This does not mean that invariably childhood trauma is responsible for psychiatric illness a person may have in adult life. Nonetheless, children do learn to experience pleasure, pain, and so on, within the context of a family and slowly develop personality traits, a sense of self, and what they expect from others.

Another central theme to psychodynamic or insight-oriented therapy (terms that will be used interchangeably) is the resolution of conflict. By conflict we mean basically two opposing forces that cannot be reconciled and that produce a lot of psychological turmoil in a person's mind. People who are seeking psychiatric treatment are generally enmeshed in conflict in many ways, and the battle of these opposing forces consumes a tremendous amount of energy, leaving the individual quite distraught and incapable of functioning effectively. Some of these conflicts can get internalized and produce pain or depression, and in certain specific types of depression psychotherapy is a very effective means of treating this pain. One of my patients who was distressed about her marriage had a conflict about the marriage based on her feelings towards the marriage of her parents. Her mother had been married three times, and my patient felt a tendency to "run away" from problems in her marriage, just as her mother had seemed to do. She eventually realized that running away from problems was something she had learned early in her life. She also realized that as an adult, she had choices and could in effect carve out her own destiny and confront rather than run away from her problems.

People who practice psychodynamic psychotherapy must first gather a fair amount of information about their patients' present situation, their past experiences, their relationships with important people, and how they have behaved in a variety of different situations. As sessions proceed, the patient generally brings up these issues in the safe surroundings and reassuring environment that the psychiatrist is careful to cultivate. As discussed earlier, the patient's relationship with the psychiatrist is a very powerful tool; since patients bring into therapy the same set of unconscious conflicts and style of relating and dealing with other people as they employ elsewhere in their lives, they invariably recreate many of their psychological patterns in therapy. The two most important goals of psychotherapy are interpreting these patterns in a way that does not produce further trauma and putting these patterns and behaviors into perspective.

The Bio/psycho/social Perspective to Therapy

Health care professionals today conduct therapy with three factors in mind, an approach called the bio/psycho/social perspective, which treats the whole person. Before a treatment plan can begin, the psychiatrist needs to learn who this person is biologically, and this involves assessing the medical, physical, and genetic state of the patient. Does she have a predisposition to certain physical illness, for example, high blood pressure, heart disease, diabetes? Is she on medications? Has she inherited any medical illnesses from family members, espeically her parents? Are there ongoing medical or surgical problems that contribute to her present emotional state? For example, is this woman with postpartum depression someone who had a C-section delivery from which she is still recovering, or did she have a normal vaginal delivery and then develop complications of episiotomy?

Psychologically, what does the patient's personality profile seem to suggest? Is this person highly dependent? passive-aggressive? histrionic? Does she tend to be withdrawn and antisocial? How would she be likely to handle crisis, including a psychiatric illness? Perhaps she is at high risk for psychiatric illness but has been able to cope well with stressful situations because of her personality structure. For example, people who are extremely perfectionistic to a point almost of obsession tend to cope well with settled situations but very poorly when faced with a change. Moving to a new city or taking on a new job may seem extremely daunting to a person who has a well-established morning routine for leaving the house at a certain time, following a certain route, and getting to work precisely on time. The person with obsessional personality traits will find coping with change more overwhelming than will a person who does not have these personality traits.

When I look at a patient's social context, I must consider whether she is married, in a relationship, or on her own. Does she have any kind of help with her pregnancy or postpartum condition? What kind of background does she have? What was her childhood like, especially in terms of the kind of mothering she received and the kind of role model her mother provides? Does she generally feel good about herself? Is her sense of identity or self-esteem acceptable to her?

All these factors have gone into shaping the person into the individual patient who has come for treatment. Every therapist, no matter what his or her background, has to look at the person in this holistic way—not just focus on his sprained ankle, or her depression, or a marital breakup, without taking into account who the person with a depression, or sprained ankle, or broken heart is. This perspective leads to a treatment or therapy that not only addresses the immediate call for help, but considers the impact of this illness in the individual's life and assesses the long-term outcome of planned treatment.

WHAT GOES ON IN A PSYCHIATRIST'S OFFICE?

Patients Have a Choice

Doctors rarely think in terms of choosing or not choosing to see a particular patient. After all, they have taken the Hippocratic oath and accepted it as their duty to see any patient who arrives for treatment, regardless of sex, ethnic background, gender orientation, and so on. On the other hand, patients have a great deal of choice these days. You can decide whether or not you want to see a particular doctor. Once you begin treatment, you can decide whether or not you want to return to this doctor. Even at an early stage, when the doctor is still a complete stranger to you, you need to feel absolutely sure that you can talk to and trust this person.

What Should You Look For in a Psychiatrist?

Most often, it is the patient's family doctor who suggests a particular psychiatrist. In deciding whether to see, and then continue in therapy with, this psychiatrist, you'll need to decide whether he or she has the expertise that is required and, almost more important, whether you feel there is enough rapport between you and this individual.

You can begin by getting some basic information from your family doctor: Where did the psychiatrist train? Does she or he have additional specialized training in the area of your concern? How long has the psychiatrist worked in your community? The answers to these questions, as well as your family doctor's experience in working with this person, will offer you some guidelines.

Other information, which your family doctor can provide, will help you begin to assess whether this particular psychiatrist is someone who can understand your values, someone with whom you can expect to establish a sense of trust. Is this doctor a male or a female? How old is the doctor? This is not to say that a psychiatrist must be your age and your sex. However, different patients have individual comfort levels, and personal attitudes need to be taken into account. Consulting a psychiatrist, after all, is not as straightforward as having a broken leg set. In the course of your therapy you will be opening your innermost, perhaps darkest, thoughts and feelings to this person.

On the other hand, in selecting a psychiatrist you're not choosing a personal friend. Some people feel more comfortable with the idea that they are talking with a stranger—a professional person whose job it is to help them, rather than a friend whose time and good will they may be imposing on. Certainly this is true of the professional nature of the relationship, but there must be a basis for a frank and empathetic exchange between the two of you.

Is the "Chemistry" Right?

In individual supportive or insight-oriented psychotherapy, the rapport between patient and therapist is of crucial importance. Whether this "chemistry" exists or not will be evident in the first few visits—in fact, researchers in this area believe that it will be evident in the first session. What goes into the chemistry is not easily definable and has to do with both the psychiatrist's and patient's personalities. The patient may feel uncomfortable about a certain kind of doctor—a 40-year-old woman, recently postpartum, may feel uncomfortable with a male therapist ten years her junior who has never been a father. The psychiatrist in turn may have reactions to specific types of personalities that may make it unworkable for him or her to treat these patients with certain kinds of disorders.

If a decision is made that the "chemistry" is not right, this is more often a decision made by the patient rather than by the psychiatrist. However, the psychiatrist will be deciding in your first meeting whether your illness actually requires a psychiatrist's care and whether he or she is the appropriate therapist to treat you. In some cases, it may seem probable that other trained therapists such as psychologists or social workers might be better matched to your needs. In addition, a psychiatrist may feel that if psychiatric care is indeed called for, a colleague who has undergone specialized training may be a better choice.

The first interviews, then, will establish whether the psychiatrist's services are needed and, if so, whether a relationship of mutual trust can be developed. Once these become clear, the therapy develops in a four-part sequence:

- Establishing a structure
- Developing a therapeutic relationship
- Working through emotions
- Terminating therapy

Establishing a Structure

At the first interview, the psychiatrist and patient need to contract together on a structure for their professional relationship. The "ground rules" need to be discussed frankly and agreed to by both parties. First of all, payment for professional services needs to be clarified. In most parts of Canada and the United States, fees for medical doctors are covered by insurance plans, and the services of a psychiatrist qualify for insurance coverage. Sometimes, the fees for a counseling psychologist who has a Ph.D. degree will also be covered. On the other hand, a patient may wish to or be required to pay privately.

Secondly, the doctor needs to estimate the possible number of visits the patient may require and the amount of time that will be spent on each session. The doctor will also outline his or her policy in regard to appointments—how much notice is required for a cancellation and whether a fee will be charged if the patient does not provide sufficient notice. This is not simply a bureaucratic rule; other patients may be waiting for appointments with this doctor and, with enough notice, could be contacted to take the cancelled appointment.

IN MY OWN PRACTICE: A TYPICAL TREATMENT PLAN FOR POSTPARTUM DEPRESSION

The general treatment program a psychiatrist describes at the first visit of course depends on a number of things—the type of illness, the seriousness of the patient's condition, as well as the factors I discussed in the section on the bio/psycho/social perspective. As an example relevant to the issues in this book, let me describe how a patient with postpartum depression might be treated.

At the initial interview, there are three general possibilities to be examined. First, the woman might be severely ill and obviously require immediate hospitalization. Second, her condition may be treatable on an outpatient basis. Third, the particular expertise of a psychiatrist might not be required, in which case I might suggest that she see a psychologist or nurse-clinician or other available trained therapists.

Let's assume that this woman can be treated on an outpatient basis. After the initial assessment, I would plan to see her weekly for the first six weeks. During these early weeks, the focus is on the woman's psychiatric condition and how that affects her family. She must be followed closely because I want to ensure that her condition does not become worse, and that, if it was decided not to start her on a medication, this continues to be the correct decision.

Also during these first few weeks, I want to interview the husband and other significant members of the family if they are involved. It's important to take time with these family members, particularly the woman's partner, to be sure that they understand the woman's illness, the treatment that is planned, and the likely duration and outcome of the illness. As I discuss in Chapter Eight, the woman's partner can feel very overlooked in this process, and he must be allowed to discuss his feelings and the situation he is coping with. Giving him the support he needs so that he is supportive of the patient is important both for his well-being and for the woman's recovery.

Once her condition has stabilized, I would want to see her once a month for the next three months, then every two months for the next six months—to assess her condition and the appropriateness of any antidepressant medication she may be taking. All of this assumes that the patient herself is comfortable with the time intervals; if she is not, we undertake to make a more congenial schedule. All together, the therapy for a postpartum depression usually lasts a year to eighteen months when a patient is referred to me.

In describing treatment for postpartum depression as an example of the use of individual psychotherapy, I want to point out that, as a rule, women with postpartum illness are not patients who are likely to become dependent on their psychiatrists. They have experienced a specific emotional illness, and they are very eager to become healthy again and get back to their lives, their partners, their infants. The concrete plan just described covers several issues: the type of treatment offered, approximate number of visits, and most importantly, the fact that a patient chooses to see me for therapy voluntarily and feels she or he can talk to me within the safe environment of my office.

Developing a Therapeutic Relationship

Patients can reflect on other positive relationships in their lives as models for what goes into making a good relationship—a comfortable feeling of familiarity and mutual understanding, a level of trust that allows you to count on someone, a satisfaction in working towards something together, and a sense of recognizing something new about yourself as you look at situations from another's viewpoint. These elements of regular interpersonal relationship have some things in common with the relationship between a therapist and patient.

The basis for the patient-therapist relationship, however, is mutual work toward the patient's recovery. The relationship has a specific assignment and operates within certain boundaries. Both the patient and psychiatrist need to be aware that if the boundaries are violated, the relationship can become dysfunctional. Both parties in the relationship have the potential to violate boundaries, and they must both be aware of their responsibilities.

Fromthe psychiatrist's point of view, the doctor-patient relationship is a sacred cornerstone of the doctor's professional ethics and of the successful outcome of therapy. The patient must feel that she can trust her doctor, that she is "safe" in the doctor's care. The doctor earns and maintains that trust in a number of ways—staying informed about current research so that optimum treatment can be offered, keeping the patient's private information strictly confidential, being ethical about drug therapy, and so on. Abuses of trust along these lines would not only endanger the patient's therapy, but would also be viewed very seriously as unprofessional behavior by medical bodies that monitor doctors' professional behavior.

The patient can abuse the relationship of trust in a number of ways—not turning up for appointments, not paying the doctor, phoning the doctor outside office hours about things that are not emergencies, and so on. In addition, for psychiatrists in particular there are safety issues in regard to abuse or violence they might encounter from patients who come to them with severe psychosis.

In regard to patients' safety, I hope I need hardly clarify that a sexual relationship between a therapist and patient is strictly unethical. This is a professional taboo that should just not happen. The movie *The Prince of Tides* quite glamourously portrayed an intimate relationship between a female psychiatrist and a troubled man who was the brother of one of the psychiatrist's very ill patients. Most psychiatrists would consider this relationship questionable insofar as it compromised the psychiatrist's ability to treat her patient, the man's sister, with objectivity and without conflicting loyalties. While patients and doctors can both be vulnerable to acting out mutual attractions, the doctor should indeed know better. Patients should not be or feel exploited in any way by their doctors.

Two Useful Concepts—Transference and Resistance

Psychotherapy happens within the therapeutic relationship of psychiatrist and patient. Individuals learn how to form relationships with others through the experience of their earliest relationships in infancy and childhood. These early relationships with parents or other primary caregivers form a pattern that individuals repeat in different relationships throughout their lives. They tend to *transfer* feelings from old relationships into new relationships, particularly if the new relationship has elements that were present in the first relationship with parents— for example, caregiving, teaching, disciplining. It's common, then, for individuals to have strong *transference* reactions in relationships with teachers, bosses, lovers, doctors, therapists. Most often, these feelings and reactions are unconscious and the individual is not aware, for example, that his dislike for a particular boss stems from an old negative feeling towards his father.

The safe environment of psychotherapy sessions allows patients to express their feelings, and in the course of the therapeutic relationship, the patient's feelings of transference will inevitably be expressed. The therapist can then help the patient realize the distortion that has been placed on the doctor-patient relationship. This becomes a "real-life" example of how the patient approaches other relationships in their lives, and the insight gained by the patient can have a powerful therapeutic effect.

The therapist, too, can bring feelings from an old relationship into a therapeutic relationship with a patient. These feelings of *countertransference*, which are for the most part unconscious, can in the therapeutic setting interfere with the therapist's ability to treat a patient. To understand this, therapists in training often receive specific guidance, under the supervision of an experienced psychotherapist, to recognize their own responses of countertransference.

Patients who come for therapy are in emotional distress and want to get help. Usually, this means that they want to cooperate with their therapist in their treatment and eventual recovery. However, the prospect of change can be deeply troubling. Psychotherapy offers the possibility of change in interpersonal relationships and insight into feelings, and in the course of psychotherapy, the patient will look at existing patterns of behavior and look at real feelings and attitudes. People with emotional distress have often created a personal "safety zone" to hide their real feelings from both others and themselves. They have often invested a lot of their energy, throughout their lives, in avoiding any more pain than they already have to bear. They might forget or overlook or deny what has really hurt them. They might involve themselves only in the kinds of relationships that offer no possibility for any further hurt. One of my patients, for example, came from a family with a father who had never held a job for more than a year or two at a time, and she recalls vividly the distressing times the family had because of lack of money. One of the main reasons she married her husband, a dentist who could offer her stable financial security, was to avoid the hurt, anger, and fear she felt as a child growing up in a household where lack of money was the key issue.

The process of keeping a distance from significant issues is called *resistance*, and it can take many forms. In the psychotherapeutic relationship, the patient might do things like cancel or show up late for appointments, try to use up appointment time in trivial conversation, or "forget" to bring up important things related to what's being discussed. If the real reasons for this kind of behavior are not addressed by the therapist, the therapy can be undermined. However, once addressed, the ways in which the patient expresses resistance can be illuminating because these behaviors illustrate how the patient expresses resistance in other relationships in her life.

IN MY OWN PRACTICE: DEVELOPING A THERAPEUTIC RELATIONSHIP

Generally speaking, psychiatrists do not believe in disclosing information about their personal lives to their patients. However, some psychiatrists may feel comfortable in letting the patient know to some extent "who they are" by the setting in which they see the patient. Consequently, their offices might reflect who they are as individuals.

Because of the kind of patients I see, it's often the case that patients want to know if I have children and if, when they talk about being pregnant, I understand what they are experiencing. Certainly, I don't feel that having had children is a prerequisite for a psychiatrist treating pregnant or postpartum patients—it is simply a matter of some individuals finding comfort and feeling reassured that the therapist feels empathy for their situation.

In my own office, I have pictures, plants, artwork, and as often as possible, fresh flowers. I feel that these details make the office atmosphere pleasant, give a sense of color and life, and contribute to the patients' comfort when they come to see me. Of course, one needn't put things on the wall that tell the psychiatrist's life history the moment the patient walks in. On the other hand, why have empty white walls and a space that suggests no friendliness? I think it would be more difficult for patients to talk about themselves in such a sterile environment.

I find that most of my patients have chosen to see me because of my particular expertise in the area of psychiatric illness related to reproductive events. I cannot deny the fact that many women patients feel less intimidated in discussing their intimate obstetrical or psychological problems with me because of my gender. In fact, many women patients specifically request a woman psychiatrist in this particular subspecialty.

For some patients, the ethnic background of the psychiatrist may be important. This can be an issue for some patients if they feel that someone of an obviously different background will be unable to understand their lifestyle, their religious beliefs, and so on. In fact, my bicultural background has turned out to be an added bonus in treating and understanding my patients. The fact that I was born in India and raised there for a number of years provides one viewpoint, and the fact that I have lived half my life in Canada has given me another. Coming as I do from two points of view, enables me, I hope, to be open, understanding, and accepting of people of different cultural backgrounds.

As for the trust that is an essential part in the relationship between therapist and patient, I think the initial expectation one communicates about trust is significant. I don't see a great deal of value in rigid rules about missed and canceled appointments. I expect my patients to understand that my appointment calendar is important—for them and for women like them who are waiting to receive help. I trust my patients at the outset, and I

haven't been disappointed in taking this approach. Some patients miss an appointment because their delivery date changes;
some because a baby-sitter does not turn up; at other times, a
new baby may fall sick. On the other hand, if a missed appointment symbolizes manipulation, resistance, or acting out behavior, then I personally call the patient to discuss how we should
proceed in therapy.

Working Through Emotions

The psychotherapeutic techniques used by psychiatrists or psychologists involve listening to the patient in an empathetic manner, accepting what the patient says in a nonjudgmental way, asking questions
that will help the patient clarify issues, and interpreting what the patient is disclosing. Through interpretation, the patient gains insight
into why she may be behaving in a certain way or showing persistence
symptoms. These are the basic principles in the process of what we
called *working through* emotions. Typically, the patient brings up different areas of conflict while the therapist listens. Not only does the patient use words to describe her feelings; she also gives clues to her
thinking by her nonverbal gestures and behavior. After learning about
a certain event, let's say about a traumatic birth or delivery, the psychiatrist listens, makes notes in her or his own mind, and tries to offer
support where it is needed and/or interpret what the patient is saying.
Interpretation connects thoughts and feelings and gives the patient
some clues about her current maladaptive behavior. Through interpretation, the patient is able to think about her unconscious, repressed
feelings from the past. This process increases the awareness of the patient and brings about change and cure. Thus working through is a
complex process that involves memories from the past, current life
situations, and the therapeutic relationship itself. It is hard work because even when a patient becomes aware of a new piece of information about herself, integrating it into her day-to-day life is not an
easy task.

To see working through in action, let me describe the process as it
unfolded with one patient. I have been seeing Josie, who just had her
first child over a year ago. She told me how she was distressed about a
neighbor who she described as "nosy" and "interfering." At first, it appeared to me that the whole issue of her neighbor was quite insignifi-

cant, but when it was repeatedly raised in our sessions it was obvious that her feelings about the neighbor needed more exploration. In talking about Josie's past, we touched upon the issue of her having been an only child. Her mother was extraordinarily protective and never allowed Josie to play with the neighborhood children. Until we talked about this, Josie had not realized the impact this had had on her. She had viewed this friendly neighbor, who looked forward to another baby in the neighborhood to play with her own child, as being meddlesome. When she understood where her feelings of discomfort came from, she was able to relate to the neighbor in a more open way and feel less threatened by her.

The ultimate goal of working through is to offer patients corrective emotional experience so that they are able to perceive events and circumstances in their life in a more positive, constructive way. The events and circumstances have not altered, but the patient's perception of them has changed from an unhealthy view that caused the patient to be dysfunctional to one that he or she can "live with." The process of working through helps patients perceive things differently and integrate their responses and emotions into their personality and behavior. Through this process, a patient's journey into the future will likely be free of the same kind of conflicts and will be subject to less psychological disturbance.

IN MY OWN PRACTICE: WORKING THROUGH

I believe in taking an eclectic approach to therapy. Sometimes I have to offer advice or engage in insight-oriented therapy; at other times, I may have to treat the patient with medications. My personal feeling is that when a patient is very severely disturbed, it is not appropriate to explore deep unconscious material that the patient may bring up. The patient's condition is itself a source of anxiety, and I believe that the patient must be stabilized—by supportive psychotherapy and/or medications—before deeply disturbing issues are considered. Once the patient's condition has stabilized, I give the patient the choice of looking into issues from the past that she has carried with her for a number of years, such as unresolved grief for her mother, or concentrating on day-to-day issues.

For the most part, the patients I see are coming to me because they have had problems related to pregnancy or postpartum. In fact, many of them have been completely healthy and are experiencing psychological turmoil only because of the events of pregnancy or childbirth. A number of patients I have treated for psychosis after the birth of a child have resumed their lives quite well after the episode—without becoming involved in insight-oriented psychotherapy at all. In these cases, as the patient recovers we spend time talking about readjusting to life and reintegrating socially after the episode of illness—which is a big task for patients who have had this illness. As we have seen, a psychotic break is a break from reality, a break from relatives, friends, and loved ones. Once the patient recovers psychologically, she often fears that society will not accept her again, that her family may view her differently, that her friends may think she is "mad." These are some of the issues a woman recovering from psychotic illness will face.

Some of my patients who have had several episodes of depression after the birth of each of their children choose to be treated with antidepressants until their symptoms disappear and do not become involved in long-term psychotherapy. On the other hand, I have also had patients ask to continue in therapy because they want to explore, for example, a history of sexual abuse or marital problems. When patients have expressed the wish to explore further, I will continue to see them in therapy, but we begin to look at unresolved issues from the past only when their depressive illness has stabilized.

Terminating Therapy

Typically, patients are fearful at the prospect of losing the therapist. The therapist has become a very important person in their lives and has occupied a special place in helping them recover. For some patients, the experience has been something of a luxurious one—going once a week or month to talk about oneself to someone who is absorbed in listening to you and committed to your recovery. Thus, even when the patient's recovery has signaled the end of therapy, it is often difficult to deal with the loss of this very special type of interpersonal relationship.

Patients have different needs in regard to the termination of therapy. Some patients who are more dependent may feel a tremendous "separation anxiety" about the loss of the therapist, and they may need several sessions devoted simply to talking about the termination process itself. For others, the process is less painful. As the termination of therapy approaches, many therapists will space appointments at increasingly longer intervals. This gives patients the opportunity to build their own coping skills, without frequent meetings with the therapist.

IN MY OWN PRACTICE: TERMINATION OF THERAPY

When patients terminate therapy with me, I emphasize to them that they can always return, that I am always available to them if they experience some crisis in their life and feel they would benefit from seeing me again. Indeed, some patients I first saw 15 years ago with postpartum illnesses are now returning to see me with problems related to menopause. Often the therapy they need is very short-term since they have previously been through exploratory psychotherapy.

And of course, some patients terminate therapy and never again have a need for psychiatric help.

The process of terminating therapy varies from individual to individual. In any event, the shift from a short-term therapy aimed at relieving symptoms to a longer-term insight-oriented therapy would be a matter of contracting between the psychiatrist and the patient. If a patient wants to continue in therapy, the two again go through a process of developing a structure and setting ground rules for the new phase of therapy.

GROUP PSYCHOTHERAPY

What Is Group Psychotherapy?

Group psychotherapy is the application of the methods of psychotherapy to a number of individuals in a group setting. The goals of group psychotherapy are similar to those outlined as the goals of individual psychotherapy: to alleviate psychological distress, to bring about changes in maladaptive behavior, and to encourage personal growth. The aim of group psychotherapy is to help patients experience relief of

symptoms and to bring about changes in their personality and behavior that will make interpersonal relationships easier. The group setting provides socialization to the members so that they realize they are
all on common ground, that they have common problems, and that
they can interact to solve these problems. The group experience also
provides education in the nature of the illness, the effects of medications, and preventive measures to avoid recurrence of the illness.

Many of the factors I've discussed in relation to individual psychotherapy also apply, in a slightly different way, to group psychotherapy.

How Effective Is Group Psychotherapy?

Group psychotherapy is widely practiced across North America, and
many researchers believe that it is at least as effective as individual
psychotherapy, if not more effective in some cases. Sometimes, people
receive both individual and group psychotherapy at the same time; for
example, a person in individual therapy may also attend a group on a
weekly basis.

Group psychotherapy is also very cost effective since one (or sometimes two) therapists can provide treatment to a number of people at
the same time. Many health care insurance plans limit the number of
individual psychotherapy sessions that will be paid for; since group sessions cost less, it's usual that insurable group therapy can extend for a
longer time. Group therapy is also cost effective in terms of physical
resources of hospital or clinic space.

The effectiveness of group therapy is confirmed by its popularity
and the number of specialized groups that have formed to address very
specialized problems—for example, Parents Without Partners,
Overeaters Anonymous, and the postpartum support groups we'll discuss in this chapter.

Types of Group Therapy

Therapy groups can function for both inpatients and outpatients and
are of several different types. The types of outpatient groups are:

- Groups organized by a psychiatrist in private practice or in a psychiatric clinic. Group members may be patients with a similar
  disorder, such as obsessive-compulsive disorder. Usually these

kinds of groups meet weekly, and a patient might participate for up to a year.

- Groups organized under the auspices of a psychiatric medication clinic. The patient might drop in weekly or monthly and attend indefinitely. Group members typically receive similar medication, and their groups are organized to explore issues around their disorders, the taking of medication, lifestyle adjustments, and so on.
- Behavioral group therapy focused around behavioral problems such as eating disorders. Usually group members participate for about six months.
- Groups organized by substance abuse treatment centers for members who are alcoholics, drug addicts, and so on. These groups might meet as often as once a day, and participation may go on indefinitely.
- Groups of patients with special medical conditions, such as diabetes or cancer. These groups offer mutual support and person-to-person education about how to live with the condition. Participation may go on indefinitely.
- Counseling groups to help members cope with bereavement and loss. The usual duration of participation is about six months.

Characteristics of Outpatient Group Therapies

Outpatient therapy groups are usually conducted by a therapist at a psychiatric clinic or hospital. Usually, patients have joined the group on a voluntary basis. Their family doctor or other health care professionals might recommend the group, or they might have heard about the group from friends. Groups are focused around a homogenous group of people in terms of their signs and symptoms—for example, postpartum disorders, premenstrual syndrome, menopause, eating disorders, and so on. Most types of groups meet once or twice a week.

How Does Group Psychotherapy Work?

As with individual psychotherapy, group psychotherapy is conducted by a professional therapist, such as a psychiatrist or psychologist with additional specialized training in group processes. Group psychotherapy utilizes and depends on a powerful therapeutic tool—the group setting itself. The interpersonal interactions that go on between members of the group are a key to the change that the therapist seeks to bring about in group members.

The way group members interact with one another gives insight into each person's quality of life and the way each relates to others. The personality and patterns of behavior of each individual are the result of early interactions with other human beings, particularly family members the person interacted with as a child. When interpersonal relationships are distorted, they can bring about psychological distress. The trained therapist can see where these distortions occur and can guide the group to help the individual realize the impact of their dysfunctional behaviors and the alternative behaviors they could use instead.

The sense of isolation, anonymity, and fragmentation engendered by our modern society can be extremely disruptive. The group setting provides a supportive environment from which members can draw strength. In a group setting, members can develop a sense of identity and belonging—the very core and root of every human developmental experience.

How Group Psychotherapy Achieves Results

A prominent American psychiatrist, Dr. Irvin W. Yalom, has devoted most of his professional life to the subject of group psychotherapy (see Vinogradov and Yalom, 1991). In the course of his research into how successful groups work, he has developed a list of eleven mechanisms by which groups achieve therapeutic results. These are:

1. *Instillation of hope:* Whenever a patient begins a course of therapy—even, for example, treatment for high blood pressure—there is a natural hopeful feeling that there is a path to recovery. In group therapies, this possibility for recovery is demonstrated as group members observe each other. Patients naturally make progress at different rates, and seeing improvement in others confirms the hope that continued treatment will result in a positive outcome.

2. *Universality:* Many people with emotional disorders feel that their particular situation is unique and that there is no one they can talk to who will have any understanding of their problem. The isolation of individuals in modern society contributes to this feeling; and patients may also have felt that they need to hide their problems and concerns. Patients who

participate in group therapy almost immediately feel a great sense of relief to learn that here is a group of people like themselves who do, in fact, have very similar problems and can talk to each other about them.

3. *Imparting of information:* In certain kinds of groups, factual information about the particular medical or behavioral condition is one aspect of therapy. For example, patients benefit from knowing what factors contribute to the illness they have, what role medications play, what the side effects of a particular medication are, how long they might require treatment, and so on. Another form of information is provided when group members offer each other advice on how to handle particular problems they all share.

4. *Altruism:* As the group develops, members find that they can be helpful to each other. This help might take the form of sharing experience that gives others insight into their own problems, or simply offering encouragement when one member of the group is facing a particular problem or feeling "down." In some cases, a patient may never before have been in a position to realize that he or she can be of help or value to someone else. Being aware of others' needs and extending oneself to offer help can be a powerful way to move beyond self-absorption in one's own problems.

5. *Development of socializing techniques:* Group therapy for some types of problems might concentrate specifically on learning to understand and practice basic social skills. For example, in groups for abusive fathers, the group leader will help the group focus on understanding their current behavior, learning about good parenting skills, and practicing these skills in role plays. Although other types of groups might not focus so specifically on social skills, there is always an element of learning about social behaviors in the course of the group's interactions. When the group is encouraged to give frank and open feedback about how they are interacting, group members invariably learn things about themselves—for example, a group member who constantly interrupts others is likely to have this pointed out.

6. *Imitative behavior:* Group members learn about successful and positive behaviors by observing the impact that individuals in the group have on each other. It's natural, then, that they come to imitate successful behaviors. For example, a very shy

person might observe the firmly assertive group member who challenges the person who constantly interrupts. When the group supports this behavior and the challenged individual tries to curb his interruptions, the shy member may feel confident in starting to imitate the successful assertiveness of the person she admires.

7. *Catharsis:* The term "catharsis" describes the strong expression of emotion, either positive or negative, which is followed by a feeling of relief. In group therapy, patients have a setting in which they begin to feel confident in exploring and expressing their emotions. Emotional expression itself can bring a short-term benefit, but other factors must operate for emotional expression to have long-term therapeutic benefit. The reaction of the group to the individual's expression of strong emotions can help the individual develop insights about herself or about the relationship or experience to which she's reacting. The group is a forum in which she can begin to apply these insights which, in the long term, she will need to apply in her life outside the group.

8. *Corrective recapitulation of the primary family group:* Often patients in a therapy group will bring with them a history of unsatisfactory relationships with the first group they belonged to—the family in which they grew up. Since these early relationships formed a pattern for their interactions, it's natural that individuals might begin to interact with the therapist as they once interacted with a parent, or to treat group members as they once treated their siblings. This is part of the normal group process and one of which the therapist is trained to be aware and to help group members recognize. In the course of the group's work, negative patterns of relationship are examined with the involvement of the therapist, the group members, and the individual. Individuals are assisted in realizing the results of their typical behaviors and in testing the possibilities of new kinds of behaviors.

9. *Existential factors:* Certain kinds of therapy groups are focused intensely on how individuals deal with the central issues of human existence—death, loneliness, whether life has meaning. These inevitably are key concerns of groups whose members have faced bereavement or who themselves are facing life-threatening illness. These issues may also be addressed in other types of groups, depending very much

on the individual character of a particular group guided by a particular therapist. The existential approach to therapy recognizes that there are limits to the guidance and support that can be derived from others and that the responsibility for living out one's life ultimately depends on the individual alone. The group setting provides the companionship of others who are also coming to terms with what this means. Patients who realize and accept their individual responsibility can develop great strength, courage, and compassion as they, first, take responsibility for their contribution to the group, and then accept individual responsibility in their own lives.

10. *Group cohesiveness:* Individual psychotherapy relies on the chemistry or rapport between the therapist and the individual. Group psychotherapy relies just as strongly on the chemistry or rapport among group members. When a group is cohesive, the members develop meaningful relationships within the group that are supportive and accepting of the members of the group. In a cohesive group, members gain confidence in disclosing their personal concerns and the group is able to help them work through these issues. Belonging to a group in which one is known and recognized as someone with something to contribute is itself of great therapeutic value. The skills that an individual practices in order to become and remain a valued member of the group also apply in the other social groups to which the individual belongs.

11. *Interpersonal learning:* The therapy group is a small model of the world. In a sense, each group presents its members with a fresh start in learning how important relationships are to human beings and how to make relationships work. In both individual ways and together, group members learn and practice new emotional experiences that prepare them to carry new patterns of relationships into their personal lives.

These eleven factors that contribute to treatment in a group setting operate to different degrees and at different times in the life of a group, and only a few of these factors apply in the setting of individual psychotherapy. This is why group psychotherapy is used alone in some cases and why, in other cases, some patients may be involved in both individual and group psychotherapy at the same time.

HOW PSYCHOTHERAPY GROUPS ARE ORGANIZED

The Structure of the Group

In organizing a group, the therapist must give considerable thought to the appropriate size. A group that's too large doesn't promote a comfort level in speaking up. A group that's too small will not promote the group dynamics that have therapeutic value. Generally, a group of six to twelve members works best.

For a comfortable exchange, the group needs to meet regularly in the same place each time. In a hospital or clinic, a small conference room, where the group can meet around a table, can usually be found, or perhaps a large office where chairs can be arranged informally. Sometimes refreshments are provided to help new members feel a point of focus as they get acquainted; other groups, might decide not to have refreshments.

An established frequency and regular attendance are both important. Most outpatient groups meet once or twice a week. Groups that provide support to members with substance abuse problems often meet daily, as do groups of psychiatric inpatients. The length of each group session needs to be decided in advance, as well as a time frame for the entire program of group therapy. These decisions vary with the nature and goals of the group. Often, groups will meet for an hour and a half or two hours. This allows time for people to settle in, reconnect with where they were at the last meeting, engage in group discussion, and then summarize and focus for the next session.

Ground Rules for Group Behaviors

Group psychotherapy, like individual psychotherapy, needs to be structured around a contract and ground rules. At the beginning, the therapist will outline the ground rules that apply—for example, beginning and ending each session on time, or how absences will be handled. Another important ground rule for psychotherapy groups is that members must respect each other's privacy and keep the content of group discussions strictly confidential inside the group. Groups work best when members realize that the ground rules support the healthy functioning of the group.

Other aspects of group norms will be clarified as group members begin to relate to each other. Group therapy depends on frank and open discussion, but some kinds of interpersonal exchanges can be negative. For example, a group member making remarks about another member's personal appearance would be "hitting below the belt." Also, certain types of relationships between group members undermine the group; examples of this would be group members who pair off or form cliques that exclude other group members. One of the roles of the therapist is to recognize inappropriate behaviors and relationships and then involve the group in helping individuals acknowledge and control behaviors and relationships that are clearly out of line.

The real therapeutic richness of the group comes from the participation of its members, and therefore each individual is greatly valued. Together, they are creating something very precious for themselves, and each team member must take responsibility for contributing to a group structure that will allow members to interact spontaneously and honestly and support each other in working through problems.

What the Therapist Does

Different types of health care professionals conduct group therapy—family doctors, psychiatrists, psychologists, nurses, social workers, occupational therapists. In addition to their own professional training, they will have had training in conducting groups. Sometimes, groups have co-therapists, usually one female and one male, who take part together in leading the group. This can be helpful to the group dynamics, especially when group members are of both sexes.

Basically, the therapist is a facilitator who sets up the group, involves a varied mix of personalities to make up the group, establishes guidelines, and then allows the group to function. The therapist's active participation in the group depends on how well and how long the group has been functioning together. At the very beginning, it is the therapist who realizes just how valuable each group member is, and this is a viewpoint the therapist may need to express actively to each individual until the group gels. At times, the therapist might need to interpret what's happening, or keep the group focused, but often he or she just lets the group continue to develop its own cohesive structure. The therapist also has a responsibility to maintain continuity from week to week, recalling where things were at the last session and where the group seemed to be headed. The therapist also needs to control destructive behaviors, and, if the group's effectiveness is being undermined by an individual who won't abide by group norms, to remove that person from the group.

SELF-HELP SUPPORT GROUPS

Self-help support groups are groups formed, not by professionals, but by people who have experienced particular problems, have benefited from the informal support of others with similar experience, and have recognized that the mutual support could be more widely extended through an organized group. Many nationally known groups, such as Alcoholics Anonymous and Mothers Against Drunk Driving, started in this way. While these groups are focused on education and support-ive encouragement, their benefits are in many ways similar to the eleven therapeutic mechanisms described by Dr. Yalom as factors in group psychotherapy (see Vinogradov and Yalom, 1991). Self-help groups, sometimes called peer-support groups, may be organized and conducted solely by members themselves; alternatively, members of the group may receive specialized training in facilitating group processes and become group leaders.

In connection with the issues discussed in this book, two types of self-help support groups that have proved useful in many settings are parent bereavement groups and postpartum support groups. The first type is composed of couples who have faced a pregnancy loss or loss of a newborn infant. This kind of group brings together parents who might not know any other people who have experienced a loss like theirs. They may join the support group because the immediate tragedy is past, and their family and friends have returned to their everyday lives and withdrawn the active support that was first present. In meeting with a group of parents whose circumstances are similar, the mother and father can realize that they are not alone, that others face the same problems, and that their reaction of grief is not inappro-priate.

Bereavement groups provide an environment in which others are sympathetic to one's story, to what happened, to how others reacted, and to the genuine impact the loss has had on the lives and future of the parents. Belonging to a group like this can help the parents, as a couple and also as individuals, to find a positive way to support each other. It's likely that any two people will have different paces in their adjustment process; in addition, mothers and fathers often experience grief differently. One partner may feel that the specifics have been talked through sufficiently, while the other still needs to examine just what happened and just what was most difficult to endure. In a group, there will be others who are prepared to respond helpfully to each of these needs. Bereavement groups also provide practical information and education about the nature of the grieving process, and members can help each other accept the stages of grief and move to each new phase.

Postpartum support groups are made up of women who are receiving treatment for postpartum depression. These groups, to which each woman might also bring her partner or another family member, can provide an invaluable support network especially for women who are socially isolated—a condition that is not uncommon in our modern society. In the setting of a group of women with similar experience, members can feel free to talk about feelings which they might have felt would not be understood by anyone else—mixed feelings about being a mother, feelings of loneliness and boredom, worries about the effect of their illness on their marriage, and so on.

Peer-support groups for postpartum depression are often founded by women who have themselves recovered from this condition. In other cases, a professional therapist or a community clinic may be the initial force in getting a self-help group started. Once the group forms, the professional person usually moves into the background and is consulted largely as a resource person. Groups might meet in members' homes or they might meet in a setting like a local community center. They set their own agendas for personal discussions and for educational presentations from outside experts.

In recent years, self-help groups have grown in popularity, and this is an informal measure of their effectiveness. If you decide to become involved in a self-help group, or perhaps start one on your own, you'll find it useful to review some of the issues we discussed under both individual and group psychotherapy. For example, it's always useful for group members to be very open and straightforward at the beginning about the group's structure and ground rules. The sooner that group members realize that the value of the group comes from the participation of its members, the more effective the group will be.

IN MY OWN PRACTICE: GROUP PSYCHOTHERAPY

Early in my career as a psychiatrist, I had the good fortune to receive six months of intensive training with Dr. Ferdinand Knoblock of the University of British Columbia, whose trainees come from all over the world to learn the techniques of group psychotherapy. Since then, I have considered group psychotherapy an important adjunct to the work I do with individuals, and

I regularly conduct groups for women with postpartum depression, as well as groups whose members have premenstrual syndrome. I usually have a co-therapist, that is, a nurse clinician who helps me with group therapy.

Each postpartum group has up to ten to twelve members, some of whom are also seeing me individually for monitoring of medications and depression. We meet once a week in a large office at the hospital. Noon has turned out to be a good time for meetings because it fits in well with most mothers' schedules; at one time, we tried evening meetings but attendance was often a genuine problem because the mothers were busy with the family's dinner and the care of older children.

Our groups usually run for an hour and a half per session, and the groups are structured around a twelve-week program. Members must commit to attending for at least twelve sessions because our goal of a positive change in outlook cannot be achieved in fewer than twelve weeks.

The groups have a life of their own, and each one may unfold in a slightly different way. Members might or might not want to organize refreshments. Usually, at the first meeting I distribute educational material that the members take responsibility for reading before the next meeting. This gives them information about the normal postpartum period, the types of medications they are on, and types of mood changes. Members are encouraged to write down questions or concerns that occur to them between meetings so that they can be brought up at the next meeting.

Our group discussions are very focused on the here-and-now rather than deep issues of interrelationships and dynamics. Most members are struggling to recover from their depression and to cope with issues in relation to their infants and their marriages, and these are the issues of importance to them. Women are allowed to bring one significant other to each meeting, if they wish. Often, women will bring their partner or perhaps their mothers or sisters. This is a benefit, of course, to the individuals who come as guests and, not surprisingly, the additional perspective that these people can bring to the discussion is often a benefit to other group members.

Women with postpartum psychosis are not included in groups of women who are being treated for postpartum depression. The medications for the two kinds of patients are very different, and women with psychosis often cannot fit into a homogenous group. However, group contacts have a particular benefit of their own, and some successful groups have developed when I have put individual patients in touch with each other. I began by making a list of my patients I felt would benefit from talking with others with similar psychotic illness. Then, since the doctor-patient relationship is always strictly confidential, I asked these patients if they would like to be put in touch with others. In most cases, there was a great interest in making a connection.

In this way, an informal telephone network has developed and, meanwhile, the individuals continue to see me for individual therapy. A number of these women, along with their husbands, decided that they would like to meet, and I am told that a number of couples get together once every three months for a potluck dinner at someone's house. My patients have told me that it is very reassuring when they get to know other women who are experiencing the same "scary" illness. I understand, too, that several of the husbands have found a great deal of support from meeting other men who are coping with this illness in their partners.

CHAPTER 11

"MY BABY'S HEALTH IS ALL THAT MATTERS"

Medications and Their Alternatives in Pregnancy and Postpartum

A s women have become more educated about good health practices, they have also become concerned about the possibility that the use of medication during pregnancy can cause harm to their babies. Because medications travel through the placenta from the mother's bloodstream to the baby's, medications that may help the mother may potentially harm the baby's development. Similarly, once the baby is born, a nursing infant can receive its mother's medication through breast milk, a topic that I discuss in greater detail in Chapter Six.

When a mother suffers from any psychiatric illness in pregnancy, the question of whether she should take medications must be carefully explored by the woman and her doctor. This question must be asked in regard to any type of medication and illness, whether the illness occurs during pregnancy or is a long-standing condition the woman had before becoming pregnant. With psychiatric illness the answer to this question becomes particularly complex. When an expectant mother has a serious emotional disorder, she may be unable to cope with the added experience of pregnancy. If she is not successfully treated, the progression of her emotional illness may have long-term consequences for her own health, her relationship with her partner, and her new baby. Weighed against this serious concern for the health of the mother is the equally serious concern for the well-being of the baby she carries if this baby is exposed to certain types of psychotropic medication at a critical time in its development.

Obviously, this is a topic which must be considered carefully, and it's important for women to learn as much as they can about their options and to take part in informed decision making about their own health care. In this chapter, I will outline what is known about the use of medication for treatment of psychiatric illness in pregnancy. Women who are receiving medication will see how, with their doctor's involvement, they can preplan a treatment program before they become pregnant. Pregnant women who might require medication will better understand how to weigh its risks and benefits.

WHEN EMOTIONAL DISORDERS CALL FOR MEDICATION

Psychotropic Medications in Psychiatric Illness

Psychotropic medication is a broad classification for a number of different types of drugs that affect the central nervous system. As we have discussed in earlier chapters, emotional disorders are often the result of chemical imbalances. Simply put, psychotropic medications act to correct these imbalances by changing the chemistry in specific parts of the brain.

Psychotropics are often required in the treatment of psychiatric illness. Certain disorders, such as manic-depressive disease, were virtually uncontrollable before it was recognized that they were a result of physiological problems that could be helped by specific medications. These potent medicines are often used along with other therapies such as psychotherapy or behavior therapy. Certain psychiatric disorders of severe nature, such as major depression and some anxiety disorders, cannot be successfully treated with psychotherapy alone, and the use of psychotropics has made positive outcomes possible in these cases. When psychotropic medications are prescribed, the physician meets with the patient regularly, closely monitoring his or her progress and response to the medication. In addition, individuals process medications differently, depending on their metabolism, and the doctor may need to adjust the dose of medication from time to time. Routine laboratory tests can measure levels of certain drugs in the individual's blood and serve as a guide to adjusting the dosage.

Psychotropic Medications in Pregnant Patients

Psychotropic medications during pregnancy must be prescribed and monitored with great caution. However, there are conditions under which medication is called for, and pregnant patients should be prepared to take part in making decisions about their use. Occasionally, an exception to this practice of informed consent arises when the patient is psychotic and thus out of touch with reality. When a patient is so severely ill, the doctor will talk with her partner or other members of the family regarding the use of these medicines during pregnancy. In my own practice I do this routinely, regardless of the severity of the woman's illness, and regardless of whether she is pregnant, since a woman with a psychiatric disorder who is being treated with medication might accidentally become pregnant. Involving the family members decreases their anxiety about the illness and demystifies the treatment plan.

Successful treatment of psychiatric illness, even with psychotropic drugs, is not necessarily incompatible with a healthy pregnancy. In some stages of pregnancy and with some medications, it's possible to steer a safe course that treats the disorder with minimal risk to the infant. In these cases, not only must the mother's condition and response to treatment be carefully observed, but so must the baby's—prenatally, at birth, and in the early postpartum days.

Some types of psychotropic medications appear to be relatively safe if used cautiously in later stages of pregnancy. Yet, all psychotropic medications cross the placenta and enter the baby's system, and no psychotropics have been approved for use in pregnancy by the U.S. Food and Drug Administration or the Health Protection Branch in Canada.

Given these facts, why would psychotropics *ever* be prescribed for pregnant patients? First of all, in severe cases of psychiatric illness, psychotropic medications may be the only successful way to treat the patient. Having said this, however, it must be made clear that there's a great deal that isn't known about the impact of psychotropics and the frequency of birth defects caused by psychotropics. In the Western world, the rate of birth defects is about 3 percent of live births, and in most of these cases, the cause of the birth defect is unknown or uncertain. Research shows that 5 to 10 percent (i.e., 1–2 birth defects in 1,000 births) can be attributed to teratogenic drugs (drugs that may cause defects in the fetus) but researchers have been unable to establish a measure of statistical risk in taking certain psychotropic medicines in pregnancy.

However, several factors are known to increase the possibility of risk to the infant. (1) Many medications should not be used in the first 56 days of pregnancy, a critical time for the development of the infant's major organ systems. (2) Other influences, such as the use of alcohol and tobacco, can add to the effect of medications. (3) With some medications, the risk rises with amount of the dose and the length of time it is taken. (4) The basic general health of the developing infant may be compromised owing to drug exposure. I will discuss the possible risks of specific types of psychotropic medication later in this chapter, but first I will offer a general assessment of when the benefits of medication might outweigh the risks.

ALTERNATIVES TO MEDICATION

Doctors and their pregnant patients must ask a number of questions when medication seems called for: "What will happen to the mother's health if she is not medicated? Is it essential that she receive medication or is it optional? What alternatives are available?" For a pregnant patient, most doctors will recommend that all the alternatives be tried first and medication be considered only if other therapies cannot improve the mother's condition.

For example, as discussed in an earlier chapter, panic disorder is fairly common in women. When panic disorder occurs outside of pregnancy, medication is often prescribed to relieve the most severe symptoms. In a pregnant patient, the "wait and see" approach, combined with behavioral and supportive therapy, can be a successful alternative, provided the panic disorder is mild and does not make the woman dysfunctional. Once panic disorder has been diagnosed, the woman and her doctor need to discuss in detail what the disorder is, what kind of symptoms she might experience, and the significance of using medication if necessary during pregnancy. Often, just knowing what's happening to her and knowing that she's found someone who can help will give a woman the strength and resources to carry on without medication. At the same time, she needs to see her doctor regularly and, with assistance, to explore other courses of therapy. Women with panic disorder can benefit from learning relaxation and stress reduction techniques, and if a behavioral therapist is available, can be coached in adjusting behavior to control the severity of symptoms. A discussion of relaxation techniques is beyond the scope of this chapter, but information on the subject is quite readily available. Many bookstores and drugstores carry audiotapes on relaxation techniques in general, as well as relaxation techniques in pregnancy and childbirth. A woman's doctor can refer her to a psychologist who can offer behavioral therapy for anxiety disorder.

Often these approaches reduce the intensity of the disorder, and the woman feels prepared to cope with her panic symptoms without medication. The fact that various avenues are open to her and that her condition is being addressed is itself a great relief. After the first trimester, a short course of mild doses of antipanic medication might be considered if these alternate therapies fail to improve a serious illness.

Making an Informed Decision

Mothers must take an active role in informing themselves about their illnesses and the possible approaches to therapy. They must recognize that no medications should be taken lightly, especially in pregnancy. When medication is first considered, women need to be aware of the consequences and to take part in making decisions about their therapy. If they do not feel comfortable with their doctor's advice and suggestions, they should ask their family doctor for referral to another specialist, who can provide a second opinion. If they are using prescribed medication, they must follow the dosage instructions exactly and at each visit, keep their doctor informed about the progress they feel they're making, any side effects, and whether the medication is of any help to them. Obviously, women who are able to make these decisions are not suicidally depressed or out of touch with reality. As I have discussed throughout the book, involving your partner in these decisions is also recommended. He then becomes your "helper" and is someone you can rely upon and trust. Many seriously depressed women find that their memory is at times severely affected by the depression. In such cases, a partner might remind you to take your tablets as advised by the doctor.

The responsibilities of motherhood begin even before pregnancy is planned. When a woman is being treated for a psychiatric illness with medication, she has the responsibility to explore in advance with her doctor how her illness will be treated if she becomes pregnant. Loraine is a patient who learned a painful lesson about the need to take a doctor into her confidence and to be actively involved in her own health care.

LORAINE'S STORY

I was asked to see Loraine, a 21-year-old woman, after she gave birth to a child with Ebstein's anomaly, a life-threatening condition of heart anomaly. Her obstetrician had learned from Loraine after the birth that she had been taking lithium for three years and had not discontinued it during her pregnancy.

In talking with Loraine, I learned that she had first had a severe episode of manic depression at age 18. She had been hospitalized at that time and started on a combined treatment plan of lithium carbonate and a neuroleptic medication. She continued to see her psychiatrist for the first six months after her discharge and then decided to stop seeing him. Her family doctor continued to prescribe lithium.

She had been told that lithium medication must be monitored with regular laboratory tests, but decided that since she was doing so well, she wouldn't bother with the tests. She got married and became pregnant—without realizing that lithium could be potentially dangerous to the fetus during pregnancy, specifically in the first trimester.

Sadly, Loraine was involved in a process of denial that had tragic consequences. She didn't want to accept the fact that she had a psychiatric illness, and she continued this denial by discontinuing the visits to her psychiatrist and by not following up with lab tests and visits to her family doctor. She had not even told her husband of her illness.

After the child's birth, she became extremely depressed and had to be hospitalized. Again, she was treated successfully with lithium and with antidepressants, and she continued to see me for almost a year after her discharge. In therapy, part of her task was to work through her attitudes of denial, her feelings that her illness was stigmatizing, and a rather negative attitude towards her caregivers.

Two years later, she planned a second pregnancy. Her lithium medication was gradually tapered and then discontinued before she became pregnant, and she was followed closely throughout her pregnancy. She did not have relapse of her manic-depressive symptoms during the pregnancy. She delivered a healthy baby girl this time, and she continues to do quite well. Although her psychiatric condition relapsed during postpartum, it was successfully treated.

I take a conservative approach when I am faced with the dilemma of treating a pregnant patient with psychiatric illness. The important points I want to make in sharing Loraine's story are these: First, her lithium levels should have been monitored after she had her first episode of bipolar illness. Second, the risks versus the benefits of lithium during pregnancy should have been discussed with her. Third, although a recent search of the medical literature (Cohen, Friedman, et al., 1994) questions the teratogenic effects of lithium during pregnancy, Loraine's baby with Ebstein's anomaly falls within the range of reported lithium-related anomalies. Lastly, the decision to taper and discontinue lithium in her case was based on one episode of bipolar illness. If she had recurrent episodes of bipolar illness, it would have been challenging to time her pregnancy between episodes and deal with the issue of becoming pregnant on lithium.

Trust and Decision Making in the Doctor-Patient Relationship

In discussing with the patient the role of medication during pregnancy, the psychiatrist ideally should put aside her or his own bias and present as objectively as possible the facts regarding this controversial topic. Most physicians view their role, first, as establishing an environment of trust and confidence that allows the patient to feel safe in expressing herself and asserting her own views. Then, they see their role as remaining well informed about the current state of medical research and taking the responsibility to share this information openly and honestly with the patient. Robin's story is one in which a very well informed patient continues to be involved with her psychiatrist in an ongoing review of the consequences of the decision they made together about medication in pregnancy.

ROBIN'S STORY

Robin, a 30-year-old psychologist, began to experience panic attacks in the first trimester of pregnancy. When this happened, she remembered that ten years earlier, while taking final exams during university, she had had a distinct panic attack. Now, a trained psychologist, she knew exactly what was happening with her, and she was determined to find help. With the help of a colleague, she began to work on behavioral and relaxation techniques that helped reduce the number and severity of the attacks in her first and second trimester.

In the third trimester, however, Robin's panic attacks became more severe, and she sought a referral to me. We discussed the severity of her illness and reviewed the current information on the use of anxiolytic medications in the third trimester. Together, we decided that I would prescribe a mild dose of anxiolytic medication that Robin would use only as she felt she needed it. She delivered a full-term healthy baby who is now two years old.

With her background in psychology, Robin is concerned that it may still be too early to know if the child will show learning disabilities or behavioral problems as a result of her decision. We have agreed that Robin and her husband will have a yearly appointment with me to allow all of us to review any new findings in the medical literature on this subject. Meanwhile, their happy little girl is scheduled to start preschool in another year and is being carefully observed in her play groups by her mother.

Given Robin's professional awareness, it is not surprising that this kind of concern is uppermost in her mind. She will probably not stop worrying until her child becomes older and progresses normally with her peers. At the same time, her family doctor and I do not disregard this concern or dismiss it as being overreactive. Robin and I have agreed on a sensible course of annual consultation, and I see myself as having the responsibility to share my particular knowledge and expertise with this family.

When decisions have to be made about a course of therapy, I feel the most frequent role I play is one of facilitator, helping the patient reach a decision that is comfortable for her and will address the needs of her illness.

EFFECTS OF MEDICATIONS ON THE INFANT:
THE THREE TRIMESTERS AND POSTPARTUM

What Current Research Shows

Psychotropic medications may affect the fetus differently depending on the stage of pregnancy in which they are taken. In general, there is a wide range in the type and severity of abnormalities that can occur with improper use of medications. The more serious abnormalities— fetal death, physical malformations, and growth retardation—may be related to the use of certain drugs in early pregnancy. Before drugs are approved for use, they are routinely tested on animals. Although animal studies are an important guideline, however, they have not always predicted the risk of anomaly in humans. Thalidomide is an example of a medication that did not produce anomalies in animal studies but had severe effects on developing human fetuses.

The possibility of a drug causing less obvious abnormalities as the child grows is not so easily measured. Since many psychotropics operate on the central nervous system, it's possible that the medication a fetus receives from its mother might later cause learning disabilities, behavioral problems, or emotional disorders. Several large-scale studies have been carried out to follow the long-term progress of children whose mothers used psychotropic medications in the first trimester. While these studies involved large numbers of children, they have conflicting conclusions. In some studies, there seemed to be no ill effect as the child matured. In others, there appeared to be a relationship between medications and later behavioral problems. In addition, psychotropic medications are fairly new, and for some of them, not enough time has passed for true "long-term" effects to be studied; the children involved are just not old enough yet. At present, we lack good prospective studies looking at neurobehavioral toxicity in children. Currently, the research team in which I am involved is studying these "kindergarten babies" whose mothers were exposed to psychotropics during pregnancy.

Where does this leave us? First of all, we can take extreme caution in the use of medications during pregnancy, a responsibility that applies to both women and their doctors. Secondly, we can look to continuing medical research and the possibility that future studies will be increasingly helpful in guiding choices. Thirdly, we can draw sensible conclusions based on experience. For example, certain medications taken in late pregnancy may occasionally cause the newborn to have withdrawal symptoms (jitteriness, shakiness, poor sucking reflex) or compromised health status due to toxicity ("overdose"), leading, for example, to an infant who is extremely sedated at birth. From this experience, the conclusion can be drawn that when certain medications are essential in treating the mother's illness, they can be used with considerable safety but with caution. Whether or not they are discontinued or reduced in dosage some weeks in advance of the baby's due date depends on the severity of the mother's illness. The chart at the end of this chapter gives details of how medication may affect the fetus or newborn.

Medications in the First Trimester

Remarkably, nature allows us a very brief safety zone during which a new fetus is protected from drug effects. Drugs enter the baby's system through the placenta, but in the short time between conception and the first missed period, the placenta is not sufficiently formed to carry drugs from mother to child. After these first few weeks of pregnancy, however, the placenta is fully formed and allows access to the highly sensitive developing child.

During the first 56 days of pregnancy, cells are actively dividing to form the baby's major organ systems—arms, legs, cardiovascular system, central nervous system, and so on. The fetus's exposure to psychotropic medications during this important period may have consequences, as discussed. Thus, the physician has to weigh the risk of untreated psychiatric illness against the risk of drug exposure most carefully. This is particularly a dilemma for the psychiatrist when she or he is faced with the challenge of treating a mother with severe psychiatric illness in the first trimester.

Medications in the Second Trimester

Once the baby's major body organs have developed, there is less risk that medication will affect the healthy formation and future functioning of these organs. As I have said, the question of long-term abnormalities in behavioral and emotional development is still unsettled. It appears that mothers with serious psychiatric illness can be prescribed medications after the first trimester, as long as attention is given to the amount of medication prescribed and the length of time the medication is taken. For example, when alternate therapies are not successful, the patient might be given the smallest possible dose until the patient is symptom-free.

Pat's case was one in which medication was necessary and a carefully monitored course of medication appeared to have no ill effects on her child.

PAT'S STORY

Pat was a 26-year-old woman who, after four years of marriage, looked forward to leaving her job to enjoy her pregnancy and to remain at home for her baby's first years. The long-awaited pregnancy was far from idyllic, however, since she developed a severe manic-depressive illness at about 21 weeks. When her husband, William, brought her to the hospital she was acutely manic—highly excited and experiencing bizarre delusions about her neighbors' attitudes towards her. She drifted in and out of touch with reality, but she was coherent enough for me to interview her when I was called in to see her.

In taking her history, I learned that she had no previous history of either depression or mania. However, her mother had been diagnosed with manic depression and was taking lithium, and a brother apparently had depressions from time to time although the family did not discuss this openly at home.

It was clear that Pat's condition was serious and that without medication, her symptoms might escalate quickly. Pat, William, Pat's obstetrician, and I discussed the pros and cons of medication at this stage of her pregnancy, and it was agreed that she would be started on one of the major tranquilizers. She was prescribed a low dose, which was increased slightly and gradually until she started to respond to the medication.

At the end of five weeks, Pat was completely free of delusions and no longer experiencing bizarre thoughts. She was now 28 weeks pregnant, and with William's participation, Pat and I examined the possibilities. We decided to discontinue the medication and see what happened.

I saw Pat regularly in my office, sometimes with William, too, for the balance of her pregnancy, and the baby's progress was followed carefully with regular ultrasounds. Luckily, she continued to feel well up to the birth of their completely healthy son. After the birth, she experienced acute depressive symptoms and was started again on medication. She still sees me regularly as an outpatient. Two years after the baby's birth, she had another severe episode of manic depression; she is someone who will probably need to be on lithium for a long time. At her regular visits, she has lab tests to measure the amount of lithium in her blood, and we check that she is remaining free of manic symptoms, as well as her depressive symptoms.

The little boy, Walter, is now in kindergarten and appears to be developing perfectly normally. Until I see hundreds of "Walters" in my practice, I can't say with a certainty that the medications Pat took during pregnancy had no ill effect. In her case, however, we felt that at that time her life was in danger and the decision to treat her with medication was a wise one.

Because of Pat's need for continued medication, this couple have decided not to have a second child, and Pat is looking forward to volunteering time as an assistant in Walter's kindergarten.

Medications in the Third Trimester

Some studies show that there is risk for babies born to mothers with third trimester exposure to medications. The newborn may show symptoms of lethargy, respiratory problems, excessive crying, difficulties feeding, or hyperactivity. In some premature infants, jaundice has been reported. A secondary risk, as I have discussed, is that the child might have long-term behavioral, developmental, or emotional problems as a consequence. This second possibility has not yet been confirmed in medical studies, but it remains a general precaution for the second and third trimester medication.

The first risk is addressed in two ways: either discontinuing the medication several weeks before the baby's birth where possible, or reducing the medication and having a pediatric specialist monitor the baby during and immediately after birth. In fact, babies are often closely monitored at birth as a follow-up to a mother's course of medication earlier in the pregnancy. In addition, most doctors have discontinued the once-common practice of giving tranquilizers to mothers to promote relaxation during delivery. As I discussed in Chapter One, the period immediately surrounding and just after childbirth is one of high risk for occurrence or recurrence of certain psychiatric disorders. Therefore, discontinuing medication in "high risk" patients may be unwise.

It appears that a safe course of action to address the possibility of long-term consequences is to carefully control the dose and duration of a prescribed medication. For severe emotional disorders in the second or third trimester, the doctor might suggest an appropriate dose of medication be taken for just a few weeks and discontinued as soon as the severe symptoms clear up. However, in some patients, because of the severity of the illness, it may be impossible to discontinue medication prior to birth. In such a patient, as earlier discussed, it is important for both the mother and baby to be followed by specialists.

MEDICATIONS YOUR DOCTOR MIGHT PRESCRIBE

I will now describe the general types of medication that might be prescribed for treatment of emotional disorders and provide general guidelines for their use in pregnancy. This information is also summarized in a table at the end of the chapter. As you look at this outline, remember that your doctor prescribed medication based on your individual condition and health profile. Some factors that will influence your doctor's decision are your history of psychiatric or other illness, other medications you might be taking, your past reactions to different medications, and your doctor's experience in prescribing medication in cases similar to yours. You can use this summary to get an idea of possible risks and to help you discuss alternative therapies with your doctor. If you are already taking any of these medications, don't make the mistake of comparing your own prescription to anyone else's—there are just too many individual variables for the comparison to be meaningful.

These individual variables also arise in the same patient at different times in her life. The way a woman's body processes medication changes when she becomes pregnant, and this may change the amount of medication she needs. First of all, as she begins to retain more water, the concentration of medication in her body will be more diluted and therefore have less of an effect. Also, her body may excrete some medications more rapidly during pregnancy. Other factors related to the pregnant woman's response to medications are the second trimester drop in blood pressure, the way her changing body protein "binds" to the drug, increased frequency of urination, and increased gastric acid in the stomach. In addition, since constipation is often a problem in pregnancy, her doctor may try to avoid prescribing medications that contribute to constipation. For these reasons, the dosage and frequency of medications will vary.

I will discuss psychotropic medications in pregnancy under four headings: *major tranquilizers* (also called *neuroleptics*), *antidepressants*, *anxiolytics*, and *mood stabilizers*. I discuss the effects of these medications in breastfeeding infants in Chapter Six.

Major Tranquilizers (Neuroleptics or Antipsychotics)

Neuroleptic medications are used in the treatment of psychosis. If a woman develops an acute psychotic illness, whether it is a bipolar disorder or psychotic depression or schizophrenia, she will need to take antipsychotics to get relief of symptoms. And women with a preexisting illness who conceive and continue to experience underlying psychotic symptoms in pregnancy (i.e., women with chronic schizophrenia) will also need neuroleptic medications to ensure their emotional stability.

The different common chemical names of neuroleptics include chlorpromazine, haloperidol, trifluperazine, perphenazine, and several others. Currently, many more neuroleptics are under development for increased efficacy and fewer side effects. Investigators and researchers have not yet come to a definite conclusion about the safe use of these drugs in pregnancy. There seem to be a number of individual case reports of congenital malformation (some cardiovascular) in the infants of mothers who were prescribed antipsychotics, such as the low-potency neuroleptics. However, two other larger studies involving a population of pregnant women that was significant in terms of numbers show that treatment with these types of medicines produced no adverse effects on the infants.

Some physicians either decrease the dose or discontinue the medication prior to delivery, depending on the mental state of the woman. This decision is usually made on an individual basis, depending on several variables: the mother's history of prior postpartum psychosis, multiple drugs, and dosage and timing of the drug. At times, it may not be possible to discontinue medications. In these cases, a pediatrician should be involved to treat perinatal complications if they arise. Again, although these are rare, toxic or withdrawal effects have been reported in newborns whose mothers have been on medication. These effects include jerky movements, restlessness, and drowsiness.

The major studies on long-term effects of infants exposed to these medications are somewhat inconclusive. The general consensus among researchers suggests that there is no connection between developmental abnormalities and exposure to major tranquilizers. However, not enough time has passed since the introduction of these medications to be able to follow a large number of children to adulthood.

COMMON NEUROLEPTIC MEDICATIONS

Chlorpromazine (Thorazine)   Chlorprothixene (Taractan)
Prochlorperazine (Compazine)   Droperidol (Inapsine, Innovar)
Haloperidol (Haldol, Decanoate)   Mesoridazine (Serentil)
Thioridazine (Mellaril)   Perphenazine (Etrafon, Trilafon)
Thiothixene (Navane)   Promazine (Sparine)
Trifluoperazine (Stelazine)   Promethazine (Phenergan)
Fluphenazine (Prolixin, Permitil)   Clozapine (Clozaril)
Loxapine (Loxitane, Daxolin)   Risperdal (Risperidone)
Molindone (Moban, Lidone)

Antidepressants

Antidepressants are used alone or in combination with other medications for the treatment of severe obsessive-compulsive disorder, depression, and anxiety disorders. They are divided into three general types: *tricyclic antidepressants, monoamine oxidase (MAO) inhibitors,* and the newest category, *serotonin reuptake inhibitors.*

The chemical names for some *tricyclic antidepressants* are imipramine, desipramine, nortriptyline, and amitriptyline. Research studies on the effects of tricyclics in pregnancy have found no connection between use of the medications and physical malformation of the infant. However, while it appears that their use is quite safe, some conservative physicians would recommend that they be discontinued several weeks before birth if the woman is asymptomatic and then restarted prophylactically in the postpartum. Even when medication is discontinued, these drugs stay in both the mother's and baby's systems for days, depending on the drug. There may be some withdrawal effects in the newborn, and it's common to have a neonatal specialist or pediatrician present in the delivery room to immediately assess and treat the baby's condition. It's important to have this support of the medical team because, rarely, the baby might experience withdrawal symptoms as serious as respiratory problems, abnormal heartbeat, or even seizures. More common, though, are lesser withdrawal effects such as irritability, breathlessness, cyanosis ("blue baby"), and poor sucking reflex.

Monoamine oxidase inhibitors (MAO inhibitors or MAOIs) are a type of antidepressant that has been shown to have teratogenic effects in studies of animals. Because the effects of MAOIs on newborns are not yet known, it is recommended that they not be used in the first trimester, and many doctors feel that their safety in the course of pregnancy is not known.

The newest type of antidepressants are *selective serotonin reuptake inhibitors*, which include drugs with chemical names such as fluoxitine (Prozac) or sertraline (Zoloft). Because they are so new, it's too early to document their possible adverse effects on the newborn; the numbers are simply not large enough to draw any valid conclusion. Recent data on Prozac in pregnancy show that approximately 2,000 women exposed to Prozac during pregnancy had no increased incidence of congenital malformations in their infants. A severely depressed patient or a patient with severe obsessive-compulsive disorder may need to continue to take the SSRI right through pregnancy and postpartum.

COMMON ANTIDEPRESSANT MEDICATIONS

Tricyclics
    Imipramine (Janimine, Tofranil, Tipramine)
    Amitriptyline (Amitril, Elavil, Endep, Emitrip, Enovil)
    Desipramine (Norpramin, Pertofrane)
    Doxepin (Adapin, Sinequan)
    Nortriptyline (Aventyl, Pamelor)
    Protriptyline (Vivactil)
    Clomipramine (Anafranil)
    Trimiptolyne (Surmontil)
Tetracyclic
    Maprotiline (Ludiomil)
Monoamine oxidase inhibitors
    Tranylcypromine (Parnate)
    Phenelzine (Nardil)
Selective serotonin reuptake inhibitors
    Fluoxetine (Prozac)
    Sertraline (Zoloft)
    Fluvoxamine (Luvox)
    Paroxetine (Paxil)
RIMA (reversible inhibitors of monoamine oxidase)
    Moclobemide (Manerix)
Newer antidepressants
    Nefazedone (Serzone)
    Venlafaxine (Effexor)

Mood Stabilizers

The mood stabilizers are used to treat manic depressive or bipolar illnesses and include medications with the chemical names of *lithium carbonate* and *carbamazepime*. Lithium has been related to heart abnormalities (especially Ebstein's syndrome) in infants whose mothers have taken this drug during the first trimester. Dr. Lee Cohen, my friend and colleague at Harvard Medical School, recently published an article on lithium during pregnancy (Cohen, Friedman, et al., 1994) in which he relates that although the initial information concerning the teratogenic risk of lithium treatment was derived from biased retrospective reports, more recent epidemiologic data indicate that the teratogenic risk of lithium exposure during the first trimester is lower than previously suggested. And a number of recent studies have suggested that lithium can be used safely in the second and third trimesters. The usual precautions apply to tapering or discontinuing the drug before the delivery date and closely monitoring the newborn. Some babies whose mothers have taken lithium late in the pregnancy have been born with enlarged thyroid glands (or goiters), a condition which is mild and treatable. Some babies born to mothers taking lithium have tended to be lethargic and cyanotic, and showed low Apgar scores.

Congenital defects have been linked to the use of carbamazepime (1% spina bifida) and valproic acid (another mood stabilizer) in pregnancy. Because these abnormalities are so serious and relatively little is known about the effects of these drugs later in pregnancy, carbamazepime is in general not recommended for use in pregnant patients.

Anxiolytics (the Minor Tranquilizers)

Anxiolytics are used alone or in combination with other medications in the treatment of anxiety. In pregnancy, their use might be considered for panic disorder, when labor is being induced, or when events of pregnancy or required hospitalization produce symptoms of anxiety. The chemical names for this group of medication are *benzodiazepines*, *mepobramates*, *barbiturates*, and *hydroxyzines*.

The use of anxiolytics in pregnancy is quite controversial because different studies have shown different results. Some studies show that when many of these drugs are used in the first trimester, there is a chance that the developing infant may have abnormalities such as cleft palate or cleft lip. Later on in pregnancy, the benzodiazepine anxiolytics may be used safely for a short course if it is necessary to treat severe symptoms, such as acute uncontrolled panic attacks. Long-term use is not recommended, though, because there are reports that newborns whose mothers have been on this medication for a long time are found to have low Apgar scores and show "floppy baby" syndrome. In this latter condition, the baby's muscle tone is very weak and, indeed, the baby seems to "flop" like a soft doll.

The key question, as always, remains, "Does the mother's health require use of this medication?" In many cases, alternatives such as behavioral therapy to help control panic attacks, can be found. Again, only in cases where the anxiety is not amenable to any form of therapy other than pharmacological means should these medications be used. Physicians must avoid taking a "casual" attitude towards anxiety or handing out prescriptions of anxiolytic medicines as if they were vitamins, since they do have an addictive potential if used for a long time. On the other hand, the patient's health, both physical and psychological, must be protected from severe anxiety reactions that jeopardize the overall outcome of the pregnancy. As discussed in earlier chapters, a woman with severe panic disorder experiences a significant amount of upheaval in her life, and without proper medication, she may be unable to care for herself properly and experience a safe pregnancy.

SOME QUESTIONS YOU MIGHT HAVE
ABOUT DRUG TREATMENT IN PREGNANCY

? *I am a 32-year-old woman who has had several episodes of panic disorder, for which I have had to take a course of anxiolytics. In between the episodes, I have been quite well and have not had to take any medication. I am now planning to become pregnant, and I don't know how the pregnancy will affect my anxiety disease and whether I'll have to go back on medications.*

It is difficult to predict the course of your anxiety disease, but we have a few facts. It seems likely that the course of your illness is related to stress, and is episodic, and most importantly, seems to respond well to a short course of anxiolytics. This is a good sign, because if the illness were chronic, we would have to control it by other means if it occurred again during pregnancy. The question is, if you get pregnant and your anxiety symptoms return, what kind of treatment should you anticipate?

This is a reasonable question, and the effect of pregnancy on anxiety disease is variable.

There can be several scenarios: In some women, the anxiety may completely disappear; if this is the case, you need do nothing but enjoy your pregnancy. In other women, the panic attacks either continue to be episodic, or worsen. There is always the option of consulting a behavioral therapist if the panic attacks are not too severe; if you respond to behavioral therapy, medications can be avoided completely. If the anxiety attacks become really uncontrollable, and the quality of your life is severely compromised, then we follow the rule of prescribing medications for a minimum length of time, trying to keep the dose as low as possible. Because the course of panic disorder is so unpredictable, it is advisable to discuss your prior history with your doctor, in order to make contingency plans for everyone's peace of mind.

? *With the birth of my second son I had a third-trimester depression and I had to take a course of tricyclic antidepressants and be hospitalized. I am pregnant again, after accidentally conceiving on the antidepressant I've taken for the last 18 months. As soon as I learned I was pregnant, I discontinued my medication. How serious is it for me to proceed with the pregnancy?*

I'm sure that you will have spoken to your doctor about your concern and will have received information on the effects of antidepressants in pregnancy. No adverse side effects have been known to occur in babies who have been exposed to antidepressants for a short length of time, as seems to be the case with you. However, there have been individual case reports of abnormalities in infants, which could be detected early enough in your pregnancy if you are carefully monitored.

If you decide to go ahead with the pregnancy, your obstetrician should monitor the baby carefully right through pregnancy. I would suggest that you, your spouse, your family doctor, and your obstetrician work together as a team in following the progress of your baby very closely and, most importantly, to monitor your own health now that you have stopped taking the antidepressant medication.

? *I have a history of eating disorder, but my symptoms are well controlled with one of the new antidepressants, Prozac, of which I take 60 mg a day. I have been debating whether or not I should get pregnant since I have been unable to go off Prozac for the past four years. Each time I've tried to go off this medication, my eating disorder comes back within a few months. This is a dilemma for me because my husband and I have now been married for seven years and would like to have a baby.*

Since you have been unable to go off this medication for any length of time, it seems that you require this medication to function and keep your eating disorder under control. Prozac is a medication that has a long half-life, which means that it stays in the system a long time. The ideal situation would be for you to go off the medication and try to get pregnant before your symptoms come back. If that is not possible, then you might ask your doctor to refer you to a behavioral therapist. With the additional support of behavioral therapy, you might try again to go off the medication and get pregnant before your symptoms return.

The idea is to try to avoid this medication, especially during the first trimester, since not much is known about the effects of this drug on the baby. Prozac is a relatively new drug, but the data published thus far tell us that no pattern of adverse effects has been found. If you become pregnant and then experience a return of your symptoms, it then becomes a question of weighing the risk of not giving you the medication versus the risk of exposing your baby to Prozac. If the eating disorder again becomes uncontrollable, you may have to go back on the medication, with the dose kept at the lowest possible level to control your symptoms.

? *I've been under a psychiatrist's care for several years and am on lithium therapy. My condition has been very stable, and my husband and I are considering starting a family. Should I discontinue lithium before becoming pregnant?*

It's good to hear you're aware of the possible effects of medication on a developing infant—in fact, lithium is one medication whose use should be weighed very carefully during pregnancy. The best course of action is for you and your hus-

band to arrange to talk with your doctor now, before you become pregnant, about the possible courses of action in your
case. Your husband needs to be as much aware of the alternatives as you are, and the two of you should both be involved together in making decisions regarding your medical treatment in
connection with pregnancy. With some women, it's been possible to discontinue lithium before pregnancy, but this depends
very much on their individual illness. If in consultation with
your doctor you decide that this is worth a trial, all of you—your
husband, too—will need to be closely involved in monitoring
your condition.

? *I was treated for obsessive-compulsive disorder in my late
teens. Now I'm in my mid-twenties and in the second
trimester of pregnancy. I was on a medication for awhile, and for
the past few years have attended a support group that's helped
me cope with my illness. A woman in my group developed
OCD symptoms in her third trimester. If my symptoms return at
that time, will I be able to take medication?*

The progress that you've made with your support group is a
promising sign that you could benefit from therapy other than
medication if your symptoms should return. Also, you have
made it symptom-free into your second trimester. If serious
symptoms require a brief course of medication, there are some
medications that can be taken for a short time in the third trimester. Be sure that the doctor treating you now is aware of your
past history and your concerns. You might want your doctor to
provide more information on behavioral therapy or refer you to
a specialist in this area who could help with specific techniques
that you could practice as a first line of treatment. In case all attempts at alternative therapies fail and you have severe symptoms in the second or third trimester, you may have to take
antidepressants while remaining under the care of a specialist
knowledgeable in this area.

WHAT I TELL MY PATIENTS

Your doctor's office should be a place where you feel safe and feel confident in expressing yourself. You should not feel overpowered or intimidated by the idea that the doctor knows best and is going to make your decisions for you. As we've seen, there are many issues involved in the treatment of pregnant women for psychiatric illnesses for which the answers are not black-and-white. Your doctor can, and should, provide you not only with information but also the guidance gained from his or her experience. However, you must be your own advocate for good health care for yourself and your family, and you and your partner must take an active part in evaluating the choices and making the decisions.

Many pregnant women with psychiatric illnesses take a "suffer in silence" approach because they are determined not to take medication under any circumstances. Keep in mind that no doctor wants to expose a woman or her baby to medications unless it is necessary and that your doctor will be working with you to explore all the possible options for treatment.

It's heartrending to think of the generations of women who suffered psychiatric illnesses in pregnancy or postpartum before these conditions were recognized and before treatments were available. These women had no choice but to try to cope alone, without real understanding or support, with what was happening to them. Today, we know much more, and there are many alternatives for supportive therapy and treatment programs that are effective and safe.

Your responsibility for your child's health begins from the time you decide to conceive. If you experience an emotional illness during pregnancy, you need to get the best medical advice you can and follow through with decisions made about your therapy. To hide your illness or avoid treatment is also to avoid taking the responsibility for your own health—and your family's well-being.

GUIDELINES FOR USE OF PSYCHOTROPIC DRUGS IN PREGNANCY AND LACTATION

Drug	Stage	Significance	Guidelines
Lithium	1st trimester Newborn	1. Ebstein's anomaly. 2. Toxicity reported in some newborns—cyanosis, hypotonia, bradycardia, thyroid depression and goiter, atrial flutter, hepatomegaly, ECG abnormalities, cardiomegaly, G.I. bleed, DI, shock (self-limiting, 1–2 weeks).	• Discontinue if possible 1 mo. before conception. • If relapse + benefit outweigh risk, restart. • If conceived while on Li, gradually taper. • Detailed scanning, monitoring—ultrasound, echocardiography. • Renal clearance increase during third trimester but drops abruptly; therefore reduce dose by 50% at onset of labor.
	Breastfeeding	3. Excreted in breast milk 40% of serum, no toxic effects noted, long-term unknown.	• Use with caution in the 2nd and 3rd trimester. • Contraindicated during breastfeeding.
ANTIDEPRESSANTS			
TCA	Throughout; esp. 1st trim.	1. Several studies have not shown increased frequency of fetal malformations.	• Probably of low teratogenic potential; more studies needed. Monitor carefully if used.
	Newborn	2. Withdrawal symptoms—irritability, cyanosis, hypotonia, poor sucking, tachypnea, varies with drug.	• One week wash-out period (discontinue TCA or taper if possible one week prior to estimated due date).
	Breastfeeding	3. Breast milk levels about 10%; no long-term studies.	
MAOI		• Limited use because of dietary restrictions.	• Not recommended for use during pregnancy or lactation.
SSRIs	During pregnancy	• Recent reports on fluoxetine (Prozac) in pregnancy. • Effects unknown.	• Too early to recommend guidelines. • Further studies are needed.
	Breastfeeding		• Contraindicated during breastfeeding.
Newer Antidepressants 1. Nefazedone (Serzone) 2. Venlafaxine (Effexor)	}	Recently released in Canada and the United States. Not recommended during pregnancy and lactation.	

BENZODIAZEPINES

1st trimester	1. Association with cleft lip + cleft palate in some studies.
Near term	2. Neonatal withdrawal—tremor, irritability, hypertonicity, over-active sucking reflex.
Breastfeeding	3. Excreted in breast milk. Neonatal jaundice Day 1–4 due to immature liver conjugation.

- Not recommended in 1st trimester unless benefits outweigh risks.
- Single or low-dose therapy in 2nd and 3rd trimesters controversial. If benefit outweighs risk, use in smaller doses for short duration.
- Still controversial.

ANTIPSYCHOTICS

Throughout, esp. in 1st trimester	1. Numerous studies: Edlund (1984) studied 19,000 infants showing 2.2% increase in congenital anomalies over control group (3.2%). • Variation between neuroleptics.
Newborn infants	2. Extrapyramidal symptoms persisting up to 6 months.
Breastfeeding	3. Breast milk concentrations about ⅓ of plasma levels. • May show sedation. • Long-term effects unknown.

- Mortola (1989) suggested a trial withdrawal of neuroleptics prior to pregnancy to see if patient can tolerate.
- Use high-potency neuroleptics in 1st, 2nd, and 3rd trimesters with close monitoring.
- (Ananth, 1970) less evidence of malformations, with thioridazine, perphenazine, trifluoperazine, haloperidol (high-potency).
- Discontinue or taper prior to delivery—depending on individual cases, e.g., past history of post-partum psychosis, drug dose.
- Most women elect not to nurse.

G. G. Briggs et al., *Drugs in Pregnancy and lactation: A reference guide to fetal and neonatal risk*, 3rd ed. (Philadelphia: Williams & Wilkins, 1990).
W. F. Rayburn and Zuspan, *Drug therapy in obstetrics and gynecology*, 3rd ed. (St. Louis, MO: Mosby-Year Book, 1991).
S. Misri, The use of psychotropic drugs in pregnancy and lactation: A review, *Canadian Family Physician*, 32 (Oct. 1986).
S. Misri and R. Sivertz, Tricyclic drugs in pregnancy and lactation: A preliminary report, *International Journal of Psychiatry in Medicine*, 21 (1991) (2): 157–171.
L. Laegreid, G. Hagberg, and A. Lundberg, The effect of benzodiazepines on the fetus and the newborn, *Neuropediatrics*, 23 (Feb. 1992): 18–23.
L. Laegreid, G. Hagberg, and A. Lundberg, Neurodevelopment in late infancy after prenatal exposure to benzodiazepines—a prospective study, *Neuropediatrics*, 23 (Apr. 1992): 60–67.
M. J. Edlund and T. J. Craig, Antipsychotic drug use and birth defects: An epidemiologic reassessment, *Comprehensive Psychiatry*, 25 (Jan.-Feb. 1984): 32–37.
J. F. Mortola, The use of psychotropic agents in pregnancy and lactation (review), *Psychiatric Clinics of North America*, 23 (Mar. 1989): 69–87.
J. Ananth, Side effects in the neonate from psychotropic agents excreted through breastfeeding, *American Journal of Psychiatry*, 135 (1970)(7): 801–805.

CHAPTER 12

"I DON'T KNOW—IT SOUNDS SO STRANGE"

Electroconvulsive Treatment in Pregnancy and Postpartum

In addition to counseling, behavioral therapy, and medication, there is another kind of therapy for treatment of severe psychiatric disorders—*electroconvulsive therapy (ECT)*. In this therapy, a patient, who is placed under general anesthetic, receives a low-voltage electrical current through electrodes placed on his or her temples. It is unclear exactly how ECT achieves an improvement in the patient's depression, but it is thought that the low electrical current produces a positive change in the brain's biochemistry. Indeed, the brain chemical changes that occur with the use of antidepressant medication are identical to those that occur with the use of ECT. Patients for whom this therapy might be recommended are those with acute depression and suicidal ideation and severe psychosis (complete lack of interaction and response). A small number of postpartum depressions or psychoses may progress to the point where ECT is required. ECT is usually considered when medication has made little difference, and in cases of acutely suicidal patients, it can truly be a lifesaving measure.

ECT (which was once commonly called "shock therapy") has had a troubled history and its use has been sensationalized in the North American media. As it is administered today, it is a safe procedure that plays a valuable role in psychiatric treatment. I would like to explain how this therapy is used.

302

HOW IS ELECTROCONVULSIVE THERAPY GIVEN?

ECT is performed while a patient is under general anesthetic. As with any medical procedure performed under general anesthetic, patients must sign a consent form beforehand, indicating that the procedure has been clearly explained to them and they agree to receive it. Since ECT is used most often in patients who are severely ill, they may be too removed from reality to understand the illness and the therapy. In these cases, the patient's partner or a family member when applicable may be the person to make the decision and to sign the consent form.

Before the procedure, the patient's general health condition is assessed with a physical examination. The examination might include laboratory tests, an electrocardiogram, and X rays. The patient is then given a short-acting anesthetic and a muscle relaxant through intravenous injections. The muscle relaxant reduces the severity of muscle contractions that are triggered when the electrical current is administered. When the patient has been sedated, electrodes are attached to the temples. A low level of alternating current (70 to 130 volts) is applied for 0.1–2.0 seconds. The patient may appear to have mild twitching and curling of the toes and then a slight tremor. The procedure lasts less than a minute, and the patient generally remains asleep and under observation for another 5 to 30 minutes. Patients usually are given six to ten treatments, with one treatment a day on alternate days.

Patients do not experience any pain during or after the procedure. A few patients have reported some short-term memory loss but normal memory functions return within a short time—a matter of days to months.

FEARS ABOUT ECT

It is unlikely that your family doctor or psychiatrist would discuss electroconvulsive therapy as the therapy of first choice when you discuss your emotional problem. Statistically, only a small percentage of psychiatric cases require ECT. To present ECT as one of a number of treatment options would be something like a doctor telling a patient with a sore throat that she might need surgery on her vocal cords—unlikely and rather frightening. In most of North America, there is a widespread public reluctance to even consider ECT as an acceptable therapy—an attitude based on fears about the misuse of ECT and misinformation about how it is administered today. Tragically, misinformation and the resulting fears about ECT can stand in the way of objective decision making when this therapy is indicated.

Today, we readily accept the idea of extremely complicated and delicate surgery on vital body organs—surgery that would have been unthinkable before general anesthesia was available and modern techniques to monitor and control vital signs were developed. Just as early surgical procedures were primitive, so were the early days of ECT. Variable voltages of electric current were administered to patients without general anesthetic. This was indeed true "shock therapy," which was portrayed horrifically some years ago in the movie *One Flew Over the Cuckoo's Nest*. It's important to understand that *the shock treatment shown in this movie does not in any way whatsoever represent the way electroconvulsive therapy is performed*. Patients and their families who are faced with decisions about ECT should not imagine that this film reflects reality.

Other fears about ECT are related to the use of electric shocks to punish individuals in countries ruled by politically repressive regimes. In these countries, a primitive form of "shock treatment" has been used as a form of punishment for political prisoners, and the administration of electric shock has been used as an instrument to extract information from the repressed. Neither of these bears any resemblance to responsible electroconvulsive *therapy*—just as the misuse of drugs, hospitalization, and surgical procedures in repressive regimes bears no resemblance to contemporary medical practice in North America. The misuse of medical techniques in oppressive regimes is frightening and continues to cause concern in our civilized world, but the legitimate and professional use of these techniques should not be disregarded because unethical people have used them irresponsibly.

Finally, some people are afraid of psychiatric care and psychiatrists in general. Nearly all of us have gone to a family doctor since childhood, and as patients, we have a good idea of what goes on in a doctor's office. We have a great deal of common information about how a broken arm might be treated, or how long the flu might last—whether or not we have ever had these particular problems. This type of familiarity does not extend to psychiatric and psychological disorders and their possible treatment. It's natural to fear the unknown, and many people simply don't want to know about "mental illness." They'd prefer to see people with emotional disorders as people who are different from their family and friends. These are the people for whom it's a real test to make the adjustments and decisions necessary when a family member—or they themselves—develop an emotional disorder.

WHEN SHOULD ECT BE USED?

Much of the controversy about electroconvulsive therapy began to clear up when guidelines for its use were developed in 1985 by a task force of the U.S. National Institutes of Health Consensus Conference. This task force clarified the specific indications for use of ECT. In pregnant or postpartum women, ECT is considered the treatment of choice for:

1. An acutely suicidal postpartum patient
2. A patient in postpartum depression with superimposed obsessional and suicidal thoughts, in whom treatment with antidepressant medication has failed
3. An acute postpartum psychotic patient in whom the use of major tranquilizers has not been effective
4. A patient with postpartum psychosis who has a history of chronic psychosis and is not responding to conventional treatment
5. A patient with postpartum psychosis who has been successfully treated with ECT for prior psychotic illness
6. A pregnant patient with suicidal depression in whom medication has failed or is contraindicated

As these guidelines show, it is not the norm in North America to use ECT as a first line of treatment. In some European countries, however, modern ECT might be used as an early treatment for depression because patients usually show very quick recovery from their symptoms, and, in the case of breastfeeding mothers with psychosis, this may mean that nursing can continue in spite of the therapy. Since the response to treatment is relatively quick, in some less developed countries, where medications and psychiatric care are not widely available, ECT is used as a cost-effective way to treat depression.

GUIDELINES FOR THE ADMINISTRATION OF ECT

Safe and consistent guidelines have also been developed for the techniques involved in administering electroconvulsive therapy. Dr. Remick, a personal friend and colleague of many years, along with Dr. Maurice, suggest excellent guidelines when ECT is prescribed for a pregnant or postpartum mother. In addition, I have incorporated recommendations from more recent literature.

1. The mother will have a complete physical exam beforehand to detect any irregularities in her general health.
2. ECT should usually not be given to mothers with high-risk pregnancies unless proper monitoring is provided.
3. The mother's condition should be continuously monitored during ECT with an electrocardiogram.
4. Low-dosage electrical current should be used.
5. All of the usual procedures applying to surgical patients under general anesthesia should apply—for example, continuous monitoring of blood pressure. Insertion of an endotracheal tube may be considered for advanced pregnancies.
6. With a pregnant mother, fetal monitoring should begin some hours before the procedure and continue for several hours afterwards. During ECT, the fetal heart rate should be monitored with Doppler ultrasonography, and it is important to assess how the fetus is doing on a weekly basis by means of non-stress tests.
7. Although the risk to the fetus from barbiturate anesthesia is not well understood, brief exposure to these agents is not likely to be problematic.

SAFE USE OF ECT DURING PREGNANCY AND BREASTFEEDING

As we have discussed, most psychiatrists would consider ECT as a "last defense" therapy in specific instances to treat a pregnant mother—for example, a woman who is acutely suicidal. In addition, ECT presents no risks for a breastfeeding infant, since the medication used for general anesthesia is excreted from the mother's body quite quickly. However, since ECT is used only in severe cases, the mothers likely to require ECT are usually unable to focus on breastfeeding because of their acute illness.

The same precautions apply in a family's decisions about ECT as to treatment with medication. The mother (if she is able) and her partner need to become fully informed about her condition, the risks of treatment, the possible alternatives, and the long-term prognosis for her illness. Again, I encourage families who are involved in these decisions to get reliable medical advice, to gather all the information they can, and to be as objective as possible about the options before them. When your family's health is at risk, you must look beyond stereotypes and popular assumptions and make a truly informed decision.

Laurie's story illustrates the extreme illness that might require ECT.

LAURIE'S STORY

Laurie, a 33-year-old nurse, had developed depression in the fourth month postpartum. She was treated at first as an outpatient and for three months was on antidepressant medication. This appeared to make little difference, and she began to have obsessional thoughts of committing suicide. I admitted her to hospital when her obsessional thoughts increased in severity and she became a suicide risk. She became increasingly unmanageable, even on the ward.

Laurie's husband, a school teacher, had been involved in earlier discussions about her medication and hospitalization. I met with him again and talked about the resistant nature of her illness and the possibility of electroconvulsive therapy. He understood how ill Laurie was and wanted her to be treated. Because she was too ill herself to understand events, it was her husband who agreed to the treatment and signed a consent form for the therapy.

Every other day, Laurie received what is called a course of "eight-unilateral ECTs." She stayed in the hospital about eight weeks all together and was discharged when her symptoms improved. At first after discharge, she complained of some problems with her memory, but most of these problems have disappeared. She is now functioning again, meeting the full challenges of being a "working mom."

SALLY'S STORY

Sally was a 32-year-old "full-time" mother, married to a retail salesman in a store that sells high-tech equipment. Sally first came to see me when she was 20 weeks pregnant, having developed a bipolar illness during pregnancy. In her case, I decided not to use ECT when she was psychotic during her second trimester—first, because she and her husband refused to consider it, and secondly, because she luckily responded to neuroleptic medication quite well and became asymptomatic in a few weeks.

Once the symptoms subsided, I stopped the medication, fully aware that if Sally required treatment again, I would restart it. She continued under my care, and with her husband, we discussed the possibility that she would again experience symptoms in the postpartum period. I also talked with them about the possibility of ECT as an option for treatment after the baby was born. Sally had not wanted ECT because she was concerned that the baby would be "exposed" to the general anesthesia that is required. In addition, she herself was not keen to have general anesthesia three times a week for the purpose of receiving ECT. These feelings were quite understandable, and since fortunately she responded to neuroleptic medication, there was no need to reconsider the choice of therapy.

However, Sally's course of illness changed after the baby's birth. She became acutely psychotic, with manic features. I again prescribed a course of neuroleptics and lithium. For months, Sally was in the hospital, separated from her baby, and it became quite obvious to her husband that ECT would now be an appropriate course of treatment. The delay in Sally's recovery was affecting the whole family, most importantly, the baby. The baby was brought in to visit Sally on a daily basis, but Sally was missing out on the special experience of the early months of motherhood because of her illness. Her husband also realized there was no point in prolonging her illness if indeed ECT was going to work.

With informed consent, eight-unilateral ECTs were performed on Sally in the hospital, and she did recover. After discharge from hospital, Sally continued to see me for two years. Even now, she comes to see me occasionally, although she is primarily under the care of her family doctor. She continues on lithium therapy.

Sally's experience illustrates two points. The first is that while ECT is an option for treatment of severe disorders during pregnancy, it is understandable that expectant mothers may be reluctant to consider it. The second is that, once the baby is born, the main emphasis must be on the mother's health and recovery. In Sally's case, the delay in using ECT prolonged her illness unnecessarily. In fact, this patient later came to feel guilty for having delayed ECT treatment and thus being unable to really take part in her baby daughter's first days and weeks, and these feelings of guilt had to be explored in therapy.

SOME QUESTIONS YOU MIGHT HAVE ABOUT ECT

? *I am a 32-year-old woman who has had two postpartum depressions. I was hospitalized after the birth of my second child and was given ECT because I was suicidal and depressed. I received eight-unilateral ECTs, and after that I felt well. I did not need to have any antidepressants after that, and I have continued to feel well for the past three and a half years. I am pregnant again and expecting the baby in about three months. Will I need ECT again?*

The fact that you have had a medication-free period for three to four years means that you have been free of depression all this time and did not have a relapse. A person who receives ECT once does not necessarily need ECT again if the depression returns. Some people receive ECT under specific conditions; being suicidally depressed is one such condition. You will not necessarily have a suicidal depression after the birth of your next child. Most people get treated with antidepressants when they are clinically depressed, and each case must be treated individually. I would suggest that you not worry right now about the kind of treatment you might receive, since many questions remain unanswered: The chance of recurrence of depression during postpartum is 60 percent. If you become depressed, your response to the newer type antidepressant medications will be tried before ECT will be considered.

? *I have had bipolar illness for about sixteen years. It started in my teens, and now I am in my thirties. I have never been pregnant, but I am now married and am thinking about having a child in the near future. I've had ECTs five times in the past few years during my illness, sometimes during my manic episodes and sometimes when I was depressed. I'm afraid that if I again have a manic or depressive illness after the birth of my baby, I may need to receive ECT.*

You seem to be very well aware of the progression of your illness over the past few years. The fact that you continue under psychiatric care and that you have taken the time to plan ahead for a pregnancy and birth are both good signs. The chances of your having either a manic episode or a depressive episode are high, given your history, but that does not automatically mean that your manic episodes, or for that matter, your depressive episodes, will be treated with ECT. Again, there are specific conditions in which ECT is appropriate, and unless you are one of the candidates in whom ECT is indicated, you will be treated first with either neuroleptic medications or lithium when you become manic, and antidepressant medications when you become depressed. Your decision to become pregnant should not be affected by the fear that you might require ECT.

? *I am married to a man with bipolar illness, for which he has received ECT in the past. I have never experienced depression, but my mother had postpartum depressions after the birth of each of her three children. My husband's treatment with ECT and my mother's history of postpartum depressions makes me wonder about the chances of my having postpartum depression and receiving ECT.*

Your husband's bipolar illness and treatment with ECT has nothing to do with whether or not ECT would be required for you, should you become depressed.

Your mother's history places you in a high-risk category for developing postpartum depression yourself; nevertheless, it's impossible to predict whether or not you will experience this illness.

Whether or not a psychiatrist would prescribe ECT is not dependent on the occurrence of bipolar illness in your husband or the occurrence of postpartum depression in your mother. What's important is whether or not you yourself suffer symptoms of depression after your baby is born. If you should have depression, the question of what treatment is used in your individual case will have to be considered at the time.

WHAT I TELL MY PATIENTS

Although the concept of electroconvulsive therapy is frightening to most people today, and for understandable reasons, ECT has its place in treating certain psychiatric disorders. In fact, I would recommend it as the first line of treatment in certain specific types of patients, when not prescribing this treatment would be detrimental both to the mother and her family. When I discuss ECT with my patients, I try to alleviate their fears by answering their questions as openly as possible. Many times, I have personally accompanied my patients and their partners or family to the room where the therapy takes place. This helps to demystify the experience and relieve their anxiety.

It's helpful for patients to see the ECT room ahead of time, to see the furnishings of the treatment room and look at the equipment that is used, so that they see in advance where and how they will be treated. I've also found it worthwhile to ask a patient who has already received ECT if she would be willing to talk about her experience with the family who is trying to decide whether to accept this type of therapy. The realization that another woman like oneself has had similar experiences and has gone through this therapy successfully can be very supportive.

Should your family's case be one in which medication therapies are tried and make little difference, your doctor might recommend that electroconvulsive therapy be tried. The popular misconceptions about this treatment can make this a difficult decision for you. I would encourage you not to refuse ECT outright if it is recommended to you by a psychiatrist. Remember that you may always seek a second opinion. If ECT is recommended in your case, you should feel confident that it is safe for you.

Your doctor is both your advocate and your resource, and you should expect that sufficient time will be spent with you to explain exactly what this therapy involves and to answer your questions about it. Once again, one of the most important things I have to do in early conversations with my patients is to help them step beyond the fears and misunderstandings they may have about emotional illness and feel confident in the course of treatment before them.

CHAPTER 13

"WILL I EVER BE HAPPY AGAIN?"

A General Perspective on Women's Emotional Health

When a woman experiences emotional illness, it's not surprising that she holds a very personal perspective on what is happening and what the future holds. Women with emotional illnesses related to pregnancy and childbirth find themselves in the particularly painful position of being ill at the very time in their lives when they had expected to be their happiest. No wonder women in these situations ask themselves questions like "Why me?" "Is there anything I've done wrong?" "Will I have this illness for the rest of my life?" and "Will I ever be happy again?" In this final chapter, I would like to suggest how women can place those very personal questions into a broader context and find hopeful answers.

RETURNING TO THE BIO/PSYCHO/SOCIAL PERSPECTIVE

Why Me?

In Chapter Ten I described the bio/psycho/social perspective on treating patients. Taking these three factors together provides a holistic view of the individual patient, and to some extent this perspective helps answer the question of why one individual develops an illness while another one remains healthy. There is also a role played by traumatic events, crisis, or stress. Medical science is only beginning to sort out why individuals respond differently to crisis or stress, but a very

312

general equation can be used to suggest the combinaton of factors that contribute to emotional illness:

The individual	+ Life events	= ???
Biological factors	Crisis	Emotional
Psychological factors	Traumatic event	health or
Social factors	Stress	Emotional
		illness

The three factors can be applied very specifically to each individual. I would like to expand these concepts to look at women's emotional health and illness in North America today. After all, individuals live out their lives in a very broad context shaped by history and culture. Both history and culture contribute to the definition of terms as basic as "good health," and they affect both an individual's view of herself and society's view of the individual.

Biological Factors: The Brain's Biochemistry

While the exact causes of emotional disorders are not clear, it is known that they involve changes in the brain's chemistry. Research has been able to identify specific chemicals that are involved in the brain's function and to track increases or decreases in the levels of these chemicals in connection with specific emotional disorders. This is a fairly new development in medical science, and there is still much to learn in this area. However, this understanding has made a great change in how emotional illness is viewed and treated.

First of all, this is clear confirmation that certain emotional or mental disorders are *medical* conditions which can be categorized, diagnosed, and treated. Depression or psychosis is no more the result of a "character flaw" or a "bad personality" than is heart disease. Secondly, once scientists began to understand the brain's chemistry, they were able to develop medications to correct chemical imbalances. As research continues, more mysteries will be cleared up and more valuable medications developed.

This understanding and approach to emotional disorders is only a few decades old and is not fully known outside the medical profession. Just think, though, what a difference this understanding makes to our centuries-old prejudices against "crazy" people.

Biological Factors: The Reproductive Cycle

Women are at greater risk than men of developing depression, obsessive-compulsive disorder, and seasonally related disorders. With some disorders, the risk for women increases with age. The identification of this gender pattern, along with the awareness of biochemical changes in the brain, has led to research on whether there is a close association between a woman's reproductive cycle and mood disorders. Different studies have shown that there indeed appears to be a link between the reproductive cycle and emotional disorders, although the specifics are unclear and continue to be a focus of research. Nonetheless, even preliminary information suggests a positive avenue for the recognition and treatment of emotional disorders.

Consequently, more is becoming known about the role of the reproductive hormones in affecting the brain's chemistry, and this has allowed us to identify both women who are at high risk at certain stages of their reproductive phase, such as menopause, and the possible impacts of medications like oral contraceptives and estrogen replacement. Moreover, in looking at the psychiatric histories of women from the perspective of the reproductive cycle, researchers are beginning to see relationships that can help predict individual risk factors and suggest when preventative treatment is appropriate.

Several general findings have emerged in the last several years. In general, it appears that mood elevations may occur at the same time as the level of certain reproductive hormones is high. For instance, a woman feels "wonderful" for a few days prior to ovulation during the menstrual cycle and usually during the second trimester of pregnancy. This seems to relate to the fact that in some women, preexisting emotional disorders may actually improve or vanish during pregnancy. The opposite also appears to be true: depression is more likely at the phase of the cycle when hormone levels are low. These conditions are present in the premenstrual phase of the monthly cycle, in the postpartum period, and during menopause. Now, this does not necessarily mean that high levels of reproductive hormones *cause* mood elevation, or vice versa, and the exact relationship between hormones and mood changes continues to be studied.

Depressive symptoms are observed in some women who take oral contraceptives, and studies on the older form of oral contraceptives showed that 30 to 50 percent of women reported some symptoms of depression. Again, I emphasize that it is not known whether hormone changes cause emotional disorders, but it is very valuable for women to be aware of a possible relationship.

As we have seen, in some individuals depressive symptoms have been connected with the premenstrual period and with the onset of menopause. Depending on different studies, at least 20 percent and up to 80 percent of women report mood changes of irritability, hostility, anxiety, sleeplessness, and loss of appetite in the premenstrual phase. The seriousness of these symptoms seems to be linked with age, with the onset of symptoms in adolescence and the highest prevalence of symptoms in the twenties to thirties. Women who are within two years of either side of menopause show a distinct increase in mood fluctuation compared to men of the same age and to women of other ages. They commonly report feelings of insecurity, lack of confidence, anxiety, difficulty making decisions, poor concentration, forgetfulness, and sleep difficulties.

The fact that serious research is being done in these areas is a promising sign for our future understanding of how women develop emotional illness. For example, it appears that women who had had a lifetime history of depression have also experienced extreme premenstrual symptoms. It is also known that 10 to 40 percent of women who have had depressions before pregnancy can be expected to develop postpartum depressions, and 50 percent of women with a prior psychosis will develop postpartum psychosis. It appears that emotional disorders during pregnancy may suggest that the woman will develop emotional illnesses related to the reproductive cycle later, such as extreme mood changes with menopause. While the exact hormonal and neurochemical factors involved are still unclear, the relationships suggested by these studies give us better information to help diagnose and treat individuals.

HISTORICAL ATTITUDES TOWARD POSTPARTUM DEPRESSION

A look at emotional illness from a historical perspective should offer women and their families a great deal of hope. In recent years, tremendous progress has been made in understanding and treating emotional illness. This progress, and the change in historical perspective, are particularly dramatic in the instance of that most puzzling of women's emotional illnesses, postpartum depression.

Emotional disorders in the postpartum go back to the first recorded medical studies—the fourth century B.C. writings of Hippocrates, the "father of medicine." He observed and documented the illness of a new mother of twins who developed restlessness and insomnia in the sixth postpartum day, became delirious and then unconscious on the eleventh day, and died on the seventeenth day. Over the centuries, doctors have tried to understand what causes emotional disorder in the postpartum period and, as modern psychiatry developed in the twentieth century, to determine whether postpartum emotional illness is a distinct type of emotional illness.

Until we get to the nineteenth century, there are only fragmentary records on postpartum disorders. In the Western world, the treatment of emotional illness in general has had a very dismal history. In some periods of history, patients were thought to be "evil" or "possessed" or "criminal." Shockingly, it seems that when the prisons were opened after the French Revolution, some perfectly normal women were released—women who had been thrown into prison because of their symptoms of postpartum depression or psychosis, from which they had since recovered. In Europe and North America, the treatment of the "insane" has been grim until only very recently. People who now can be recognized as having emotional disorders—and are treated successfully—would at one time have been locked away for life in "asylums" that offered little or no treatment and, more often than not, terribly inhumane conditions.

In the nineteenth century, two French doctors took a great interest in postpartum emotional illness. In the early 1800s, Dr. J. E. D. Esquirol carefully documented the cases of 90 women and divided their illnesses into three types: those that occurred during pregnancy, those that occurred immediately after childbirth, and those that occurred six weeks or more after the birth. These women had severe symptoms that had brought them to the attention of medical professionals, but Dr. Esquirol was the first to recognize something we know only too well today—that many more women were suffering in silence, afraid to reveal their illness for fear that they would be misunderstood, stigmatized, perhaps even removed from their families.

In the mid-nineteenth century Dr. Louis Marcé conducted similar observations of over 300 French women. Dr. Marcé was one of the first to try to come to grips with the question of whether women's postpartum depression is a unique condition or whether it is like any other depression and occurs by coincidence in the postpartum period. He, too, divided his cases into three groups: illness beginning in pregnancy, illness occurring within six weeks of childbirth, and illness occurring six weeks or more postpartum. His conclusion was that the types of emotional illnesses he observed in pregnancy were no different from those in nonpregnant or male patients, but that those that occurred in the postpartum had a unique identity of their own. He was convinced that something in the body's physical mechanism was at the base of postpartum illness, although he could not identify it.

Dr. Marcé's conclusions have become important cornerstones of modern thinking on postpartum illness. Since his time, the endocrine system (the body's system of organs that are responsible for hormone production) has been discovered, and researchers are beginning to explore the possible connections between the endocrine system and emotional disorders. In addition, his conviction that postpartum illness was a unique type of depression is now widely shared by many psychiatrists and offers a useful way to approach and treat this particular disorder in women.

Perception of postpartum depression was nearly derailed in the early twentieth century, when psychiatry was beginning to take shape as part of medical science, and there had to be some common agreement on terminology and classification. An influential psychiatrist, Dr. E. A. Strecker, wrote that postpartum depression and postpartum psychosis were no different from these same disorders experienced outside the postpartum period—and the terms themselves actually disappeared from medical textbooks! Only very recently has there been a turning point. In 1980, an English psychiatrist, Dr. Ian Brockington, organized an international conference on postpartum psychiatric illness. When physicians and researchers from around the world came together, they discovered that many of them were pursuing similar work that pointed in the same direction that Dr. Marcé had taken over a century earlier. Psychiatrists still have not reached a unanimous decision on how postpartum disorders fit in the larger classification of depressive disorders, but postpartum disorders are now being actively investigated as a distinct entity. The result for women today is better diagnosis and treatment as well as the realization, which the public is coming to share, that certain types of postpartum disorders are temporary, treatable medical conditions that can be followed by a healthy life.

CROSS-CULTURAL VIEWS OF THE POSTPARTUM PERIOD

I began this chapter by talking about the bio/psycho/social model of therapy. As we look at our own biological, psychological, and social profiles, it's worth noting that many of our views of ourselves and others are influenced by the culture in which we live and the historical time in which we find ourselves. I discussed the way modern medical research is clarifying the biological basis of emotional disorders and how, historically, emotional disorders have come to be understood as treatable conditions. However, there are still many questions unanswered and thus many active areas for scientific inquiry.

One of the fascinating areas that continues to be studied is why postpartum disorders do not occur consistently across cultures. If postpartum depression occurred solely because of biochemical changes, then one would expect to find a similar percentage of women with this disorder from culture to culture—and this is not the case. Recent cross-cultural studies show that although the physical processes in childbirth and postpartum are of course the same, women's attitudes towards them and the way that they experience these processes emotionally differ from country to country. One of the clear cultural differences is that family life in the industrialized West is quite isolated. Nuclear families are breaking up, and there is little support from extended family. In this setting, even small mood changes may be perceived as "depression." In addition, the nature of stress may be different and may be perceived differently in North America than in some non-Western countries.

SOME STUDIES IN MEDICAL ANTHROPOLOGY

Studies in the field of medical anthropology show how cultural perceptions shape attitudes towards disease and illness in different societies. Dr. Laurence Kruckman, an anthropologist who has gathered information on how various cultures view childbirth and the postpartum period, notes that when the perinatal period (that is, the time around birth) is discussed in the Western world, there is a tendency to overlook completely the idea that this period extends beyond the mother's release from hospital. Even the week's stay in hospital, which was the tradition twenty or thirty years ago, has now been shortened to a day or two. In contrast, other cultures have developed rituals and myths that acknowledge the idea that a woman who has given birth needs a recuperation period set apart from normal life.

Some cultures' rituals are directed toward protecting the vulnerable new mother. In rural Guatemala, the new mother's ordinary activities are curtailed during the eight days after birth, and attention is given to keeping her warm. It's believed there that the woman is susceptible to cold and wind, and that exposure to these can thin her breast milk and make her child sick.

A similar seven- to eight-day period is observed in some parts of the Philippines. The new mother is given a special diet, heat treatment, and herbal medications, and she is confined to her home and expected to rest. New mothers among the Ibibio people of Nigeria retire to a separate hut called the "fattening room," where they are cared for by older women and devote themselves only to eating, sleeping, and caring for their babies. One anthropologist has called these rituals of support, "mothering the mother."

Many cultures also have special rituals that accord distinct recognition to the mother. For example, after a period of rest in the "fattening room," the Ibibio mother with her infant is welcomed out of seclusion with a feast in her honor. The baby's father presents the mother with a new dress and plants a palm tree for the infant.

Dr. Kruckman's conclusion as an anthropologist is that North American women experience postpartum blues and depression because (1) the postpartum period is not structured in society as a distinct event that happens for a specific time period and has particular needs; (2) there is little social recognition of the woman's transition to the role of mother; and (3) mothers receive little meaningful assistance, including information about caring for themselves and their babies.

What Can We Learn from the Anthropologists' View?

As I have pointed out in other chapters, the causes of emotional disorders are complex and are not yet fully explained. I do not feel that cultural factors alone cause postpartum depression. However, these studies support the findings that women who have weak social support systems and/or a poor marital relationship are at greater risk of postpartum depression.

It is interesting that in recent decades, women have been able to "reclaim" the experience of childbirth because they did not want the increasing medicalization of the birth experience. As a result, prenatal classes have fostered a very participatory approach to pregnancy and childbirth. Even so, the postpartum period has not yet been "reclaimed," and the fact is, once the new mother walks out of the hospital, she's virtually on her own. More and more, health care professionals are recognizing the distinct demands of the postpartum period, and postpartum support groups have formed in some communities. Perhaps, in addition, women themselves need to consider how the postpartum period could be meaningfully acknowledged and supported within the context of our North American society.

WILL I EVER BE HAPPY AGAIN?

The question of happiness is a very interesting one, and one that must be answered from a very personal, even very private, perspective. One person can be unhappy surrounded by people he or she loves; another person can be happy living alone, in complete isolation. Happiness is an intangible state, and no one can tell from the outside whether or not another person is truly happy. Happiness is a feeling of individual experiences from *within*.

When one considers the possibility for happiness in a person with a serious illness or a chronic disease, one needs to recognize that it is not the external events that account for happiness, but the individual's perception of life events or illness. No one chooses to have a psychiatric illness, any more than they choose to undergo a debilitating surgery. Over time, conditions change—the patient may recover, or may experience relapses or flare-ups. Although events themselves may seem beyond control, one always has a personal choice in how to respond to them.

MARGO'S STORY

I first saw Margo, a woman now in her early fifties, when I was a resident in psychiatry in the mid-1970s. Margo's story represents one of the most important messages I have for my patients, because it was Margo who first asked me, in the midst of her postpartum depression at the age of 29, "Dr. Misri, will I ever be happy again?" Let us use Margo's experience to explore how this question can be answered.

Margo had experienced postpartum blues after the births of her first two children. After the birth of the third, she became severely depressed and had to be hospitalized. We did not have some of the antidepressants we have now, but she responded very well to a medication called Elavil, which is still in use today, and was discharged from hospital within a few weeks.

I continued to see Margo for about a year, which proved to be a very devastating time for her whole family. Although she resumed her normal activities, she had great uncertainties about the effects of her moods on the two older children, who were ages three and five. Her husband was generally supportive, but he was also worried about the children and exhausted by the confusion in their family life; their marriage was quite troubled for most of that year. Eventually, Margo's depression improved, and her therapy was terminated.

When her youngest was about four years old, Margo came back to see me. Now in her thirties, she was finding that she had severe premenstrual mood changes. From the time of ovulation to a few days into her period, she was experiencing a state much like her postpartum depression. At that time, PMS (premenstrual syndrome) was little researched, and the course of treatment was unclear. We tried several things—special diets, lifestyle changes, vitamin B, and also evening primrose oil. I referred her to an endocrinologist for hormone studies and to a dietitian who revamped Margo's diet and put her on an exercise program. All this was to little avail, and she continued to have severe symptoms.

At age 37, Margo had a miscarriage and decided against more children. After her tubal ligation, her premenstrual symptoms became even more severe, although she could still function as a full-time mother and homemaker. In the 1980s, we began to see more research on premenstrual syndrome and decided to try Margo on a tricyclic antidepressant. She took a small dose daily for the first half of her menstrual cycle, then increased the dose in the second half. Most of her symptoms were alleviated.

Now in her early forties, Margo found that after a year of therapy, she felt much more energy and felt well even without antidepressant medication. Her children were all in school now, and she began to concentrate on establishing herself as an artist. Margo had painted for many years, and her paintings vividly depict her mental state. The evolution of Margo's paintings paralleled her evolution as a person. Her different episodes of depression, her experience with PMS—all these are quite powerfully evident in her work. She has become, in fact, a well-known Canadian artist.

This was a very stable and fulfilling time in Margo's life. Her children were growing up, her husband was very proud of her achievements, and she was gaining worldwide recognition as an artist. In 1991, now around age 50, she again returned to see me. She complained of hot flashes, occasional breast tenderness at midcycle, increasing insomnia, a gradual weight gain of 20 pounds over two years, and irregular menstrual periods. Her family doctor established with blood tests that she was indeed going through menopause. She went to the menopause group at the hospital, received educational material, and it was decided that she was a good candidate for hormone replacement therapy.

Early in 1993, Margo returned to me with full-blown symptoms of depression. While she was managing her menopausal symptoms very well, she was unable to sleep, she had no appetite, and she had lost 35 pounds. She appeared very sensitive and vulnerable, and she cried throughout our session. Her oldest child had moved overseas, and she said her heart ached for him. She felt that her second child, a daughter, had always been her husband's favorite, and she felt very distant from her. Margo felt very guilty about the youngest, because she had always been convinced that she had been adversely affected by Margo's postpartum depression. I had a chance to meet this child and found her to be a stable, sensitive, good-natured young girl.

Margo and I agreed that she should try one of the newer types of antidepressants and continue with her hormone replacement therapy. Her severe depressive symptoms cleared up within six weeks. Her paintings now are focusing on older women—women who are slightly overweight but radiant-featured, women who give an entirely different message to the world about womanliness than do those on the covers of fashion magazines. We recently decided that it was time again for Margo to terminate therapy, and when she left, she shared these thoughts with me:

> When I first came to your office almost twenty years ago, I asked you, "Will I ever be happy again?" You had

only started your training then and did not know what to say. But now, having been with you for so many years, I know the answer.

Whether or not I will be happy again has little to do with you and little to do with the medications. You have helped me thorugh crisis every time, but you cannot make me happy! Whether or not I will be happy again has really to do with myself. I didn't give up when I had a major depressive illness when my baby was born, I didn't give up through those years of monthly premenstrual upsets, I didn't give up when I had a major brush with depression during menopause. I know that I may have to take hormone replacement for a few years, as you've told me, but I am going to paint now with more zest than ever.

This time, Dr. Misri, I'm not going to ask you, "Will I ever be happy again?" Because in spite of it all, I have been happy throughout all of this! Really, in spite of all the problems I've gone through. After all, isn't that what life is meant to be?

REFERENCES

Abrams, R. (1992). *Electroconvulsive therapy* (pp. 103–104). New York: Oxford University Press.

Alder, E. M., Cook, A., Davidson, D., et al. (1986). Hormones, mood and sexuality in lactating women. *British Journal of Psychiatry* 148:74–79.

Alder, E. M., & Cox, J. L. (1983). Breast feeding and post-natal depression. *Journal of Psychosomatic Research, 27*:139–144.

American Psychiatric Association. (1990). *The practice of electro convulsive therapy: Recommendations for treatment, training, and privileging*. A Task Force Report. Washington, DC: APA.

Assor, A. & Assor, T. (1985). Emotional involvement in marriage during the last trimester of first pregnancy: A comparison of husbands and wives. *Journal of Psychology, 119*:243–252.

Berchtold, N. & Burrough, M. (1990). Reaching out: Depression after delivery support group network. In NAACOG, *Clinical issues in perinatal and women's health nursing*, Vol. 1, No. 3. Philadelphia: J. B. Lippincott.

Berkowitz, G. S. & Kasl, S. V. (1983). The role of psychological factors in spontaneous preterm delivery. *Journal of Psychosomatic Research, 27*:283–290.

Brandt, K. R. & Mackenzie, T. B. (1987). Obsessive compulsive disorder exacerbated during pregnancy: A case report. *International Journal of Psychiatry in Medicine, 17*(4):361–366.

Brazelton, T. B. & Cramer, B. G. (1990). The attachment of fathers to be. In T. B. Brazelton & B. G. Cramer (Eds.), *The earliest relationship: Parents, infants, and the dramas of early attachment* (pp. 33–42). Boston: Addison-Wesley.

Brockington, I. F. & Kumar, R. (Eds.). (1982). *Motherhood and mental illness*. London: Academic Press.

Brown, E. & Barglow, P. (1971). Pseudocyesis: A paradigm for psychopsychological interactions. *Archives of General Psychiatry, 24*, 221–229.

Buttolph, M. G. & Holland, A. D. (1990). Obsessive compulsive disorders in pregnancy and childbirth. In M. A. Jenike, L. Baer, & W. E. Minichiello,

(Eds.), *Obsessive compulsive disorders: Theory and management*, 2d ed. (pp. 89–95). Chicago: Year Book Medical.

Button, J. H. & Reivich, R. S. (1972). Obsessions of infanticide. *Archives of General Psychiatry, 27*:35–240.

Cherr, S. H. (1985). The incompetent cervix. In S. H. Cherry, R. L. Berkowitz & N. G. Kase (Eds.), *Medical, surgical, and gynecologic complications in pregnancy* (pp. 408–419). Baltimore, MD: Williams & Wilkins.

Clinton, J. F. (1986). Expectant fathers at risk for Couvade. *Nursing Research, 35*, 290–295

———. (1987). Physical and emotional response of expectant fathers throughout pregnancy and the early postpartum period. *International Journal of Nursing Studies, 24*, 59–68.

Cohen, L., Rosenbaum, J. & Heller, V. (1991). Psychotropic drug use in pregnancy. In A. J. Gelenberg, E. L. Bassuk & S. C. Schoonover (Eds.), *The Practitioner's Guide to Psychoactive Drugs* (pp. 389–405). New York: Plenum.

Cohen, L. S., Friedman, J. M., Jefferson, J.W., Johnson, M. & Weiner, M.L. (1994). A reevaluation of risk of in utero exposure to lithium. *Journal of the American Medical Association, 271*(2), 146–150.

Cohen, L. S., Sichel, D. A., Dimmock, J. A., et al. (1994). Postpartum course in women with preexisting panic disorder. *Journal of Clinical Psychiatry, 55*(7), 289–292.

Cooper, P. J., Murray L. & Stein, A. (1993). Psychosocial factors associated with the early termination of breast-feeding. *Journal of Psychosomatic Research, 37*(2), 171–176.

Cox, J. I., Murray, D. & Chapman, G. (1993). A controlled study of the onset, duration, and prevalence of postnatal depression. *British Journal of Psychiatry, 163*, 27–31.

Diagnostic and statistical manual of mental disorders, Fourth Edition. (1994). Washington, DC: American Psychiatric Association.

Drotar, D., Baskiewicz, A., Irvin, N. et al. (1975). The adaptation of parents to the birth of an infant with congenital malformation: A hypothetical model. *Pediatrics, 56*, 710–717.

Edwards, D. R. L., Porter, S. M. & Stein, G. S. (1994). A pilot study of postnatal depression following caesarean section using two retrospective self-rating instruments. *Journal of Psychosomatic Research, 38*(2), 111–117.

FitzGerald, C. M. (1984). Nausea and vomiting in pregnancy. *British Journal of Med 57*, 159–165.

Gitlin, M. J. & Pasnau, R. O. (1989). Psychiatric syndromes linked to reproductive function in women: A review of current knowledge. *American Journal of Psychiatry, 146*(11), 1413–1422.

Golbus, M.S., Conte, F. A., Schneider, E. L. et al. (1974). Intrauterine diagnosis of genetic defects: Results, problems and follow up one hundred cases in a prenatal genetic detection centre. *American Journal of Obstetrics and Gynecology, 118*, 897–905.

Goldstein, D. J. & Marvel, D. E. (1993). Psychotropic medications during pregnancy: Risk to the fetus. *Journal of the American Medical Association, 270*(18), 2177.

Hamilton, J. A. (1992). Patterns of postpartum illness. In J. A. Hamilton & P. N. Harbeger (Eds.), *Postpartum psychiatric illness: A picture puzzle* (pp. 5–14). Philadelphia: University of Pennsylvania Press.

Harper, P. S. (1983). Genetic counselling and prenatal diagnosis. *British Medical Bulletin, 39*(4), 302–309.

Harris, B. (1993). A hormonal component to postnatal depression. *British Journal of Psychiatry, 163*: 403–405.

Hewast, R. J. & Ellis, D. J. (1984). Breastfeeding as a maternal child team effort: Women's perceptions. *Health Care Women International, 5*, 437–452.

Inglewood, D. G. (Ed.). (1985). *Recent advances in postpartum psychiatric disorders*. Washington, DC: American Psychiatric Press.

Jacobson, S. J., Jones, K., Johnson, K., Ceolin, L., Kaur, P., Sahn, D., Donnenfield, A. E., Rieder, M., Santelli, R., Smythe, J., Pastuszak, A., Einarson, T. & Koren, G. (1992). Prospective multicentre study of pregnancy outcome after lithium exposure during first trimester. *Lancet, 339*, 530–533.

Jordan, P. A. (1990). First time expectant fatherhood. In NAACOG's *Clinical issues in perinatal and women's health nursing* (pp. 311–316). Philadelphia: J.B. Lippincott.

Kay, J. (1987). Pregnancy loss and the grief process. In Wood, J. R. & Esposito, J. L. (Eds.), *Pregnancy loss* (pp. 5–19). Baltimore: Williams & Wilkins.

Kessler, S., Kessler, H. & Ward, P. (1984). Psychological aspects of genetic counselling, III: Management of guilt and shame. *American Journal of Medical Genetics, 17*, 673–697.

Klaus, M. H. & Kennell, J. H. (1983). *Bonding: The beginning of parent-infant attachment*. St. Louis, MO: C. V. Mosby.

Klerman, G. L., Weissman, M. M., Rounsaville, B. H. & Chevron, E. S. (1984). *Interpersonal psychotherapy of depression*. New York: Basic Books.

Kruckman, L. D. (1992). Ritual and support. An anthropological view of postpartum depression. In J. A. Hamilton & P. N. Harberger (Eds.), *Postpartum-psychiatric illness: A picture puzzle* (pp. 137–148). Philadelphia: University of Pennsylvania Press.

Kumar, R., Marks, M., Wieck, A., Hirst, D., Campbell, I. & Checkley, S. (1993). Neuroendocrine and psychosocial mechanisms in postpartum psychosis. *Progress in Neuro-Psychopharmacological and Biological Psychiatry, 17*, 571–579.

Lamb, M. E. (1981). *The role of the father in child development*, 2d ed. New York: John Wiley.

Mack, S. A. & Berman, L. C. (1988). A group for parents of children with fatal genetic illness. *American Journal of Orthopsychiatry, 58*, 397–404.

Majerus, P. W., Guze, S. B., Delong, W. B. et al. (1962). Psychotropic factors and psychiatric disease in hyperemesis gravidarum: A follow up of 69 vomiters and 66 controls. *American Journal of Psychiatry, 32*, 636.

Marchetti, F., Romero, M., Bonati, M., Tognoni, G. and the Collaborative Group on Drug Use in Pregnancy. (1993). Use of psychotropic drugs during pregnancy. *European Journal of Clinical Pharmacology, 45*, 495–501.

Martell, L. K. (1990). Postpartum depression as a family problem. *American Journal of Maternal Child Nursing, 15*, 90–93.

McGorry, P. & Connell, S. (1990). The nosology and prognosis of puerperal psychosis: A review. *Comprehensive Psychiatry, 21*(2), 157–171.

Murray, L. & Stein A. (1989). The effects of postnatal depression on the infant. *Baillieres Clinical Obstetrics & Gynaecology, 3*(4), 921–933.

Myers, M. F. (1984). Treating troubled marriages. *American Family Physician, 29*, 221–226.

Myers, M. F. (1989). Marital upset after the baby. *British Columbia Medical Journal, 31*, 483–485.

NAACOG (1990). *Clinical issues in perinatal and women's health nursing: Psychological Aspects of Pregnancy and Postpartum*, Vol. 1, no. 3. Philadelphia: J. B. Lippincott.

Nurnberg, H. G. (1989). An overview of somatic treatment of psychosis during pregnancy and postpartum. *General Hospital Psychiatry, 11*(5), 328–338.

O'Grady, J. P. & Rosenthal, M. (1989). Pseudocyesis: A modern perspective on an old disorder. *Obstetrics and Gynecology Survey, 44*, 500–511.

O'Hara, M. W., Schlechte, J. A., Lewis, D. A. & Varner, M. W. (1991). Controlled prospective study of postpartum mood disorders: Psychological environmental and hormonal variables. *Journal of Abnormal Psychology, 100*(1): 63–73.

Osofsky, H. (1982). Expectant and new fatherhood as developmental crisis. *Bulletin of the Menniger Clinic, 46*, 209–228.

Palomaki, G. E. (1986). Collaborative study of Down's syndrome screening using maternal serum alpha-fetoprotein and maternal age. *Lancet, 2*, 1460.

Pastuszak, A., Schick-Bosehetto, B., Zuber, C., Feldkamp, M., Pinelli, M., Sihn, S., Donnenfield, A., McCormack, M., Leen-Mitchell, M., Woodland, C., Gardner, A., Hom, M. & Koren, G. (1993). Pregnancy outcome following first-trimester exposure to fluoxetine (Prozac). *Journal of the American Medical Association, 269*(17), 2246–2248.

Pederson, F. A. (1980). *The father-infant relationship: Observational studies in the family-setting*. New York: Praeger.

Phillip, C. & Anzalone, J. (1982). *Fathering: Participation in labour and birth*. St. Louis: C. V. Mosby.

Pool, S. R., Sharere, D. R., Barbee, M. A. et al. (1983). Hospitalization of a psychotic mother and breast feeding infant. *Hospital Community Psychiatry, 31*, 412–414.

Remick, R. A. & Maurice, W. L. (1978). Electroconvulsive therapy in pregnancy (letter). *American Journal of Psychiatry, 136,* 761–762.

Rohde, A. & Marneros, A. (1993). Postpartum psychoses: Onset and long-term course, *Psychopathology, 26,* 203–209.

Seiden, A. M. (1976). Overview: Research on psychology of women. I. Gender differences and sexual reproductive life. *American Journal of Psychiatry, 133,* 955–1007.

Severing, S. K. & Moline, M. L. (Eds.). (1989). *Premenstrual syndrome. A clinician's guide.* New York: Guilford Press.

Sholomskas, D. E., Wickamarathe, P. J., Dogolo, L., O'Brien, D. W., Leaf, P. J. & Woods, S. W. (1993). Postpartum onset of panic disorder: A coincidental event? *Journal of Clinical Psychiatry, 54*(12), 476–480.

Spirito, A. & Williams, C. et al. (1989). Psychological impact of the diagnosis of gestational diabetes. *Obstetrics and Gynecology, 73,* 562–566.

Steiner, M. (1990). Postpartum psychiatric disorders. *Canadian Journal of Psychiatry, 35,* 89–95.

Swerts, A. (1987). Impact of genetic counselling and prenatal diagnosis for Down syndrome and neural tube defects. *Birth Defects, 23,* 61–83.

Tamminen, T. (1988). The impact of mother's depression on her nursing experience and attitudes during breastfeeding. *Acta Paediatrica Scandanavica, 77,* 87–94.

Van Gent, E. M. (1993). Puerperal affective psychosis: Is there a case for lithium prophylaxis? *British Journal of Psychiatry, 162,* 564–575.

Vinogradov, S. & Yalom, I. D. (1991). A concise guide to group psychotherapy. Washington, DC: American Psychiatric Press.

Whiffen, V. E. & Gotlib, I. H. (1993). Comparison of postpartum and non-postpartum depression: Clinical presentation, psychiatric history, and psychosocial functioning. *Journal of Consulting and Clinical Psychology, 61*(3), 485–494.

Winnicott, D. W. (1964). *The child, the family and the outside world.* London: Tavistock.

Wisner, K. L., Peindl, K. & Hanusa, B. H. (1993). Relationship of psychiatric illness to childbearing status: A hospital-based epidemiologic study. *Journal of Affective Disorders, 28,* 39–50.

Wisner, K. L., Perel, J. M. & Wheeler, S. B. (1993). Tricyclic dose requirements across pregnancy. *American Journal of Psychiatry, 150*(10), 1541–1542.

Wynn, R. M. (1983). *Obstetrics and gynecology: The clinical core.* Philadelphia: Lea S. Febiger.

Zaslow, M., Pederson, F., Kramer, E. et al. (1981). *Depressed mood in new fathers: Interview and behavior correlates.* Boston: Society for Research in Child Development.

INDEX